Into

D0589669

KATE ADIE

Into Danger

Risking Your Life for Work

HODDER

First published in Great Britain in 2008 by Hodder & Stoughton
An Hachette Livre UK Company

First published in paperback in 2009

1

A CIP catalogue record for this title is available from the British Library

ISBN 978 0 340 93322 0

Typeset in Plantin by Hewer Text UK Ltd, Edinburgh
Printed and bound by Clays Ltd, St Ives plc

Hodder Headline's policy is to use papers that are natural, renewable
and recyclable products and made from wood grown in sustainable forests.
The logging and manufacturing processes are expected to conform
to the environmental regulations of the country of origin.

Hodder & Stoughton Ltd
338 Euston Road
London NW1 3BH

www.hodder.co.uk

To my sister Dianora

Acknowledgements

To Nigel Churton, Tim Cross, John Davidson, Didy Grahame, Jennifer Leybourne, Denis Murray, Martin Narey, Georgina Perry, Guihua Li and Wim Robberechts for help and advice, and to Jessica and Charles Thomas for the most peaceful garden in which to write.

To Rowena Webb and Juliet Brightmore and Esther Jagger at Hodder & Stoughton for their wise suggestions, and also to Kerry Hood, and to Louise Greenberg and Brenda Griffiths for endless encouragement.

Contents

Introduction

A young man in a white shirt and black trousers, clutching a carrier bag, stands in front of a huge tank which could crush him like a caterpillar under an enormous boot. The image of this lone citizen, stopping the Chinese Army in its tracks on the edge of Tiananmen Square in Beijing in 1989, went round the world. Why did he do it? Why did he put himself in danger?

On the hull of a capsized ship, a diver descends into a pitch-black space through a smashed window. Below is chaos, people thrashing around in rising water, freezing cold, unable to see anything. He stays there for over three hours, hauling them to safety. Why do such a job?

Washing off the dirt of days in a river in the African bush, a young lieutenant looks up to see the enemy looming into sight. Without a second's pause he crosses the river ahead of his men, destroys one tank, damages the second and attacks the third. His men follow and win the day. He is never seen again. What made him pay the ultimate price?

We live in times when strenuous efforts are made to protect and insure ourselves against every kind of threat in our increasingly long lives. We do not expect to be eaten by wolves. We have learned how to avoid being struck by lightning. We will not be consulting a witchdoctor. Life has many hazards, but we are getting better at avoidance. 'Fate' is a giggle at the newspaper astrology column rather than an almighty and universal sense of doom.

For centuries, the power of myth and superstition and magic suggested that most dangers were unavoidable. In an uncertain world, where natural disasters were not understood, disease was a mystery and famine lay beyond the control of the majority of the population, fate loomed large. Legend and religious belief crystallised the threats and gave them form, perhaps the most potent being the Four Horsemen of the Apocalypse. Thundering out of the pages of the last book in the Christian New Testament, they suggested that danger was brought down on to people in specific ways – War, Disease, Famine and False Belief (and a dozen variations and interpretations on this theme).

Different theologians gave the horses and their riders expanded roles; novelists and Hollywood embellished them. The Red Horse represents war, its rider's sword standing for every kind of destruction and the spilling of blood. The Pale Horse (actually green – not grassy and vibrant, but the greeny-grey tinge of ill-health) had his powers enhanced to cover not only sickness and death but hunger, plagues and all-round decay. The scythe, later a sword, carried by his rider lives on as a symbol of death. The Black Horse stands for pestilence, bringing barren fields and famine, resulting in unfair trade and leading to crime. His rider carries scales. The White Horse is a more disputed animal, the subject of learned treatises on his crown-wearing rider. To many he was the Anti-Christ, or a false prophet. His symbolism is difficult to delineate in the modern age, but when the clergy used to rule ordinary lives and mortal souls mattered more than earthly life it was a warning about the danger of straying from the straight and narrow path of accepted belief.

Show the scythe, the scales, the sword and the crown today and there will still be a notion of what they stood for. We know that sickness and war, crime and belief, drive danger towards us. However, we are far removed from the societies who could ascribe all danger to divine will or destiny. Few of us see life in terms of rigid fate. We challenge dangers, we endlessly pursue solutions to problems, we prepare for disaster and we think up ways of cheating death. Or at least the human race in general does, confidently hoping for progress and a better standard of living.

But individually, we are rather more cautious. Few would get out of bed very willingly if the day's work appeared to involve facing real danger – the sort that puts your heart in your mouth and poses the question: why are on earth am I doing this? I will admit that at times in my working life I have found myself caught in crossfire, or stunned by a grenade, or trying to ask directions from a corpse during a gun battle, and the first response of this reporter has been 'Why am I doing this?' rather than 'What's going on?' To be honest, there have been many such moments, but none of them was on the cards at the start of the working day. Reporters make mistakes, get stuck in the wrong place, have accidents, blunder into trouble, and get to meet the most interesting people (but armed, drunk, fanatical, intolerant or very angry) at the wrong time. Danger occurs by mistake. And I had certainly never planned to take on a dangerous job.

I

Into Danger

In the whole of my post-war childhood in Sunderland I never encountered a journalist, save for a procession of spotty individuals who turned up at school to jot down the names of annual prize-winners and sports champions, resulting in a number of girls having their names spelled as anagrams. Nevertheless the local paper, the quaintly named *Echo*, was the unquestioned bible of hatches, matches and dispatches, a chronicle of worthy civic events and a sniffy observer at the magistrates' court, forever using a tone of resigned endurance for the trail of petty criminals up before the beak. Drink figured largely in these cases, but was regarded as inevitable, with only the occasional reference to someone who had had more than fifteen pints, as if in wonder at the man's capacity to get a couple of gallons of Vaux's Ale into a bantam Geordie body. Wearside, for all its poverty and hard living conditions round the shipyards and pits, resolutely refused to commit seriously interesting crime. A streak of Nonconformist Puritanism ran through the bleakest housing estates, and the middle classes appeared to be irredeemably decent and dull. If they did get up to anything, they made sure it didn't get into the papers. Admittedly there was domestic violence, but not yet aired in public: the shipyard workers' wives limped into our family chemist's shop blotched with bruises and never made mention of them; the bourgeoisie would rather have been seen naked in the High Street than give a hint of strife at home.

4

Living opposite us was the only citizen I knew who possessed a gun. Weekends saw him heading for the Northumbrian moors for a legitimate pot at the grouse. He saw this as a wry comment on his trade: he was the *Echo*'s chief photographer, and he reckoned to spend Saturdays joining shotgun parties in the afternoon, following a morning of shotgun weddings. Indeed, the only hint that journalism might produce a smidgeon of trouble lay in his photographic Rules of Discretion: in the *Echo*'s extensive wedding coverage, no bride appeared below the waist – otherwise, he said, the family could get a bit nasty.

As to my joining the people who practised the mysterious craft of journalism, such an idea never arose. My school magazine charted the Old Girls' lives every year, and in the 1950s those of us in the prep school could see the future projected in the phrases 'Jean Bruce-Low – only married' or 'Nina Sawyer, working at the Medical Research Council Hospital, Bathurst, Gambia, British West Africa'. Wife or colonial pioneer. A splendid achievement after years of genteel education, 'deportment lessons' and brutal hockey. In between were a great swathe of teachers, physiotherapists, orthoptists, nurses and librarians, and lots of girls in vicarages, from Nyasaland to India to the rectory in Kue Kue, Southern Rhodesia. If any idea ever entered our young heads, it was that nothing would change very much. And life would be peaceful and well ordered; our parents and grandparents had both endured dreadful and lengthy wars, but those were in the past and we were full of free orange juice, school milk and sensible over-boiled British food.

For me as a child, danger belonged to the past, in particular to the war which had ended in 1945 just before I was born. And that war and all its dangers were hardly mentioned. As a result, it was difficult to connect the conventional people who passed through my childhood with any kind of frightening events. We lived in a neat suburban cul-de-sac of semis, with a gap at the bottom – 'A firebomb from Jerry in '41,' said the neighbours in passing. Buddleia bushes and lumps of brick and concrete made it an interesting playground. The rockery at the bottom of our own garden was forever yielding shards of rusty iron – those that had not made it into our sideboard and bureau. 'A 500-pounder,' said the neighbours knowledgeably. Landing smack-bang on the concrete of the back lane, it had magicked our greenhouse to powdered glass. People had died – something that was mentioned in a matter-of fact manner: 'Whole town caught it that night in '43.'

But there were no descriptions of what it had been like to go through such raids and there were shrugs of indifference when more was requested. I was made to understand that everyone was 'in the same boat. There was nothing special.' Occasionally I heard a reference to the curious routine of 'fire-watching', but as there were no high-rise flats or flat roofs in this part of suburban Sunderland I was at a loss to know where anyone perched to look for smoke and flames. And whatever emotions might have swirled around as people stared into the sky on cold nights for approaching bombers and the flash of explosions, there was never a hint of them.

Our dining room had housed a Morrison shelter. I was fascinated: it seemed just like being on the front line somewhere – perhaps a trench ran to the kitchen and out into the garden? I was at a loss to know exactly what it had looked like (a large chicken coop apparently, intended to withstand the house collapsing on to it); however, it was recollected and dismissed with a grimace ('You could never get a good night's sleep in that thing') and I was referred to the smart dining table which stood in its place. So what had it been like – lying awake listening for the drone of the Luftwaffe? Was there a sense of great apprehension? Of being a sitting duck? Of being the unlucky target? Of being in mortal danger? None of the residents of this bombed street seemed to recall such thoughts. It was over. Let's not drag it up – let's put that behind us.

The drama of war, its extremes of fear and despair, had been packed away. My home town was pitted with bomb sites, but they were empty of emotion, ignored by a generation uncomfortable with feelings expressed too publicly, known as 'making a right show of yourself'. Asked if there had been danger, they made little response.

Further probing brought the comment that the boys overseas had had it far worse. Atlantic convoys, Alamein, the Japs and the Burma Road – heavens, what was a little bombing compared to that? So childhood in the fifties was a pleasant, sunny place, the calm after the storm, with no suggestion of seeking a thrill or upsetting the apple cart. And the spotty lads who chewed their pencils and scribbled weird symbols in their notebooks under the suspicious eye of the headmistress hardly held out the promise of an exciting world entered through journalism.

For a start, we were headed for the traditional roles considered suitable for girls. Nursing, teaching, something secretarial. 'Career' was an unknown concept. What lay ahead was a path to security, whether it be the haven of marriage or the comfort of a steady, respectable job. Boys had adventures. Girls did something useful, then 'settled down'. Words such as ambition, success and money were not polite. Adrenalin would have been considered rude. If danger had ever been mentioned, it would have been regarded as a totally unacceptable intrusion into normality. 'Rather unnecessary' would have been the reaction.

Even at university, which was suddenly opened up to so many more of us in the sixties, most of the women were clustered in the Arts Faculty, with teaching held out as the ultimate goal. This would provide the all-important 'security' – especially if you hadn't landed a husband yet. Huge generalisations, I know, but late-night conversations with other female students from miners' lasses to landowners' gels echoed with the same worries from home: you mustn't be left on the shelf, you need a safe and reliable job, you need 'some security'. And many happily headed for such a future. However, even the bolder souls who set off on the hippie trail to Australia or seized a placard and joined the huge student protests across Europe still belonged to a country that was no longer involved in an all-consuming war which brought danger and death into everyday life.

Perhaps we would have been a good deal less sanguine if we had been aware of the dangers which lurk in everyday jobs. We had never read the lengthy lists compiled by gloomy statisticians which catalogue the misfortunes of a working life. Before you go out of the door, these doom-mongers note, even a housewife is prey to death by, among other things, falling on bread knives, skidding on abandoned roller skates, entanglement in window blind chords and being struck by lightning. A quiet and orderly life can be full of hazards. Admittedly, these examples appear in a modern American review and the data is a bit sketchy, but they could happen any time, anywhere. So it might be safer to pop into the world of work outside the home. Insurance companies, government statistical bureaux and university researchers regularly publish annual lists of risky occupations, though based on hugely varying principles: reported fatalities, accident statistics, days off work, frequency of incidents, workplace environment, and deaths and injuries per capita in any given group. Given this last criterion, then the one job you wouldn't want in the United States, if you want to see your pension, is President. Four dead, two injured and a dozen assassination attempts among just over forty men is not a good advertisement for a safe job. Statistically, it's a much better bet to be a British monarch. Lion tamers and elephant trainers are also in this category – there aren't a lot of them, but their survival rates aren't good.

Worldwide, there are common threads to dangerous work. Casual behaviour around buildings and trees brings widespread misery: lumberjacks and construction workers everywhere are greatly at risk. So are those who burrow into the earth or head for the sea: Mother Nature can be ruthless with miners and fishermen. Even so, carelessness, negligence, lack of training and above all poor working conditions turn what should be routine into a death-trap: appalling conditions in Chinese mines – where several thousand men die every year – could be rectified, and elsewhere in the world mining is no longer recorded as especially dangerous. However, daily bread has to be earned, and millions everywhere have no choice about taking a risk in a badly run industry, where the work itself may not be particularly hazardous but the lack of safety precautions and an attitude which sees life as cheap make it seem so. However, I and my contemporaries in

Britain half a century ago were not driven by such considerations when looking at our career prospects.

To be honest, I was merely driven by a kind of gentle desperation arising from having obtained a degree in Scandinavian Studies which qualified me for a massively important national role – should the Vikings ever invade us again. Serendipitously, the BBC came to my rescue by launching an experiment in local radio, and accidentally locating a station in my native north-east (we were meant to be Radio Manchester, but something went wrong). I joined Radio Durham, and having done all the significant jobs such as sorting the record library and feeding the station cat I progressed from technician to producer before heading for Radio Bristol. At no time did I think of slipping into the local radio journalism stream. That was in the hands of ex-local newspapermen. Women ('girlies') were not entirely welcomed at that time, and anyway. I knew nothing of the trade. But I wouldn't have thought it dangerous, and when I finally got tipped into a post in BBC Plymouth, finding myself filling the role of news reporter very inadequately, and none too willingly, I still thought it a broadcasting job like any other. Not for one moment did I think I had stepped into a world of danger.

Journalism was spoken of in many terms, some of them none too complimentary, but there was no sense of it having the glamorous cachet of 'life-and-death' situations.

When I began reporting from the national newsroom in London, the seasoned old hands who had been through conflict in the Congo, Rhodesia and Vietnam never talked of the work in terms of danger. They had had their scary moments, been through some very nasty lethal incidents, but didn't rate this as the defining character of their journalism. There was the driving hunt for the story, the camaraderie, the adventures, the alcohol hidden in the expenses' claims, the foul food, the dreadful journeys, the hair-raising encounters with very angry people and . . . yeah . . . danger? Well, suppose so. A bit.

And if you met fellow members of the press who seemed bent on finding a lot of trouble, you gave them a wide berth. That wasn't what the job was all about. Bringing the story back is what's important. And to do that, you need to be in one piece. We are not warriors. We don't do danger. It's just that occasionally, almost invariably by accident or unexpectedly, danger tries to do for us.

The job, in itself, isn't inherently dangerous. It has to be admitted that we find common cause with those who have chosen to head for war zones, the military. The hours are rubbish, the conditions in the field are one degree above slum-dwelling and the pay is average. We actually enjoy spending hours in muddy ditches telling jokes and tales while lots of hot metal flies around above us (well, the journalists enjoy the jokes, at least). We sense that we both have a purpose in the midst of chaos, one to bring order, the other to witness this process and spread the information back home. But at that point, the jobs divide. We have different attitudes to risk and different objectives.

On the battlefield, in the war zone, the assumption seems to be that journalists and soldiers face the same dangers and therefore share the same decisions about risk – after all, the bullets and shells and bombs don't have little computers in them programmed 'Not Intended for the Non-Combatant Press'. But we have different obligations. The military are under orders, with a duty to deal with the enemy. The media have no parallel set of orders, even though they may feel a duty to report (and they worry the military with the suggestion that they might even want to interview the enemy). But in most cases, journalists are merely under an obligation to turn in some work in return for money. Even freelancers, roaming at will and independent of editors, are rarely skirting mines and living on horrible rations for the good of their soul: they would like to be paid for the results of their self-induced trouble.

No one orders the journalists and camera crews forward. The stories of the men going 'over the top' from the trenches in World War I induce a particular shiver among reporters. At the blast of a whistle, you wouldn't find the world's finest hacks clambering eagerly out of the muddy ditch towards the barbed wire. No, thank you: we'll just wait in our little foxhole and see what happens. And for a very good reason. The military system not only demands that you follow orders, it lays down that your duty is to head towards 'the objective', however unreasonable it may be. To do or die. The hack has a completely different objective which lies in the opposite direction: to get the story back, way behind the lines, to the readers, the viewers, the listeners. And if you decided to do (in a soldierly manner) and were to die, then you would have failed in your objective. No story.

And the journalists have the bonus of taking their own decisions. They may be working for a monster on the news desk back home, but even the most ruthless editorial beast (whose idea of personal peril is being run over by an uninsured mini-cab driver in Islington) is unable to winkle a terrified reporter out of a cosy foxhole in a foreign land. Particularly in the age of the mobile phone, when a threat to terminate employment can be answered by holding up the tiny metal amulet to transmit the explosions and whizz-bangs back home, along with a shouted suggestion about insurance. Pressure to deliver a story may reach great intensity, but it is highly resistible in the face of your own demise. The fashionable jargon for this situation is 'being in control', even though you wouldn't normally use such a phrase to describe a gibbering hamster of a hack trying to dig to Australia via the foxhole. But it is a kind of control: because you, the representative of the press, have made that decision. You're not moving, you know what's good for you, and if there's going to be any sort of story at the end of the day you need your vital bits and breath in your body in order to write it. You don't have to face the soldier's danger.

And this curious opportunity to exert a lever on your fate, when there is obvious danger all around, is a comfort. You are not being propelled by others into the jaws of death, you won't be facing a court martial and you're going to live to tell the tale. It will be a measure of your ethics and your personal virtue if, while telling that tale, you remember in your heart of hearts that you have been saved not by any personal heroism, but by the blessed dispensation of needing to file the story. You might write about danger, but you have no duty to tackle it. Perhaps this is why journalists seem a less traumatised crowd than might be popularly expected. Having been addressed more than once about war zones, by concerned members of the audience at literary events, with the words, 'Miss Adie, you of course must be a very damaged person . . .', I am aware of the general suspicion that the hack pack is a mass candidate for the funny farm. (We might as well use the language which hits home.) We see war, disaster, tragedy, grief – all the stuff which is the tsunami of news, unexpected and overwhelming. Surely the witnesses to such bad news end up in splinters as the wave buffets them relentlessly?

Well, a few don't come out of things too happily. But they tend, in my experience, to be those who went in with an equivocal attitude or quite a lot of unresolved personal baggage (those who would make a mess of being a chartered accountant, never mind a war correspondent). The rest of us are firmly in the common-sense groove which heads both the story and ourselves back to home and safety. There is a real misconception that adrenalin and a 'buzz' are the drivers when it comes to a difficult assignment. Apart from the fact that it is difficult to do anything sensible and coherent when on a 'high' achieved through fear, the business of journalism just doesn't get done when the hack is a dog of war, straining at the leash. . . .

Twenty journalists stuffed behind a farm wall in Croatia one Saturday afternoon in the early 1990s, cameras trained on a distant village being pounded by Serb tanks, were joined by an eager-beaver American youth fresh off the plane to Zagreb.

'OK, you guys waiting for someone, or do we just walk in?'

The silence was filled with the gut-wobbling roar of a fat piece of Soviet hardware crabbing through a field of part-harvested sweet-corn. We stared at the tank. Not one of us had seen a tank fire in anger in a European field, neat and tidy corncobs being scattered by churning tracks as the monster made its way past little barns.

'Come on—'

The tank lurched to a halt and its long snout traversed nastily, sweeping the odd standing corn stalk, coming to rest with the village church squarely in its sights.

Some of us behind the wall ducked as the barrel did a tell-tale nod. Others continued to stare and were rewarded with a horrendous boom which brought them to a crouch like everyone else.

'Hey, see *that*!' said the newcomer.

We had seen. Most of us were not feeling too good. The wall was a stone wall, probably built with the same stone as the church. The church tower now had a large hole in it. And a fire had begun. The distance between us and the tank was probably the same as from the tank to the church.

'So we go take a look, yeah?'

We had no idea who this bloke was. He had a rather swish professional camera and a large back-pack.

At some point my cameraman and I decided we should put on flak-jackets, which we hadn't really got used to. However, tank fire is more than impressive, it's bloody scary, and we needed to do *something*. That something did not involve going any nearer, which our new companion found truly amazing.

'So you're journalists? So there's a war going on? So what's it all about, guys?' He hunched himself under his back-pack into Action Man on the Starting Blocks, camera at the ready. We sat on the ground behind our wall.

'*Bon voyage*,' said a French TV correspondent from the depths of the farm building.

Then the small arms fire which had chattered all morning started up again – from everywhere. Those of us who had spent a few months in the country already recognised the sound of the domestic AK47 – the handy little weapon which lived in the cupboard next to the vacuum cleaner in any respectable Croat household. Every farm and barn was busy with chattering sounds. The odd bullet zipped overhead with a curious veeeeeep.

'Where's all that coming from?' asked Action Man.

'Everywhere,' we replied, flat on the ground. 'They've *all* got guns.'

'Hey, I did some stuff in Central America but I've never seen, you know, tanks and things. . . .'

The bullets veeped and hissed.

'Look, the way back to the town, are the farms on the way full of guys firing?'

'Oh, yes,' we said, still flat on the ground, the more pessimistic reporters wondering if they should ask his name – just to get his obituary right.

A short while later he realised that no one had any intention of storming the battlements, as it were. He quietly collected his camera and back-pack and melted away, having seen – perhaps learned – that journalists may encounter danger but don't necessarily have to face it, deal with it or rid the world of it.

But who are the people who do?

2

The Snake Venom Collector

'Welcome to the nation's first and finest planned retirement community for active seniors. Everything under the sun in this Master-Planned Community: from Lizard Acres to Lush Oasis.' Forty thousand 'active seniors' have read the advertisement and are now enjoying their sunset years in Sun City, Arizona, having moved to a development which boasts more than 325 days of sunshine per year. There are eleven golf courses, spas aplenty, and seven mildly active leisure centres, nearly all of which suggest a nice quiet way of life punctured by lengthy snoozing on a smart patio which just thirty years ago was virgin desert.

What I remember about the place was the silence. Sun City is a suburb (in the American sense of the word – miles from the centre of town) of the ever-sprawling city of Phoenix. It was in its infancy in the early eighties when I saw it, but appeared to be a sun-bleached paradise for the living dead. Any journey – to the neighbours, the supermarket, the large hospital – was undertaken in a gently humming golf buggy. Any exercise, such as hauling up the garage door, was avoided by using electronic buttons. Aggravating activity, like watering the garden, was bypassed by acquiring a fully grown monster saguaro cactus which needs the watering can only once every seven years.

However, there's always a little trouble in paradise. The city limits pushed into the Arizona desert with that can-do American confidence and well-sprinkled lawns, ensuring that the residents felt they had moved somewhere that wasn't in the slightest bit wild. Even so, there were hints that every so often the desert bit back. Like a newly minted urban myth, the tale of the 'stiffs on the patio' was doing the rounds. It appeared that one of the unexpected sights in this manicured 'Master-Planned Community' was that of a pair of turned-up toes stretched out on the barbecue terrace, bereft of the usual signs of violent urban crime. The perfect murder? Ask the smooth realtors about this rumoured phenomenon, and they denied all knowledge: 'Gossip,' they said, as they set off to flog yet another 'mountain view and three-car garage des. res.'. 'Anyway,' they added, 'the median age of our community *is* seventy-five.' However, their enticing advertisements did say from Lizard Acres to Lush Oasis; but no one had had a word with the lizards – and their friends.

Today, the internet is more forthcoming. Next to the local news items such as 'Fabric artist stitches way to national final' and 'Sun City flings open its doors to spring' there are bloggers curious to know whether life in Arizona might be for them: 'My husband and I would like to move to Phoenix. The only thing that worries me is having snakes in my garage and trantulas [sic] and scorpions in my house. Is that really a good reason not to move there or is that stupid?' Reply, from Phoenix: 'Wow, we are alike. I hate creepy crawlies. I think Phoenix is a great place to live, even if you have big phobias . . . but we have so few of the ones that bug you – I'm from the north-east where spiders that look like they've swallowed a cat hang out in your basement. So here's a really OK place to live.'

Reassuring stuff. Yet the local Fire Department has a wonderfully lengthy list of things that the unobservant and accident-prone might like to familiarise themselves with, from Terrorism Preparedness to Getting Lost. A fair amount of their practical advice involves a word I hadn't previously encountered: what to do should you become 'envenomated'. There are seventeen different sorts of rattlesnakes in Arizona and some of them haven't come to terms with the idea that they should share the desert with retirees snoozing gently on the rattlers' place in the sun. Hence the urban myth, the mysterious sudden deaths on the patio – but like so many such stories, not entirely without foundation.

Rattlers are the stuff of the movies: the snake which has to be dispatched swiftly by the hero after the cinema audience has experienced that curious sound like a pair of raspy maracas being shaken. A sound intended to warn off anything that's come too close. And with good reason. Snakes get mad when disturbed. Also frightened, and their venom rises. And they move like lightning. Should you become envenomated, having disturbed a rattler on its preferred bit of former desert, its toxin can kill.

But why would you venture close? Most people run a mile at the sight of a grass snake worming through an English meadow. Nevertheless, despite the danger one or two people are drawn to snakes, and for the very reason the rest of us take to our heels: the two fangs dripping poison. For someone has to harvest the venom which makes up the vital antivenom. Someone like Bill Haast.

Bill makes it clear that he is not a snake charmer. He sighs as he describes the miserable creatures which wobble up out of baskets for tourists to gawp at. 'De-fanged and dyin',' he says, with exasperation. We're staring out at his garden on the west coast of Florida: not a snake in sight. His home is in a rural part of the state that used to be much wilder, and teeming with snakes. Now farms and large houses dot the landscape, edging out much of the wildlife. However, Bill stares out through a huge plate-glass window at a gathering of red-headed vultures flapping over some food that his wife Nancy has thrown for them; he laughs at their antics and at the dainty-pawed raccoon that sets about them and muscles in on the meal. But what he would really like to see is a little slither of movement through the grass: now that's worth watching 'cos snakes are *innerestin'*.'

He sits in a large house full of herpetological images: there are mammoth gold Egyptian ornaments, wooden carvings, pottery nicknacks, fangs and beady eyes printed on tiles, and a monster concrete king cobra statue rearing above the swimming pool. Serpents stare at you from everywhere: in the loo, tiny ones curl round the handbasin taps. Clearly, Bill is not tired of snakes – though he's been around them for a long time.

'When I was about eleven years old, I was collecting garter snakes – a very harmless species – near the river which went by our home in Patterson, New Jersey. I used to make pets of them. Since then, I don't think I've ever been without a snake in captivity. I like them for what they are – animals, natural things.'

The next year he went off to scout camp, and while everyone else was whittling wood, tying knots and sitting round the camp-fire, young Bill was down in the undergrowth busy amassing 'a nice collection of rattlers and copperheads'. Which he insisted on taking home. No wonder his mother fled their third-floor apartment that night when she found out what was in the box her boy scout had plonked on the floor. Thankfully, she returned, but not before setting out some rules about a secure box – and never opening it when she was around. She had a son utterly hooked on snakes, despite the fact that he already knew they could be dangerous.

'From when I was a kid, I knew *how* dangerous they could be, but maybe I felt impervious – you know what kids are. But it didn't hamper me in any way. I didn't think about it. It's just in the nature of the snake, and if he's dangerous, I guess if I'm foolish enough to get caught then it's my problem, not his.

'The first time I was bitten was at Greenwood Lake, New York, when I was twelve years old and at the scout camp – hey, this is about a hundred years ago. I was bitten by a timber rattlesnake – I was pushing the brush aside, and he was very, very quick and struck out at my arm, and I didn't see it until I felt it. If you're not looking right spot on where he is, you'll miss him, he's so fast. The arm swelled up, but there's all grades of snake bites. If they bite hard and hang on, you get more venom. If it's glancing, you get less.'

Bill is laughing a lot at this point and one throwaway remark he's made is not far from the truth, for he was born in 1910 – and is looking forward to his first century very soon. And now he's off on his favourite subject, snake bites.

'A coral snake will hang on religiously – it's in its nature to hang on, because its fangs are very small, so it wants a good chance to deliver a full dose of neuro-toxic venom. Cobras will hang on as well, if they've a mind to – one got his fangs in my arm once and that eventually put me in a respirator. . . .'

It's a wonder Bill has precise recall of specific bites. Admittedly, the first one must have been memorable – at twelve years old. The second bite occurred later in the same year, this time from a lanky copperhead, four feet long and 'as big as you'll ever see one of them'. He grabbed it by the tail. Wrong end. It whipped round and sank its fangs into a finger, putting Bill in hospital for a week. His long-suffering mother went out and bought him a book about snakes. He sat in bed reading about the beastie that had nipped him, learning that its venom will make you ill but is rarely fatal. 'That's the very moment,' he says, 'when I began to think about venoms and their possible value.'

These first two encounters had not put him off in any way: since then, Bill Haast has been bitten 171 times. He doesn't look to see if he's in any of the record books, because no one seems to have survived even a fraction of that number which includes bites from the deadliest varieties on earth. As a teenager he spent his spare time learning how to handle them, helping them shed their skin, noting just when a rattler 'rattled'. At fifteen, his pocket money and casual earnings went straight on a ten-dollar diamondback rattler bought from a catalogue. He was thrilled when it arrived and thought it enhanced his collection enormously. However, with this snake his curiosity about the venom led him to see it not so much as a pet but as a creature whose true fascination lay in its ability to deliver poison in a split-second strike – swiftly, elegantly and often fatally – and one which might be harvested.

It would be wrong to say that the diamondback merely obliged. Extracting venom does not occur under congenial conditions: toxic juices flow when the snake is either terrified or mad as hell or both. In his Florida sitting room, Bill reaches for one of dozens of videos collected in racks on the wall – programmes in which he has figured over the decades. He spools quickly through several, most of which have a sequence in which a glamorously attired TV reporter – mainly favouring safari-wear – chats animatedly to Bill and then looks suitably intrigued as he slides out a tray in a cabinet in his laboratory-cum-workroom. Out comes a dangly coil. Reporter looks serious as Bill waves one hand in the air and then deftly grabs the back of the snake's head with the other as the jaws rear open and the fangs come into very sharp focus. At this point, most of the reporters have gone into reverse safari and are flat against the door. Including this one on the sofa, watching the video. Watching an enraged snake straining every muscle, fangs quivering with poison and fury and with the nastiest look in its tiny beady eyes, is something you should only do from a sofa at a safe distance from a TV screen. The 'strike' is always a split-second movement, the snake using speed, power and agility. It is shocking, transforming a seemingly dozy bit of rubber hose into a stiff, strong, hissing weapon, doing its utmost to deliver as much poison as possible.

The usual reaction is to rear back yourself, getting your head as far away as possible. Mr Snake is merely logical, though, and goes for the hands that are left outstretched in defence. Bill's fingers work the video button with some difficulty: his hands are a rather odd, waxy yellow, with tapering fingers – those that are left, that is. Several are thin stumps, the flesh having been rotted away by snake venom over the years. 'Guess I was just a little too slow on occasion,' he explains with a smile. 'A Malayan pit viper made my index finger kinda hooked. An eastern diamondback left one hand curled into a claw and a cottonmouth bit the tip of my right pinkie – its venom dissolves tissue, so the finger lost all feeling and there was just a bit of blackened bone sticking out. My wife, Nancy, cut that off with a pair of garden clippers.'

Teenage Bill probably gave little thought to the likely fate of his fingers, but set out on a working life as a snake handler for a travelling fair. He had wanted to join a prestigious zoo, but didn't get hired, so a variety of jobs ensued, including the fair, bootlegging 'moonshine' in the Florida Everglades during the Depression – and all the time collecting more snakes. In the first of three marriages, he settled down to study aviation mechanics and eventually joined Pan Am as a flight engineer. His work took him all over the world during World War II, and while others admired the landscapes of Asia, Africa and South America Bill saw countryside stuffed with puff adders and cobras. And brought them back, hidden in his toolbox. He also hatched a plan to turn his hobby into a business: he would open a 'Serpentarium'. The attachment to the idea ended one marriage, but found a set of buildings rising on a plot of land facing Route 1 south of Miami. With his second wife, Clarita, he gave up the aviation job and worked all hours to open the attraction at the end of 1947.

The new venture was part snake-park, part laboratory, for behind the Serpentarium lay the curiosity about venom. The snakes were not pets on show, they were regarded by Bill as workers. To the fascination and awe of visitors, Bill and Clarita hopped into one of the pits and hooked up large specimens to demonstrate their characteristics. However, the main attraction was Bill choosing a 'snake *du jour*'. While it had a good writhe and hiss, with a circle of faces twitching back as it reared up and got good and mad, Bill would wave his left hand to distract it and suddenly seize it with his right. Very quickly he would press the head with its bared fangs down on to a rubber membrane stretched over a test tube – and the snake would speedily empty out a stream of amber venom. This would be repeated many times a day, for it can take a hundred extractions to produce a gram of powdered venom. The Serpentarium flourished, the visitors gawped and Clarita narrated the process, though she was on tranquillisers for some of the time . . .

Bill was bitten again. And again. However, ever since his second bite as a teenager he had been aware that the antivenom he had been injected with then had consisted partly of venom itself. 'So in 1948, I started immunising myself with cobra venom. Why did I start? Well, that's just me, I guess. It's a big step, but I don't think I did it for protection – I just did it. It was venom from a Cape cobra, diluted. I filled a syringe with an almost infinitesimal amount and injected myself. I didn't tell anyone – not even my wife. I mean, everything is a challenge, especially when you're young.' It is a technique known from Roman times as mithridatism, though its usefulness tends to be confined to those who insist on working closely and frequently with venomous animals, a category into which Bill Haast fits snugly. And by now he needed all the help he could get, because he was frightfully keen on king cobras.

Cobras in general exert a fascination: myth, legend and worship are attached to them, and a number of supposed characteristics. They are supposed to be smarter than your average snake, docile enough to be 'charmed' and tame enough to be 'kissed' on the head by a woman. What most of the stories omit to mention is a trail of dead people who attributed human emotions to a coil of muscle that packs enough venom to fell an elephant. However, it is true that they look terrific, rearing up with their hood spread wide, a signal that means anger, readiness to strike and a large reservoir of poison as ammunition – an irresistible animal for Bill Haast:

'I'm impressed by them – especially the king cobra, which is my favourite one to work with because it sits up and is a challenge each time I catch one. They're the largest poisonous snake, for one thing – they've reached twenty feet in length. And when I had the Serpentarium, I worked with them every day. It's a very, very fast snake when it moves. But they're at a little bit of a disadvantage when they strike, because they sit up: if they didn't, they'd be much faster. They take this defensive, frightening attitude – you know, like when the rattlesnake rattles, "Don't tread on *me*." The cobra sits up and spreads his hood and makes himself look more formidable.

'When you think of the character of a snake, you could say that they ain't friendly – but some are more offensive than others. There are some you can pick up, carefully, gingerly, and they won't strike or bite. But others, you can't get near 'em – rattlers are that way. But there's no snake I wouldn't approach, though. Cobras, mind – cobras are . . . unpredictable.'

He starts to enumerate encounters with cobras in which he came off worse. They are meticulously catalogued. Bite Number 26: 'Thailand cobra. I was trying to throw it off balance to catch it and it sort of went against the wind.' It got Bill on the forearm, leaving eight clear fang marks and putting him in hospital, eventually in an iron lung for two days. 'Bite Number 33: king cobra, 1962. Fourteen foot long and able to deliver thirty drops of venom at a go, enough to kill thirty men. A clever boxer . . . shifting stare . . . he got me just above the knuckle of my right index finger. It happened so fast, nobody thought I was hit.' He agreed to go to hospital, mainly because everyone at the Serpentarium was in such a state – his wife had been describing the process to the visitors and a photographer had been present to record the cobra's strike. Even so, Bill had never liked too much fuss to attend these 'incidents'. 'When I was bitten, I *guess* it affected me, and I'd get to a clinic – and then we'd sit outside, just to see how it was going to develop. And if it was serious, I'd go in. But if it didn't seem too bad, we'd go back home.'

This time, Bite Number 33, the king cobra's reputation spurred things along a bit. Although its venom is slightly less lethal than that of its common cousins, it delivers so much more. After mild swelling and few obvious signs of trouble, suddenly Bill's entire system nearly ground to a halt and his pulse disappeared. He was pumped full of antivenom, then cortisone, and for several hours appeared to be dying. Then his blood pressure improved, and within half an hour he felt 'recovered'. He went home, and twenty-four hours after his mauling was back extracting venom from cobras. One of his doctors at the hospital remarked that if he was back at work, maybe the bite didn't so much affect his body as his mind . . .

And in one way it had: it had convinced Bill that he had achieved 'immunity'. Half a century ago, much less was known about the extreme complexity of venom and the widely varying effects of a bite. Different species, human reaction, size of snake and amount of poison all contribute to a complex picture. Nevertheless, Bill felt that at the Serpentarium they were dealing with something very potent, and in the early fifties he supplied venom to the University of Miami during the intense hunt for a vaccine against poliomyelitis. The experiments were encouraging, but when the successful

Salk vaccine appeared the trials involving venom were abandoned. However, his own blood has been used successfully to treat acute cases of snake bite in others: after a dramatic flight to the bedside of a critically ill boy in Venezuela who had been bitten by a coral snake, a pint of Bill's blood was pumped in and the patient recovered consciousness. The next day the country made him an honorary citizen. Considering that an estimated 5 million snake bites occur worldwide every year, and over a hundred thousand people die, there is an obvious need for antivenom. However, there are still precious few sources of venom for medical use – no one has yet found a way to 'milk' a snake without risk.

I watch Bill move around his house – a little stiff now, but a slim healthy-looking man, with extraordinarily smooth skin and few wrinkles. His good head of hair is not completely grey and he has a healthy appetite, according to Nancy, who fuels him with an enormous sandwich mid-morning. As his third wife she inevitably had to acquire snakes along with marriage. The Serpentarium was hard work but, along with the sale of venom to pharmaceutical companies, gave them a good lifestyle. She seems *almost* content with so much snakiness, happily informing me that she still responds to calls from Florida neighbours when something ripples into their backyard. Armed with a snake hook ('Bill's hands won't let him do it, so I suppose it's up to me . . .'), she will go and relieve hysterical families of their unwanted guest, pop it in a case and find it another home in the wild. She had picked me up in her scarlet Rolls Royce Corniche, lovingly cared for and utterly superior to all other traffic, a status reinforced by Nancy's regal driving diagonally across a many-laned highway.

'It's true,' she admits, 'I'm not the world's *greatest* snake enthusiast, but I'm an *admirer* of snakes and their qualities. Our purpose in having them was for what the venom can do. It's not picking up the snake for the snake's sake at all, and not because you like them. In fact, if anything we have a terrible conscience about having had to use so many animals, keeping them against their will. For whatever good purpose, it's on our conscience.'

After they had sold the Serpentarium (not one of his three children wanted to inherit it) and ended up at Punta Gorda, they landscaped their small estate to include a huge snake pit where they could raise rattlesnakes and still supply venom. 'Part of the reason we had the special propagation area to raise the rattlesnakes was because it was enjoyable to see the animals in their natural environment – they were free.' Most people would not have a rattlesnake pit near the back door, but, just like her husband, Nancy doesn't countenance the idea that it's dangerous.

'It's a matter of knowing the animal, knowing that they're terrified. I mean, we loom so much larger than them and they're scared to death – so we have to respect the power they have and that they will try to defend themselves. And we have to work with them in a way that distresses them the very least. It's just a matter of understanding the basic nature – like working with sharks. Just a matter of respect and familiarity. Because most people don't understand them. I sympathise with snakes – they're so maligned, and we think of them as the lowest link in the chain of life. They may not be wise – but they're clever.' We drive past the pit which is now empty, for the Haasts are thinking of moving nearer the coast. I have to admit that I'm not overly disappointed not to see several hundred rattlesnakes, even if they were deliriously contented and happy in their pit, while Nancy mowed the grass round them.

Bill doesn't miss them too much. He has never seen snakes as pets and doesn't even have much affection for them. He is intrigued and impressed and at times in awe of them – and still longs to know what their venom might do for us. Antivenom for polio, arthritis, multiple sclerosis, lupus – there's a lengthy wish-list of conditions for which he believes snakes might hold some of the answers. He is aware that in his long life he has not been formally educated, and that if you become famous for working with snakes you are labelled a showman. However, you can't argue that he is not a long-living example of a healthy human being, claiming never to have had a cold or flu or any serious disease. Apart from the occasional trip to the edge of death, thanks to a snake, and the subsequent intensive care, he says he has never taken any medicine, not even an aspirin. He laughs a lot – and has enjoyed life.

I ask him why he took such a dangerous, snake-strewn path. In the name of what?

He answers immediately: 'Venom production for venom research – and *I* produced it. I've been giving myself venom from over thirty-two species since 1948. When I reach a hundred – and that's not far off and I still feel the same – it will have been proven to me that the venom's had a good deal to do with it.'

I asked the question, 'You do this in the name of what?' to draw out the reason for doing dangerous work.

I asked it of people who clearly want a challenge, an adventure. Also those who have a sense of duty or professionalism; and others with humanitarian ideals, together with people for whom a faith is enough. Everyone I asked 'In the name of what?' responded eagerly. They all knew why they did their work.

3

The Food Taster

It could be argued that knowingly courting danger is not good for you. However, dig out the statistics on dangerous jobs and the World Health Organisation will tell you that sheer physical inactivity kills about 2 million of us every year. So doing nothing is not an option. I encountered energy, enthusiasm, satisfaction and joy when I listened to stories of danger experienced and danger dealt with. For all these people, it was worth going into danger. But curiously, what is probably the most dangerous job in the world stands in class of its own. It doesn't require any of the motivation evident in all of the other jobs I explored. Indeed, motivation of *any* kind is truly lacking in those who have had to take up such work, with the possible exception of an unthinking and even self-sacrificing sense of duty. It is work for which you cannot train, nor can you take precautions. You won't have chosen or volunteered to do it – you have probably been coerced. There's no excitement to be had, only fear. And it's work which is literally a poisoned chalice. But unlike Bill Haast, who knows perfectly well that the snake he's holding is lethal, the food-taster can only ponder about the poison which might be on the plate in front of him.

A Short History of Food Tasting
Yum yum.
Aaaaaaaargh . . .
The End.

Despite the above, it's one of the world's older professions. Nor is it exclusively a tale of medieval banquets and ancient crones grinding up weird roots and leaves to pop into the goblets of kings. George W. Bush, Saddam Hussein and the members of any up-to-date list of the Rich and Powerful play their part.

It's worth defining in modern terms why a food taster's job is so dangerous: it seems that risk assessment, so beloved of the Health and Safety experts, can't really cope with it. Food tasting sneaks further up the scale into the lethal zone known as direct hazard assessment. You're not looking at the *likelihood* of something nasty happening. Your experience counts for very little. And you're not *speculating* on the outcome. You either taste and live, or it's your last dinner.

Let me make it clear that we are a world away from the tasting that occurs in the modern food industry, which only has consumers on its mind. The more traditional tasters have always had poisoners and assassins in their thoughts. The earliest references appear in ancient literature and religious texts. Even the innocuous-sounding 'cup-bearer' who appears frequently in the Bible would not have held the position merely to ornament his master's household. He would have been a trusted servant, the guardian of the drink, preventing others from slipping a little something into it – and usually expected to take a good sip before setting it before his boss.

The Greek Republicans, the Imperial Chinese and the Romans all had leaders who feared that death would come not on the battlefield but at the table. Powerful men could surround themselves with bodyguards, avoid the public, pass draconian laws, wear armour and make frequent sacrifices to the gods – but every one of them had to eat. So someone would be given the food-tasting post – or have it forced on them, more likely. The only alternative was not very satisfactory: give your dinner to the dog. Sadly, this was not foolproof: many a dog turns up his nose at fillet steak in favour of some rubbish lying about on the floor. Additionally, some dogs will bolt anything and none has yet mastered the art of saying to his master, 'Well, I ate it, but it tasted very funny' . . . before disappearing to a distant corner of the garden and turning up his toes three hours later.

Having money and influence at least enabled the fearful to try to seek out possible precautions in addition to the hapless taster. Over a thousand years ago, Chinese emperors lit upon the very modern idea of 'choice': provide so many dishes at each meal and the assassin gets little inkling of which will be set before the great man. On the other hand, it was the Chinese who came up with the cunning twist to the poisoner's modus operandi: never mind the food on the plate – why not embed something dangerous in the plate itself? A nation well versed in the art of porcelain didn't find it difficult to make crockery which released something deadly when hot food was placed on it. Later from the seventeenth century, Qing dynasty emperors put small silver pieces into their food, convinced that these would change colour on contact with poison. This proved to be unreliable, so the emperors fell back on the food-tasting system, deciding that they could lose a court eunuch or two. But even in the early twentieth century the Dowager Empress Cixi, renowned for her cunning and suspicion as the long reign of Imperial China came to its end, was still putting her faith in silver: a complete dining set survives with silver spoons and chopsticks 'for the detection of poison by the Empress' food taster'. And she too had continued the tradition of confusion – demanding 108 dishes to be prepared for every meal.

Should your modern host grandly bring in the entrée on a salver, just remember that it dates from the use of a silver dish at the Spanish court and was intended to 'salva' or protect you from unpleasant consequences. All this assumes that you trust the cutlery as well: eat at the Persian court two millennia earlier and you would have been unwise to accept a slice of meat carved by the queen – carved with a knife edged with poison. This was a little trick the Medicis revived in Italy in the sixteenth century – for a slice of delicious cake for their rivals.

You could always wear the odd charm or amulet to ward off ill effects: toads suffered disproportionately for several centuries, due to firm beliefs in their magic properties. Swelter'd venom of toad may have been fine for Shakespeare's witches' potion, but 'stone of toad' – a calcified lump found nestling in the unfortunate creature's stomach – was thought to be of great value in combating poison. Mary Queen of Scots kept 'a little silver bottle containing a stone medicinable against poison'. Her great adversary, Queen Elizabeth I, elected for a different approach, regularly dosing herself with antidotes and having all her many gloves and handkerchiefs minutely inspected for traces of poison. And she could also afford, and was expected to have, a food taster.

Make it to the end of the meal, having survived the food, the tableware and the cutlery, and you might relax for a moment and toast your success. You would be well advised to have brought your rhino-horn drinking vessel with you: prized for various reasons, it was once thought excellent for neutralising toxins – though you would probably have been sold it with the claim that a fabulous unicorn had been de-horned. King Louis XIV, not trusting everyone who dined at the French court, had an 'Officer of the Goblet' to take the first gulp. It might be wise, therefore, to clink glasses with your neighbour before you drink. Clink energetically, so that wine spills and mingles in the two vessels, and you would be following in the tradition of the Borgias' guests in Renaissance Italy, who were extremely wary of hospitality from the princes of the poisoning world. Whether or not Lucrezia, Cesare and their kin were as murderous as history paints them, their reputation as the worst-ever dinner party hosts has never deserted them. But it wasn't all one-way. Even the Borgia pope, Alexander VI, was despatched in dubious circumstances involving a cardinal and a box of sweetmeats.

So if a pope can fail to make it to the end of the meal – and two others went the same way – it is perhaps not surprising that one of the institutions still having a food taster on its payroll at the start of the twentieth century was the Vatican. In the late 1960s, during major reform of the papal court, it stated that the office of food taster 'had been vacant for years' – but then omitted to mention the job in the list of posts to be abolished. So now it's merely assumed that there's no one answering to the description of Papal Taster in the Vatican. However, if there is he's not alone in the modern world.

Kings and emperors are in shorter supply these days – but tyrants, dictators and all-round monsters continue to proliferate. And as ever, although they surround themselves with armed guards, electronic fences and surveillance cameras they still need to eat.

The two horrors of the twentieth century, Hitler and Stalin, both feared being poisoned, part of their near-paranoid lack of trust in those closest to them. The Russian dictator also had a huge appetite – something of a disadvantage, particularly for the frightened men who used to taste his food. Hitler's suspicious nature was more on show when he travelled abroad – often an awkward situation for those who do not want to advertise the elaborate precautions which protect them at home. For refusing food, or just questioning its goodness, is one of the oldest insults. Hospitality, sharing whatever little is in the larder, is one of the great gestures of civilised life. Even leaving food on the side of the plate, pleading satiety, is unacceptable in many cultures. Handing it on to a minion to test it – well, how rude can you get?

Hitler and Stalin got away with it, because they belonged to an era when private lives remained resolutely private. However, as more recent world leaders have increasingly had their public activity minutely scrutinised the scope for a spot of tasting has shrunk. It has become harder to keep eccentric behaviour under wraps, especially at international gatherings. TV crews, reporters and feature writers poke their noses into the most interesting places they can find – and kitchens and dining rooms are always good for a story.

Absolute dictators who don't like travel fare rather better, but these days there are few in that category. One of them, though, manages to generate lurid stories. Kim Jong Il of North Korea rules a country of wretched drabness and oppressive ideology. His cult is everywhere, as even the smallest children are taught to revere and love the 'Dear Leader'. Tales of famine and poverty have been common. So has the Dear Leader had to tighten his belt and live on plain food? According to one reliable source he shows all the signs of being a party animal – and not in the political sense. And guess who uses silver chopsticks? Not, as some observers have thought, as a mark of ostentation, but in the old belief that prodding a nice fat freshly boiled lobster with silver will ensure that it's fit to eat. He's reportedly fond of lobsters. And Hennessy VSOP cognac. He is also big on banquets, though not a word to his hungry citizens. The source for this seditious stuff is his chef for thirteen years until 2005, a Japanese not keen to have his name publicised, and referred to as Fujimoto.

He had been taken on because of Kim's liking for sushi. Tuna, eel and sea urchin were his favourites, along with boiled giblets and steamed abalone with wine. The chef travelled to Japan to buy fresh fish – and everything he brought back was checked by the 'poison tasters'. Even the rice was inspected and tested – grain by grain. However, he was only following his father, the 'Great Leader', Kim Il Sung, who had clearly been bothered by the idea of nasty germs and ill-intentioned people and used to make all diplomats scrub their hands with disinfectant before they met him. His food tasters were always on hand, though they clearly failed to keep him on top form as he died with a grapefruit-sized growth on the back of his neck. No one ever mentioned this – their own death would have ensued.

So, having given an insight into the Dear Leader's private life (naked women, drunken pranks, platform shoes and bouffant hair to boost his minute stature), and with due regard to the perilous nature of serving the Kims, Fujimoto is now in hiding in Japan, fearing that his revelations will lead to assassination. Revealing that your master lives hedonistically in a land of deprivation is one thing. Saying that he needs his food to be tasted for poison when the entire nation is meant to adore him is another.

Romania's late President Ceaucescu, who had that discomfiting habit of being horrible to his people but nice to dogs, owned a black labrador. Originally called Gladstone, it had been given to him by the former British Liberal leader, David Steel, and came from his own labrador's litter. Ceaucescu renamed it Corbu – Raven – and grew so fond of the creature that he promoted it to the rank of colonel in the Romanian army. The dog then acquired its own house, a telephone, a TV and a motorcade – presumably for inspecting military manoeuvres – and streets were closed as its car swished down the streets of Bucharest.

However, all dogs must eat, regardless of rank, and the labrador was given its own taster, a doctor. My colleague John Sweeney was told by a maid at one of the many official residences that the dog's dinner was cooked and brought to the bowl wrapped in clingfilm just in case something was slipped into it. Spaghetti Bolognese and sausages were favourites on the menu, supplemented with Winalot and dog biscuits sent in the diplomatic bag by the Romanian ambassador in London, who had the task of making the weekly trip to Sainsbury's. The doctor dutifully tucked into the meat (always best-quality, often steak) and the Winalot and biscuits.

Munching Col. Labrador's bowlful might possibly have been accompanied by slightly less angst and apprehension than that experienced by the President's own tasters. There were many who served in that post during Ceaucescu's long and unpleasant rule, and they seemed to lack the status of Corbu's man. I was assured by many people I spoke to in Romania that at least one, or perhaps two, are still alive. However, I couldn't locate either of them. And the more I enquired, the more I was told that anyone who was prepared to admit that they had been instrumental in keeping the old beast alive (the President, not the dog) was likely to get a hard time from rather a lot of people.

At Christmastime in 1989 I was handed a video in the chaos and darkness of Bucharest's TV station. I never saw who gave it to me, but managed to find a local technician who stuck it into a machine. Up came pictures of an elderly pair meeting their end at the hands of an informal firing squad. It was the President and his wife. The sensational emotion which coursed round the TV building underlined the fear that had permeated the whole country for years. Fear of having your village bulldozed, fear of being forced to bear five children (abortion, birth control and divorce having being banned), fear of arbitrary arrest, of torture, of the omnipresent secret police, of another mad idea worming its way out of the brain of the appalling Ceaucescu.

Nevertheless, had his miserable citizens been allowed near him they would have also seen their President's fears: horror of most things foreign – especially foreign people. Ceaucescu was convinced that foreigners might try to kill him, so he developed an aversion to shaking hands in the belief that they might infect him with some fatal disease. He made one exception when abroad, having received an honorary knighthood from the Queen at Buckingham Palace. But as soon as possible he raced off to wash his hands with alcohol. He had also brought his own bedlinen to the palace. Why he didn't expect the aforementioned labrador puppy (very foreign) to explode or deliver a dose of anthrax has never been explained. . . .

On this occasion any unpleasantness over food seems to have been avoided, or at least a matter of No Comment. But from his earliest days in power Ceaucescu travelled with a taster, though in most instances, mindful of international incidents involving hospitality, the Presidential Sampler managed to operate relatively discreetly. However, in the mid-seventies the Hungarian leader Janos Kadar offered lunch to Ceaucescu during a visit to repair rather strained relations between the two countries. A dish was placed in front of the guest, whereupon the Romanian taster emerged like a jack-in-the-box from behind his President and dug his fork into the food. The Hungarians were appalled. Official talks followed – inevitably still rather strained – and the Hungarians had a little brood about the insult. At dinner, as another delicious plateful appeared in front of Ceaucescu, Kadar lunged forward and swapped the dish for his own. International stand-offs don't usually occur at the dinner table, but the Hungarians glared their way to victory this time, with Ceaucescu's taster caught between a rock and a hard place, unable to work out where he should stick his fork.

Not that this cured the President of his little habits. He managed to appal the Greeks a few years later, arriving at the Hotel Grande Bretagne in Athens accompanied by two food tasters – plus three doctors and two ambulances.

Cuba's Fidel Castro probably likes his cigars more than this food. It's muttered that someone who likes beans with everything *needs* a food taster. However, it has to be realised that the American CIA have tried to finish him off so many times, in so many ways – the exploding cigar, the poison pills in tea and coffee, the bacteria in the handkerchief, the plot to put fungus in the diving suit (aborted), never mind the bullets, the bombs, the toxic gas and the syringe full of poison posing as a ballpoint pen – that he'd be wise to take precautions.

At a Caribbean summit in the early 1990s, with prime ministers and presidents sitting down to dine, there were the usual special dietary requirements of powerful men. But one delegate made a specific request, no doubt needing fuel for one of his legendary nine-hours speeches. Castro would like flying fish and cou cou, came the message. No big deal – traditional Caribbean and the national dish of Barbados.

Large kitchens are tense places at the best of times, and just as the temperature was rising the crowded space was augmented with a delegation of 'special people': quiet Cuban gentlemen who didn't introduce themselves, and their interpreter. They were all very interested in flying fish. First, they wanted to see the bills for its purchase. Who had supplied it? Where had it come from? Then they wanted to know how it was to be prepared. All the ingredients had to be lined up for inspection: the fish – to be poached in white wine with a little onion and dill; then the cou cou – a mixture of cornmeal and okra. The little team followed the chef around the kitchen, tasting at every stage of cooking. Just a nibble, a savouring, a pause – and a thumbs up.

Needing to go to the loo, the chef found the team there, checking it out. (The Americans, who also had a VIP delegate, didn't bother with the loos – they had posted sharp-shooters on the hotel roof. It all depends on where you think the threat lies . . .) The flying fish and cou cou were assembled and presented: a final nibble, nibble, and the plate was whisked through. Later, back came the comment: 'Delicious – he really did like it.' The chef was thankful, but left wondering what kind of threat the loos presented.

At least Castro's tasters demonstrated a confidence that any toxic substance would show itself instantly. Here lies a major hurdle for all tasters – especially those with impatient and hungry masters. Much has been made over the years of slow-acting poisons, delivered in tiny doses, but accumulating in the body and finally having lethal effect. Assassination, though, tends to demand a quick result – otherwise the coup or the power struggle gets muddled and delayed by a lingering exit. And you don't want doctors ruining your efforts by having time to find the antidote. Even so, only a few poisons produce the spectacular thud on to the tablecloth just moments after having touched the lips. Most people's digestive systems take a little time to realise that they've been invaded by a fatal dose. This begs the question: what's the point of tasting the dainty dish *just before* it's set before the king?

Trying to discover whether paranoid dictators, or men whose opinions are set in iron, or those who are universally mistrustful, ever have meaningful discussions with tasters on the subject of methodology is something of a challenge. Actually, it's not. It's near impossible. Secrecy, embarrassment, today's obsession with 'security' – all conspire to shroud the details in mystery. On the other hand, common sense and history would suggest that tasters are traditionally expected by their employers to keel over loyally within an unreasonably short time.

One man who did put some thought to the matter was the founder of modern Turkey, Kemal Ataturk. He died relatively young in 1938, aged fifty-eight. However, he had been wounded thirteen times in battle and survived numerous assassination attempts before finally succumbing to cirrhosis of the liver – caused undeniably by his convivial private life: all-night dancing and drinking and smoking rather adds to the pressure of running a country. But even though he delivered a secular, progressive nation out of the ruins of the old Ottoman Empire, he clung to the very traditional Turkish habit of using a food taster. Unusually, his administration was relatively open about it: the post was official and paid $15,000 for what was described as 'fifteen minutes' work per day'. Mohammed Mouhi tasted all the food and drink intended for his master – but with one caveat: after tasting, the whole meal was placed in a hotplate for *one hour* while Mouhi was observed. If he didn't die, then the meal was served. It's hard to know whether this cut down the risk substantially, or merely offered a little extra reassurance to the great man. Though it does suggest that Ataturk, for all his vision and influence, never had a really hot meal in his presidential life.

Mouhi survived his employer. A man named Kamel Hana did not – but for all the wrong reasons. Life in the presidential circle surrounding Saddam Hussein in Iraq could be short, brutish and terrifying. Curiously, for all his supposed toughness Saddam shared with Ceaucescu the weirder aspects of personal fear: he was a scaredy-puss about germs. But Saddam, as in most aspects of dictatorship, was a cut above Ceaucescu's obsession with shaking hands. Even before a delegation got to see him, he was taking precautions. He had his own military advisers stripped down to their underwear so that their clothes could be washed, ironed and X-rayed. Eventually he took to having people X-rayed, believing they might have a stomach full of explosives. How he thought they might be detonated has never been explained. At least Ceaucescu only fussed about his own apparel, putting a special guard to watch over an isolated storage area for his clothes – he wasn't going to have anyone impregnate them with poison, thus rendering his very skin vulnerable. It's not clear where he got this idea from. Perhaps he read scary Transylvanian fairy tales as a child.

Saddam Hussein had a more up-to date approach: apart from the X-ray machines, he got his country's nuclear scientists to investigate deliveries of choice imported lobster for traces of radiation. You never can tell with lobsters – they change colour rather dramatically on boiling – and one can only presume that Saddam thought they glowed rather too red at times. In common with the Chinese emperors he employed the confusion technique, owning a number of palaces across the land and having meals prepared in them simultaneously to baffle any would-be poisoner.

And, of course, he had a taster – thought to be the son of his chef. A neat bit of thinking – the father would have to risk dispatching his own son if he served tainted food.

This was the kind of logic natural to Iraq's ruling family: a number of relatives were on the receiving end of his murderous wrath, and even the nearest and dearest only survived because they shared his cunning. His two sons, Uday and Qusay, were chips off the old block: violent, mean and frightening, though they appear to have missed out on what passed for unctuous greasy charm in the old man.

The tale of the food taster's demise crawled out in an atmosphere of fear and whispered horror. As a result there are several versions, embellished by the kind of details which are added when no one dares tell the truth. But the central story is traditional enough: a woman, an affair and family feuding, ending in theatrical violence. Kamel Hana had been with Saddam and his clan for many years; to say he was trusted would probably be taking it too far – such a quality hardly existed in the Tikriti clan, whose jealousy and in-fighting thinned their ranks regularly. However, he had the title of food taster and was seen at many functions carrying out his task. He was not a young man and Saddam used him for various personal tasks, including the classic function of go-between in matters of the heart – or possibly just matters of sex. At some point in the late 1980s, one particular name was whispered more frequently – the ex-wife of the former chairman of Iraqi airways and a member of an important Baghdad family. It would seem she had become Saddam's mistress.

This reached the ears of Uday, the elder son, who already had an impressive record for beating to death anyone to whom he took a dislike. To say he was furious probably does not do justice to his mood – his rages were spoken of with awe, and witnessed by people who were wise enough not to use words such as 'disturbed' or 'homicidal'. His rage appears to have arisen from a sense that his mother had been insulted – though it is hard to gauge what constituted insulting behaviour in Saddam's family. But even Uday had enough instinct to know that attacking his father might be inadvisable. So he sought out the man who had facilitated the meetings with the mistress: his father's confidant, the food taster, who was attending a diplomatic reception on an island in the River Tigris, hosted for the Egyptians by the Iraqi vice-president.

Into this formal gathering of grandees, ambassadors and foreign VIPS nibbling their canapés barged Uday and his henchmen. Uday either used a baseball bat and clubbed Kamel Hana to death, or beat him with a piece of wood, jumped on his spine and crushed his skull, or battered him with a stick and then stabbed him with a handy electric carving knife from the buffet table. Whatever version, murder most foul occurred in front of a large number of people. Who did nothing but stare as Uday wiped away some spots of blood and left to attend another party.

Responses in the family were typically extreme, from matter-of-fact (it was nothing new, after-all) to a sentence of death. Eventually Uday was put on a plane to Switzerland – whereupon he promptly drew a gun in a nightclub and was arrested. After his arrival back in Baghdad the talk in the bazaars was that his father had welcomed him with the words: 'That's my boy!' It may not be true, but at least it's in character. And of course the food taster was quickly replaced – though there's no record of anyone *applying* for the position.

It might be thought that in the modern world the opportunities for food tasters are in decline. Surely we are now, with a few notable exceptions, more democratic, more sophisticated, and such work should be banished to the realms of the crude assassin and medieval superstition? The more benign modern leaders – the popes, the Japanese emperor, the Jordanian royal family have all abolished the post in living memory. Nevertheless, references occur rather more frequently than might be expected, even at a UN summit in South Africa in 2002. And then there are the Americans.

Usually a forthcoming nation in publicising their president's health, his food preferences, even what the First Dog has in his bowl, the Americans are coy about food tasting. Information leaks out via the traditional sense of insult, when a host's hospitality is questioned. And being sniffy about French food is tantamount to declaring war, especially if you are President Ronald Reagan and are being offered the finest cuisine the nation can provide.

Gastronomic rage growled through the French press when Reagan arrived at the Palace of Versailles. Perhaps the French should have been warned that the former actor put no great store by exquisite menus: this was a man whose favourite meal was pot roast, macaroni cheese and custard flan. The first inkling that all might not be to the liking of the White House corps was the replacement of bottles of French water with American supplies brought from Air Force 1. Then the French chefs were asked to retire to the pantry as a special team inspected the kitchens. Eventually two food tasters, members of the Secret Service, insisted on sampling everything intended for the President, having no qualms in explaining that Mr Reagan wouldn't eat anything that hadn't first been tasted. The chefs headed out for a little chat with the press, stating proudly, 'Our own president has no food tasters. He trusts French food.'

More frosty moments were in store across the Channel at Windsor Castle. The Secret Service advance party had already checked out the seating arrangements, the helicopter landing pad, the press centre facilities – and the light bulbs. Suggestions that Nancy Reagan should have breakfast in the Queen's private quarters, that the castle's shrubbery be lit to look like a Hollywood backdrop, and that armed presidential bodyguards might lurk in every cupboard – and in the Queen's car – had already been quashed. Perhaps mindful of the contretemps at Versailles, the Queen's chef had already put down a few markers. The American special inspection team arrived – four of them, designated 'food coordinators'. It swiftly became clear that they were not going to be allowed to interfere with the royal kitchen routine. All domestic arrangements, announced Buckingham Palace, would be looked after by Royal Household staff. The Americans made worried noises. The Palace went deaf. It doesn't 'do' food tasters.

George W. Bush, on the other hand, doesn't 'do' foreign food. And he and his staff are not embarrassed to admit it, saying, 'He's a little suspicious of such things.' Although he hails from an extremely wealthy family, George W.'s tastes are Main Street USA: hot dogs, burgers and presumably a lot of ketchup. Noses have been frequently wrinkled in the White House at the notion of providing 'fancy dining' for visiting heads of state. But he, too, found the British Royal Family hugely unamused when it came to a banquet given by the Queen in 2003. There was much speculation that the usual huge armoured motorcade would contain the requisite number of 'food coordinators'. Menus had been planned and discussed, wines chosen and meticulous preparations made to measure precise spacings for plate and cutlery and glasses. The press enquired about 'special arrangements'. Buckingham Palace replied, 'There is no formal procedure for food tasting. The inhouse help is fully vetted.' And that would seem to be that. Until the night of the banquet, when several men arrived in the kitchens and identified themselves as the 'nutritional inspection team'. Silent consternation was broken by a senior member of the Household saying, in firm and precise tones, 'Her Majesty will be pleased to have this food and so will *everyone* else.' The 'inspection team' slunk off.

Help may be on hand, though. Rather than have a human food taster hanging around tables and kitchens rather obviously, the Thai government has come up with a more discreet solution: get yourself a tasting-mouse. Shortly after his perilous dining experience in London, Mr Bush travelled to Thailand for the summit of Pacific Rim nations. The Thais were insistent that all due precautions should be observed – they were also hosting Vladimir Putin of Russia, President Hu Jintao of China and the Prime Minister of Japan, and the poisoning business has often featured in the history of their nations. Time to send for the mice: ten splendid rodents selected for being 'particularly healthy' and apparently with a track record of analysing food in poisoning scares in schools. Samples of the dishes planned for the heads of state were to be fed to the mice under laboratory conditions; and some food would be 'injected into their intraperitoneal cavity'. Something which even Ceaucescu and Saddam held back from. . . .

The mice go some way to solving the problem of time, because their small bodies are likely to react much faster. Arsenic would probably do for them within seconds, thought Mr Somsong, the director general of the Health Ministry's medical sciences department. 'Bacterial poisoning, though, might take up to fifteen minutes to affect them.' A great improvement on Kemal Ataturk's hour-long wait.

Everyone survived the summit, including the mice, and the Chinese went home to introduce the mice to the Beijing Olympics. So now we know what to look for – not the shadowy nervous figure hovering near the plate, but the little squeaking cage under the table.

Food tasters have figured just behind the world's most powerful people for over two thousand years, but it's a measure of the job's dangerous nature that there are virtually no memoirs describing the work. Either you died in the execution of your duties, or you lived in fear of disclosing your real feelings. Your very closeness to the king or president may have marked you down for retribution from those resentful that you played even an unwilling part in keeping a monster alive. And these days, the modern obsession with security means that officials who might throw light on the job work in anonymity and obscurity. As a result, the public remains as ignorant about their leaders' personal fears as any medieval peasant about his emperor. Nor have the rules of hospitality changed. There is still awkwardness and embarrassment, perhaps even an 'international incident' when precautions are revealed which show one head of state to be less than trustful of another. Refusing food is probably the monopoly of billionaires who own successful football teams: Roman Abramovic, the Russian owner of Chelsea FC, has minders who bring his food with them.

One small wheeze that the powerful now employ is the simple precaution of the buffet meal: the favourite form of dining amongst the Middle East's emirs and sultans – and also with President Clinton and his Secret Service minders. It's the Chinese confusion factor updated: who knows which dish you may select from? The poisoner is faced with a dilemma: risk killing everyone, or give up?

And because all of us must eat and drink, there's no automatic sympathy for someone who thinks it may be lethal to do so. What's the alternative? Starvation – or a food taster. Not an option for an ordinary citizen. And in the ordinary scheme of things, there are few reasons why any of us should associate eating a meal with danger: wielding a knife and fork is hardly an act of bravery. In the end, if you haven't spoken to someone who has been made to eat dinner simply *because* it may be poisoned, it's hard to imagine what it must be like and to realise that it's probably the most dangerous job in existence.

To hear from lips which have food-tasted 'for real' would suggest a long wait in a graveyard. Those who survive dictators tend to go into hiding, unwilling to justify their job. Those who serve modern presidents merely claim anonymity and then deny their calling. However, an inkling of what it might be like comes from an elderly retainer in a princely household – where 'duty' now means being part of the maharajah's tourist business, but for his forebears used to mean risking everything at mealtimes.

I went to meet a delightful elderly gentleman whom I first glimpsed bearing two flaming torches in a castle in Rajasthan in India. Mathura Prasad is now in his ninth decade, a handsome man who dresses traditionally with a splendid turban. He spends his evenings demonstrating a stately 'fire dance' for the tourists who come to Mandawa, an enchanting reminder of the wealth and power of princely India.

The castle has turrets and marble floors and roof terraces which overlook the town and distant villages that all used to be part of the thakur's, or maharajah's, fiefdom. There are marvellous portraits of men in elaborate costumes, swords in scarlet scabbards, and photographs of men in impressive turbans wearing gold jackets and much jewellery. Independence from Britain, followed by the actions of Prime Minister Indira Gandhi, removed much of the old system of titled local rulers, but as elsewhere they adapt and survive. Mandawa still has its maharajah, although he runs the family castle as a hotel. And his fire dancer used to work for his father – as a food taster, the third generation to serve in the post.

Mathura Prasad's son translated for his own father, who was thoughtful and reserved, still the courtier – or, at least, the very loyal traditional servant.

'My father looked after the Maharajah Jai Singh, and he even went away to college with him. He was a *personal* servant, so he dressed him and was always with him. I followed on, and always worked for the royal family – our lives were together. I was very close to the family – treated as one of them, in fact. Wherever they went, I went. I was always interested in food and I liked cooking. Therefore I had the privilege of working in the kitchen – which was important. Only certain servants were allowed to work there. Indeed, there were guards round the kitchen. The food was always brought from the kitchen with a cloth over each dish, and I was there to see that no one popped anything extra into the pot or interfered with it. Then I put the cloth over it and went with it to the dining table.

'There was a special room in the palace for ceremonial dresses; and I had to look after the jewelled cufflinks and all the many gold buttons. We travelled all over India in such style, to many palaces of princes and maharajahs and thakurs. But I always stayed close. That was what was expected, especially when food was prepared. And we always took our own cooks with us – along with the drivers and bearers and guards, of course! Our own cook supervised the food, wherever we went, and only our Maharajah's servants were allowed into the kitchen. You couldn't have anyone there who wasn't a member of his household. So often the plates were huge, when there were grand people dining: enormous platters heaped with mutton and rice and vegetables and chapatis and so many good things. Then there were wonderful sweets, with so much milk and rice. The food was always good.

'Before I tasted, some of each dish would be fed to a dog. Only then did I taste – I wanted to know that it was cooked right, because I cared about food. Then the guards also tasted, before it went to the table under armed escort. Important military men also tasted before the Maharajah – and if there were an important guest, my Maharajah would exchange bits of each dish with him. Just in case.

44

And if the Maharajah thought something tasted a little odd then I ate it, immediately. I did it out of loyalty.'

Mathura didn't elaborate on his fears or feelings: as far as he was concerned, devotion to duty and closeness to the family were everything. He comes from an ancient tradition and never thought to question the duties he inherited from his father. That the work might be dangerous was of no consequence to him. Life can be risky, he reckoned, and this was just one aspect of it. Anyway, his eyes lit up when talking about the tasty dishes. If your work as a servant involved eating such pleasurable food, intended for royalty, what was there to complain about? And then all the people they visited also had food tasters. It seemed natural and quite unremarkable. And he thought his Maharajah a splendid man.

'I don't think he had enemies here in Mandawa. But everyone has enemies, and this was an important family. Important people are separate, different. So we went on with the tradition. And the Maharajah liked my family. So we were happy.'

This was a world of tremendous splendour. Even the smallest palaces in the princely states tried to deliver as much glamour and show as possible. Moderation and restraint were not part of the tradition. What you wore, how you dined, how you celebrated public occasions: it was a glorious spectacle of colour and opulence, a parade of magnificent materials, gold and jewels. Underpinning this was a horde of servants, and I asked Mathura how many there had been in the castle. He thought back to his youth and estimated that there might have been a hundred in Mandawa, attending to the needs of quite a small royal family.

His master's son hooted with laughter when I mentioned this. The present Maharajah has a much more precise memory: 'We had *at least* four hundred servants – he probably didn't remember the camel keepers, the stable-hands, the horsemen, the gardeners. . . .' Thakur Devi Singh is every inch a maharajah: confident, outgoing and intending to live up to the family motto: 'The brave shall inherit the earth.' He's a full-time hotelier now, but even as we were talking a car-load of villagers arrived with a local dispute which they expected him to solve.

The world of his childhood was very much the old India, but he recalled it with much enthusiasm.

'Mathura's father and mother came to Mandawa along with my grandmother when she came here to get married. They were servants in her family. Mathura's whole family moved here with her, so he grew up in Mandawa. We were a small family – my grandfather and grandmother, my father and uncle and my mother and aunt, and we small children – with all those servants. We had horses stabled here and we had a farm as well. Every evening my grandfather insisted we go on "compulsory riding". There was a bit of hunting – not much, mainly partridges and rabbits, and I'd go out on a camel, sometimes in a Jeep.

'We didn't have an awful lot of guests, but at that time there were perhaps only four or five cars in the whole town, so if we were on the castle battlements in the evening and spotted headlights in the distance we knew we'd got guests and had to get the servants busy. Mind you, we were quite organised – my grandfather got electricity here before they did in Jaipur. And we provided street lights as well. But the electricity only went on at sunset, and was off promptly at 10 p.m.

'We looked after the welfare of a large number of villages round about, and we still have responsibilities now. We still command respect in this area. My father became a member of the State Legislative Assembly in 1952, then a member of the Upper House of Parliament, and my uncle was a member of the Lower House. And we're still active in politics here. Today, as you see, there are people coming to see me who have some problems and want some advice and help.'

He talked of the villagers and of Mathura's family in a benign and fatherly manner, and there was a feeling that though much had changed in the country, much remained the same. 'Mathura used to drive my mother and father around. He could repair the car, he was an expert cook, and a very good singer and dancer as well – an all-rounder, you would say. Also a bit of a notorious chap, you know. He went to my grandmother and said, "My wife's a bit dark-looking, and would you permit me to get married again?" She said, "Nonsense, get out – you've married her, that's it!" And finally he had six daughters and one son.

'He felt – and rightly – that he was part of the family, and he was expert at making the soolas – the barbecue – which takes a good two days to do. There was more than one kitchen. The main one was controlled exclusively by ladies. Then there was another where the mutton and chicken were cooked – and he was there. He supervised the food, and everyone kept an eye on what went on – not just him: And yes, he definitely tasted the food. You know, food tasting is important in India because of history. Aurangzeb, the Mughal ruler of India, came to power by getting his two brothers poisoned in the late 1600s. There are always complications with younger brothers. . . . So that suspicion has always lingered on here. Admittedly, by my father's time things had got a bit better – but the tradition remained.'

The Maharajah gleefully went into the details of difficulties caused by younger brothers, while we looked out over the castle, part hotel, part mildewed and empty owing to the complexities of family ownership. History hung in the air – family arguments used to end up with a little drop of poison. So I asked the inevitable question: 'Do you have a food taster any more?'

The Maharajah leaped on the answer: 'I trust everyone. *My* food tasters are the tourists who are staying here. Because they all have their breakfast at 7.30. So I eat at 9.30 . . .!

Mathura Prasad had answered 'duty', when I asked him 'in the name of what?' But that's unlikely to be the word used by all the others who have had to – and still do – face their next meal with fear.

4

The Diver

Food tasting would certainly have been in the saddlebag of the Pale Horse, who is sometimes just known as Death. And dicing with death, tempting fate, often sounds exciting. There are dangerous sports, record-breaking attempts, all kinds of thrilling escapism with which to spice up everyday life. However, since they are about seeking pleasure or amusement these could be termed self-indulgent. Dicing with death for a serious reason is a much deadlier business.

> The dredger *Sanderus* was dredging inwards between the New and Old Mole on the Western side of the channel. She observed the ferry pass her at about 8 knots. Several of the *Sanderus'* crew confirm that the bow doors were open. At about 18.28 the *Sanderus* observed the *Herald* sheering to starboard and heeling to port. Within 30 seconds the ferry's lights went out; she had capsized.

The Department of Transport report into the loss of the *Herald of Free Enterprise* off Zeebrugge begins with this matter-of-fact passage summing up the catastrophic events of 6 March 1987: a routine crossing from Belgium to Dover of a ro-ro ferry, the fatal negligence which left her bow doors gaping to receive an inrush of water, and her lurch over into the sea which took just one minute.

But the events of that night were anything but matter-of-fact. To a reporter who flew in a couple of hours after the capsizing, the harbour was a scene of controlled chaos. The huge ship lay on her side, bulging above the surface, a red and white whale in black water surrounded by flashing, twinkling lights from an armada of rescuers. Helicopters hovered and roared while naval vessels nudged around like urgent sheepdogs, alive with dark figures on their decks. Numerous tugs, a crane barge, a lifeboat and other ferries were searching the whole area. Boats moved urgently to and fro, laden with equipment, lights, ladders and ropes. Ambulances, medical teams and young volunteers carrying clothes and blankets crowded the dockside.

I spent the early hours listening to the survivors' tales: stories of bravery and desperation, of determination and terror. No one mentioned the word 'drowning'. The combination of freezing water, being trapped and helplessness is something which makes most people shiver and quickly think of something else.

The official report gives a picture of the remarkable resources which were deployed very quickly; the initial heroic efforts by members of the *Herald*'s crew who broke windows and lowered ropes to haul out survivors; the wider emergency operation gearing up on land. However, the report contains an error, describing a ship called the *Cowdenburg* as coordinating the rescue on board the *Herald*. There was no such ship – it was just one man, Gie Couwenbergh, and he had gone into an environment which most of us would avoid: a pitch-black space above desperate people sloshing frantically in rising water. 'It's my job,' he says laconically. 'A job I love.'

Why anyone should want to be a diver is a mystery to that part of the population – which includes me – who don't even like sliding their head under six inches of bathwater. Tell that to a professional diver and they will inform you that the bathwater test is a good measure of whether you will ever get to grips with scuba gear, never mind the full frogman stuff. Apparently some of us just don't take to the idea of being completely immersed in water. We look at goldfish swimming happily in their bowls and don't envy them.

But there are others who can't keep out of the stuff. And in the 1970s, the oil industry couldn't get enough of them.

Norway and Britain were starting to exploit the 'black gold' which is the answer to a country's economic prayers. The oilfields of the North Sea promised an extraordinary bonus from an area that had hitherto yielded just cod and haddock. In the early days, the rush to plant weird-looking platforms in very unfriendly waters went at a hectic pace. I watched these monsters, which resembled giants' tables crowded with oversized Meccano, being edged slowly out of ports on the east coast, only to fly over them later and realise they were like a speck of seaweed in an ocean. If you have ever been in a bouncy helicopter above a winter sea whose huge waves are hurling themselves at the minuscule dot on which your pilot appears mad enough to want to land, you will begin to understand what is called 'an intermittently hostile environment'. It is like trying to hit a tea-leaf from the topmost diving board. The relief you might feel when plonked on to this tiny atoll of metal, spotlights and jumbo drills is completely undermined when you realise that some people are at work *underneath* it. You pray you won't be invited to see what the divers are up to. Their realm is this cauldron of heaving, spray-fizzing power. The legs of the platform plunge down into it, supporting the complex gear that sucks out the precious oil. To keep it all going the divers are deep beneath the surface, miles from any coast and immersed in darkness, wearing heavy equipment and manipulating tools and cables with presumably only a few haddock for company. . . . And in the 1970s, many died. The official reports on how they met their end make grisly reading. Why should anyone want this job?

'I'm enjoying it – having the time of my life.'

Moss Mustafa really means it. He's been diving for decades – and he is one of those people who jumped into ponds as a small boy.

'My mother tells me that, when we lived in this house with a stream in front of it, she would dress me in the morning and I'd immediately go and jump in the stream. And then she'd change my clothes – and I'd go and do it again. I had this fascination with water, always wanting to know what would float and what wouldn't – like my mother's shoes and so on. . . . I always loved swimming, and when we went to the seaside I'd swim out a long way, frightening my parents. I couldn't just paddle. I thought nothing about swimming a mile. I've always loved water.

'I originate from Cyprus – I'm Turkish Cypriot. My father served in the British armed forces – he lied about his age and joined when he was sixteen. He served in a paramilitary police commando unit in the EOKA campaign [the movement for union with Greece] in the 1950s. He was decorated, and highly regarded by soldiers. So, growing up as a child, I loved to hear his stories. He was very strict and a commanding figure, tall and handsome, very strong – my James Bond, I suppose. And he inspired me.

'My father was posted to England when I was about three. When I was seventeen I joined the Territorial Army in Broadstairs – the Queen's Regiment – and discovered I loved soldiering. Then, because I loved water as well, I joined the Marines. And started diving. And the first time I did it – well, you spend a day with the SBS [Special Boat Service] at a swimming pool in Poole. Very basic, with cylinders on your back and a mask and mouthpiece: "Just remember not to hold your breath on the way back up – and off you go." Fifty-eight of us had joined (though only nineteen eventually made it as Marines) and I looked at them: some were nervous, some came out of the water rather soon, and with me . . . well, they were screaming and shouting at me to come out. I *wouldn't* – I fell in love with it. You're weightless, and it's the closest you can come to flying. If you think of a ship when you're on land, to get from the bottom to the top you've got to get ropes and ladders and it takes ages. Then think of a wreck lying on the seabed – if you want to get from the keel to the top of the mast you just fly up. It's a *huge* attraction.

'Having developed this passion for diving, I naturally wanted to go into the SBS. But there was a lot of red tape, courses, sign on for so many years and so on, and I was young and impetuous and just wanted to get on and do it. Then I heard about the Regiment – the SAS – and its TA regiment, 21, which had a boat troop, where you could just walk in from civvy street and go for Selection [the strenuous tests to qualify for the SAS], and I thought – great, let yomping over the hills sort you out, not the red tape. And from 21 regiment I thought I'd get into the full-time SAS – 22 regiment.

'So I left the Marines and got into 21 – great bunch of mates, still my closest friends. Mind you, my parents were horrified to see me driving a mini-cab while I was going for Selection. They were keen for me to do a sensible job and didn't want me to go into diving. But I'd looked at commercial diving, and doing a course would have cost over £4000 – a lot of money in 1981. I couldn't afford it.

'I picked up a fare one day – five fit and drunken lads. George, who sat next to me, was a commercial diver working on the Thames Barrier. Wow, I thought. So I told him my story and he said, "There's a TOPS scheme – the government training course." I said, "You've got to be kidding! For diving?" And he said, "Not many people know that – including the people working in the labour exchange. So you need to get down there, and say, 'I want to do a diving course.' And they will say, 'You want to do a *driving* course?' 'No, *diving*,' you say. And they'll say, 'It doesn't exist.' And you say, 'Yes it does.'" And that's exactly what happened.

'I'd left the Marines, having risen to all of £75 a week, and I didn't have a bean to my name. I was in a hurry and the sports diver qualification at Falmouth – where you can do it in two weeks – cost £500. So I went to see my bank manager, asked for a £500 loan for the course and he said no. So I sold my car, drew out the money via my credit card and wrote a letter to the manager, saying, "I'm really sorry, but I have to do it and I promise when I get back I'll mini-cab and pay you back." I got a very stern reply.

'So I did the course, came top of the class, went to the labour exchange to sign on the TOPS course, mini-cabbed and paid the bank off. They put us through a three-day assessment, with various tests, including putting a helmet on us and then turning off the air supply. Some of the guys freaked out – so they didn't make it. You're meant to sit there and sort of smile, and they're just testing you to see if you can hold your nerve – because this happens to divers. You lose your hat – you've got to keep calm.

'I remember, I went to the canteen and had a cigarette – and the other twelve on this assessment took one look which said, "Aha, we've got you. *You're* not going to pass . . . think you're fit?" Then there was a running test – up to the top of the hill at Fort Bovisand and back, and I took off like a bat out of hell and left the others standing – they didn't know I'd just passed Selection for 21 SAS the tough stuff across the Brccon Beacons! And while I was waiting for them to finish, I asked the instructor if he minded me lighting up another cigarette. . . .' This is a man who still smokes and is still diving.

'So I got through, and went off to qualify as a commercial diver. And through someone on the course, I got offered a job out in Abu Dhabi. My sister was getting married and I told her I had this golden opportunity – three months' work at £60 a day. I said I'd give her half the money to help towards setting up home. She said, "Stuff the money – I've only got one brother, and I want you at my wedding." I had to turn the job down. And after the wedding . . . nothing, and there were more divers around than jobs. So I decided that as the firms who ran offshore business were in Great Yarmouth and Aberdeen, I'd drive up there and go round them with a bunch of CVs. But I couldn't afford to. Then my bounty – my pay-off – from the TA came up and I organised myself with my rations and my camping gear like a good soldier and set off with a map of where all the companies were in Great Yarmouth. The first one I went to, I got a job – and later I realised that divers don't usually turn up in a suit and tie. But I was keen to make an impression, and I think they were a bit puzzled. Anyway, they asked if I could begin in the Gulf on Sunday. I said yes. "Hard work?" Yes, I said. "Three-month job?" Yes, I said. They made it sound horrendous, but I still said yes. My parents, who were still very sceptical about diving, could hardly believe it – £60 *a day*! And off I went.'

Moss has worked all over the world, and likes the freelance, unexpected nature of it – 'Can you be in Abu Dhabi tomorrow?' But there is no guarantee of a job, and divers are paid only for the days they work. There is inshore work, covering rivers, jetty, marinas, docks and the Thames Barrier, and offshore, which centres on the oil industry.

'There's two sorts of commercial diving – inspection and construction. Inspection's the white-collar job and construction's the underwater navvy, putting in clamps weighing several tons, or joining pipelines. There's a huge gap where the diving course stops and the work starts – there's no formal training programme, and it's left to you to work things out for yourself.'

Moss thinks it's very like soldiering – you have to have discipline, use your initiative, be professional and have lots of humour: 'There's no room for bluffing: it's not like an office.' Especially in the North Sea.

'The North Sea oil and gas industry grew so rapidly – money was thrown at it in the early seventies and it was a new science, especially for divers. We didn't have that much commercial experience. We learned our lesson by the mistakes we made.

'Is diving dangerous? I think it's a matter of perception. No diver *thinks* it's dangerous, but others perceive it as so. It used to have a very bad reputation, and when divers do have an accident and die it's often under horrific circumstances: they get sucked into a pipe, their helmet gets ripped off and so on. So when it does happen, it's headline news.

'For example, when I was in the North Sea there was an accident in the southern sector in 1984. You first carry out a risk assessment – and I'd challenge anyone to do one and identify what ended up killing *this* diver. He had to drill into what we call a "member" – that's a tubular steel part of the oil platform. It was flooded, so there was no difference in pressure – a lot of divers have been sucked into holes because of such differences. All had been checked, ensured safe. And he got down underwater, where you are weightless and just like an astronaut, so you have to tie yourself into the job to get some leverage, otherwise you'll be pushed backwards when you drill. He got the drill ready, put it on the point he was going to work on, told the surface to make the drill hot, pressed the button – and killed himself. How? Well, he was wearing a band mask – a neoprene hood, rather than a rigid helmet, which he'd washed and disinfected after the last job. He'd hung it up to dry with a lanyard – a piece of cord. This little lanyard was floating and somehow got round the chuck of the drill, so when it spun it pulled the hood off his head.

'The dive supervisor went through all the right actions for an emergency, getting a secondary supply of air to him, and launched the stand-by diver. He happened to be fresh out of diving school and this was his first commercial dive – once in the water, he said the tide was too strong to get to the guy in trouble. Maybe he lost his nerve. But that's how we learned our lessons.

'In Ruweis in Abu Dhabi, there was a tanker jetty that went a couple of hundred yards out to sea, with wires going down to the seabed attached to concrete blocks by shackles, and we had to change them over. We were scuba diving at about 70 feet, no contact with the surface. It's banned now for commercial diving, because so many divers have died – you now have to have an umbilical cord. Suddenly there was this explosion, a huge release of gas, and when I grabbed the gauge I saw it was going down fast. The O-ring had blown on my bottle. Your instinct is to do a Polaris to the surface – shoot up there instantly. But you can burst a lung with the pressure. Or get an embolism. Lots of unpleasant things. So I resisted the temptation and went up slowly, hand over hand on the wire. A bit shaken, I was hauled on board and the supervisor commented, "You're up early." I told him, "My O-ring blew." "Well, there's another bottle there," he said – and turned around and walked off. There's not a lot of sympathy in the game. And you do need discipline.

'In commercial diving, it's just a means of transport to your work site. Nobody pays you to *go* to work – it's the job you do when you *get* there. And you won't have much of a career if you're concerned about the environment you're in. It slows you down and you can't do your job. You've almost got to switch off and imagine you're working in air.

'I've *thought* I was in danger several times. Got caught up in a fishing net, which is unpleasant. Saw a shark in Abu Dhabi while I was inspecting the leg of a jetty, making notes on a clipboard – but it was so fast, so agile, I realised that if it decided to go for me that's it: forget all this fighting stuff, or giving it a biff. Then there are sea snakes, and stone fish and chicken fish, which are poisonous. And jelly fish, especially in warmer waters, when it's so hot and you're diving without a diving suit, just wearing overalls. And the jellyfish get up your sleeves and they're painful and scar you and they're *horrible*. . . .

'If you work onshore, in docks, it can be pitch-black. You can have a burning torch just inches away from your face and you can't see it. You do everything by feel. We do 24-hour operations and so you don't stop at night, either. But I remember diving off Libya, with a ship above me using thrusters to keep it exactly in position, hovering within a yard, at about 100 feet, and I left the diving bell and looked down – and got *vertigo*. I could see several hundred feet down. Weird. A perk of the job, though . . . amazing visibility!'

Vertigo above deep trenches just adds to the list of reasons why some people don't like even the deep end of the swimming pool. However, Moss has unabated enthusiasm for the day job – and for a long-time he was also busy in the SAS as a Territorial: 'Ten years, a member of 21. And I'd decided that I wouldn't join 22 – I had the best of both worlds, diving and soldiering. Loved it. We did a few interesting things. . . .' Like most SAS men, he doesn't elaborate. However, you do get the impression that he didn't have much of a quiet life at any time, and anyway, he emphasises that he *always* liked being under water.

Even so, for nine years he stopped diving, got married and started a family. He worked for Lloyd's Register, took a master's degree in Engineering Asset Management and did consultancy work. However, his old enthusiasm for the SAS led him to take on one of the traditional clubhouses associated with the regiment at the National Shooting Centre at Bisley in Surrey. It sports the title of Artists' Rifles – a name which carries 150 years of military history, with an illustrious list of writers, artists, poets and sculptors, who volunteered for its ranks in World War I, among them Paul Nash and Wilfred Owen.

'I didn't think I'd ever go back to diving – I was forty-seven, and *nobody* was diving at that age when I started. Then I took the clubhouse on and a friend came to see it and told me to get back into diving because running a club needs subsidising. I said. "At my age, who'll give me a job?" But it was after Hurricanes Katrina and Rita, and he said, "There's a worldwide shortage of experienced divers as a result." The one thing I wanted to do was saturation diving – it pays £1000 a day, when air-diving pays £400 a day.

'You live on the ship in a chamber – it's a bit like a caravan – for up to twenty-eight days. In air-diving, the maximum you can dive to is 50 metres or 165 feet. But some of these platforms are 500, 600, 700 feet deep. To get there, you have to breathe in a mixture of helium and oxygen. Ordinarily you can only work for a couple of hours, then you have to decompress. It's not very efficient. But they've discovered that whether you stay under pressure for one day or twenty days you need the same length of decompression. Three men go down, and you do a maximum of six hours in the water. It's weird . . . the chamber is tiny, with six of us in it. It's like a tiny submarine with bunks. The laundry and food are locked in and out. So you live in the chamber, pressurised to the level you're going to work at, with a diving bell called a "moon pool" which is lowered through a hole in the middle of the ship. It takes five days to decompress from 500 feet, so even if your mother died, or your child, there's nothing anyone can do. You can bring a man back from the moon quicker.

'So off I went. I started fitness training, got the medical, did the offshore survival course and got the inspection certificate. And I'm back into it. My first dive was 100 feet at night. I made my way over to the platform – couldn't see anything *and* I'd been out of the water for over nine years, so I was wondering if this was such a good idea. Then I started swimming and, fortunately, hit the platform. And I loved it! Maybe it's a mid-life crisis. . . .'

These days the business has much higher safety standards and divers get much more sophisticated support. But there are still accidents, and the legacy of the dangerous North Sea 'Klondike' days is that divers are very aware of the demands of commercial firms – and governments. They are conscious of safety, but have that knowing attitude to danger which is common in the military – not surprising, when more than half of Britain's divers have been in the services. And there's that love of living like a fish, being happiest in water: 'I've seen brave men – soldiers, police – who've been very uncomfortable underwater. And I've seen sixty-year-old grannies who've loved it. You either have a phobia about putting your head under water or you don't. And if you don't, you don't regard it as dangerous. We know diving's inherently dangerous – but it doesn't frighten us.'

As a small boy in Belgium Gie Couwenbergh, the hero of the *Herald of Free Enterprise* disaster with which this chapter opened, appears to have been made in exactly the same mould as Moss Mustafa. Now in his sixties and spending much of his time diving in the warm waters of the Dominican Republic, he had a career in the Belgian navy, ending up as superintendent of diving for the armed forces. He was another water baby.

'I was born in Antwerp, on the River Scheldt, and I was always attracted by water – I *wanted* to go swimming. My first memory – I think I was three years old – was of my father swimming in a pool, and I jumped into the water and couldn't swim! And I remember I was drowning. I had my eyes open underwater, and I was looking around and saw my father coming to me to take me out. And everyone thought I'd be scared of water after that – but I jumped straight back in. I was never afraid of water.

'I joined a swimming club, but I didn't want to be in competitions – I never wanted to be the first. Then I went to sea scouts, with boats, rowing, sailing and all that kind of stuff. I wanted to make a career as captain of a merchant ship, but my parents said, "You'll never be home or have a family life" and so I became a teacher of mathematics instead. But I was not the kind of man to spend my life in a classroom, and soon I had to do military service, joining the navy in '65. At the end of fifteen months I was a reserve officer and had spent six months at sea in the Mediterranean – Monaco, Malta, the white uniforms, the girls and all that. We were very popular. Of course we had to do the watch from midnight to

4 a.m. in the rain, but at the end I thought this was something I wanted to do.

'When I finished I got married and went to work for General Motors in Antwerp, specialising in computers, but I found that boring and wanted to get away. So I wrote to the navy and they said there was an opening for me – though the money was about a third of the salary I had at GM, with all my overtime. There *was* overtime in the navy – but you didn't get paid for it. But in life you can't focus only on money, and at the end of the day I want to feel happy, and you can't do that if you have to look first in your wallet. So I joined the navy again in '68 and I thought: now I'm *on* the water, but I also want to be *in* the water: I want to do this diving – and ordinarily, you have to pay to go scuba diving. But if I do it in the military, I can dive as much as I want during my work hours and get paid for it! However, they said, "If you want to dive, you also have to do EOD [Explosive Ordnance Disposal]."'

One of the advantages – perhaps – of joining the armed forces of a small nation is what is now called 'multi-tasking': you get to do a range of jobs, whether you want to or not. The Belgian navy was having trouble getting people to apply for EOD work; so diving, which was much more popular, became the bait. Similar qualities are needed – you want calm, solid people who don't panic.

'It's EOD at sea, stuff dropped by aircraft, IEDs [Improvised Explosive Devices], everything. So I had to do two years' training. But the most difficult thing was that, just as I was starting training, we had an accident with a British bomb found here in Flanders, and *seven* EOD people died. I wondered what had happened, saw pictures of it and so on, and came to the conclusion that they had made a mistake. And I made up my mind not to make mistakes. The first lesson I learned was – don't improvise. Go step by step, and never say, "*I* know." You have to go back to the books and look it up and follow the rules. Don't let anyone put any pressure on you – especially the politicians who want things dealt with as soon as possible. When a UXB [unexploded bomb] is found they say, "Come on, it's bad for the economy to have shops closed, to have to evacuate people and so on." You have to ignore it.

'And there's so much stuff still here from World War II. We have *everything* – stuff from Napoleon's armies even! If you go back in history, Belgium has been the playground for most people's wars . . . full of nice fields. . . .' He roars with laughter, a big, solid, capable man, energetic and funny. He had found his niche in life and loved every minute of it.

'We searched fishing boats capsized in the North Sea – I remember the *Gerlinda*, which sank near Ipswich, 65 metres deep, rough seas, cold, in February, and not knowing if there were bodies to find or not. And that's when you get dangerous moments – but it never took me by surprise. Cold and darkness don't bother me. And generally we know what we're looking for. But fishing boats are difficult – floating cables, nets, ropes and dead fish.

'I went into the wreck through a small hole, and I knew if I moved around a bit I'd produce a cloud and have no more visibility, so I had to be very careful. I couldn't go in with the air-tank on my back – it was too big. So I took a 15-metre hose, and knew that if I lost it I was finished. I attached the hose to my arm – I knew that if I lost visibility, I could follow the hose back out. At 65 metres, I don't have to take a breath two or three times a minute – one breath will last me five minutes because at a pressure of 7 bar you get seven times the amount of oxygen. You mustn't ever panic. If you have a lot of stress in your life, or panic easily – then don't dive. Most accidents happen through panic.'

What happened to the *Herald of Free Enterprise* was not a mere accident: it was caused by negligence and what was judged in the subsequent inquiry to be 'a disease of sloppiness' at every level of the shipowner's hierarchy. The panic occurred as hundreds of people found themselves in a capsizing vessel, plunged into darkness, just as they were starting a routine Channel crossing. There were families heading for the final leg of a journey home, lorry drivers, service people travelling from bases in Germany, and lots of day trippers enjoying a cheap special-offer ticket from a tabloid newspaper. Within seconds, with many of them already in the cafeteria for an evening snack, their world tipped 180 degrees as water surged through the open bow doors and the lights went out.

Zeebrugge harbour was busy. The crew of the dredger *Sanderus* saw the ship disappear. And at the naval station on shore, Gie Couwenbergh was in the last phase of a routine exercise involving NATO vessels.

'I was duty officer. A phone call came in to my CPO [chief petty officer]: "A ferry's gone down off Zeebrugge. Helicopters are on their way – and they're looking for divers."

'I went straight to my car, which had all my diving gear in it – I'd been diving the day before when a French ship had had an accident with its propeller shaft – saying, "Tell the helicopters to pick me up. I'll be here." Others were running towards the ships, and three of us waited to be picked up and taken to the *Herald*.

'We saw the ship on its side, and everything was dark. The only light we had was a floodlight from the helicopter, but we could see the whole ship. There was already another ship alongside, and some of their crew were on the *Herald* but just standing there, because they didn't have diving suits or equipment with them and so they couldn't do much.

'I was lowered down. There was no sign of anyone. The two others were "baby" divers – sports divers, but not fully qualified. The other seamen had already broken glass in one of the windows, and lowered a ladder. But the ship's beam was at least 25 metres, and the ladder could only go down about 10 metres. I looked down through the window and saw all these flickering things. And I could hear very little because of the noise of the helicopters and the other ships' engines. I could see a white shirt – and all these "things" moving. What's this? I thought. I've got to go down. I could see someone trying to help people out – an assistant purser, it turned out, Stephen Holmwood – and then I went down through the broken window. With just a small lamp – and I left the lamp with him. But I couldn't get right down to the water. The ladder was 10 metres above it, so I had to jump into the water.

'What I'd seen – the "things" – were the reflectors on the lifejackets bobbing around. But people weren't wearing them – they were just floating everywhere in the water. This was the cafeteria. All the tables and chairs were bolted to the deck, which was a good thing, because people could climb higher. Try to imagine what the cafeteria had been like – full of people, 25 by 50 metres. And if you turn it on its side 25 metres becomes 2 metres, so people got jam-packed together. The lockers with the lifejackets which were under water burst open and pushed people upwards – then the lockers above on the other side of the cafeteria, opened and dropped on top of them. They were the main problem we had. People couldn't put lifejackets on while they struggled in the water in the dark, and they were in the way. They had long tapes and these were sticking to people and getting wrapped round their limbs. One man managed to get one on but the tapes of his jacket were round the neck of another passenger – nearly strangled him – and I had no scissors to cut them . . . Ten metres of water, a layer of lifejackets and people and then 15 metres of air up to the window.

'At the beginning, you hardly knew where to start. I told the men on deck, "Lower a rope." And there was really only room for me to manoeuvre, so the two other divers stayed on deck. I grabbed the rope and made it like a lasso, and had to work out a signal to get it pulled up – because of the noise, I couldn't talk to the deck. It was very difficult, making sure that the people were pulled up and through the window one after another without being hurt. I always took the person who was closest to me. Sometimes there were suddenly three people or more next to me in the water – I took one, and when I turned round the others had disappeared.

'People were desperate in their struggle for life. I was very conscious of that – and there was only so much we could do. One woman was shouting, "Help me! Help me! Get me out!" and I was thinking, well, as long as she can still call out, then it's somebody else first.

'It was an indescribable scene. And yet you're so busy . . . one man, I put the rope round him under his arms and gave the signal to lift him. And then, I don't know what he did, but he slipped out and fell down right on top of me – and I disappeared with him, under water. I surfaced and still had him with me, so I said, "OK?" And he replied, "Where are my glasses?"

'The state of the people changed all the time. At first they were very active, shivering violently, but that faded away because of the cold. You could see how people faded away. I think it would be a smooth death – like falling asleep.

'It wasn't so noisy down in the ship – but suddenly, when I was busy looking to get the next person out, down came a wire with a sling, with a diver from one of the helicopters whom I knew, yelling, "Do you need any help?" I said, "No – there's only room for one rope." So he said, "I'll take one back up." Then he realised how dangerous it was, and what would happen if the helicopter moved. So he managed to get one in the sling with the words, "I won't come back." I did feel it was a race against time. And it wouldn't have helped to have either two ropes, or someone to help me. You could only get one at a time out of the window – and we didn't have a second window.

'I think I stayed there between two and a half and three hours, until there were no more people on the surface. The last few I got out I knew were dead, because they were floating on the water. I didn't count, but afterwards I was told we got about fifty people out, thirty of them OK, then ten unconscious, and the last ten were dead.

'Actually, when I jumped into the water the first face I saw in front of me was a young woman, blonde hair, blue eyes, and she had bruises on her head. She looked straight into my eyes and didn't say anything. And she was the first I got out. And afterwards, three hours later, when I got back on deck, she was still there. She was dead. That I won't forget.

'No one said thank you – because they were so exhausted. Most couldn't say a word, they were so weak.

'I never felt one moment of panic or fear. The only bad moment was when I myself had to get out of the water. The level had risen, which was a good thing because it brought the ladder nearer. But I'd thrown away my gloves when I was working because I couldn't handle the rope, so my hands had been in the cold water all of the time. The suit was OK, made of neoprene, but it cuts into your wrists, so the blood circulation wasn't 100 per cent and my hands were literally blue. And I had to climb the rope ladder again – and I couldn't feel *anything* with my hands.'

Gie Couwenbergh recalls the night in detail and recounts it without tension, though he is clearly a very humane man whose only thought was getting people to safety. He shrugs when asked about danger.

'I don't think I put my life in jeopardy. Of course I took some risks, and if someone had fallen on me while being pulled up I could have been knocked unconscious – but whatever! You can have a car accident when you just leave the house. I don't think about it a lot. I don't brood. We had a debriefing afterwards, where they warned us about nightmares and problems with erections and all that! I told them, "It's OK. No problems!"'

Now retired from the navy, he still dives for fun while running a business selling diving equipment and working as a consultant to governments on diving. 'When I get asked, "Where did you work?" I always say, "Work? No, I had a great time." I've never seen the job as work. I often didn't take holidays – it was such fun to go to the job every day.

'You float under water – no gravity, so you can't fall. I've been diving near Sark, where there's a lot of current, and when you're two metres from the seabed you watch the bottom passing under you, but you don't feel anything – you're floating. It's wonderful – a very funny feeling. Doing a job in another environment, that's what's interesting – seeing barracudas and sharks. And what I really like is to *work* under water. It's a great feeling.

In the name of what?

'Well, your Queen gave me the QGM, the Queen's Gallantry Medal, but I didn't really agree that I should get it. We all worked together. I'm not really a guy for medals – I think it should be pinned up in the bar for all the guys who are divers.

'Do I think I was a hero? No, I was just doing my job.'

And for Moss Mustafa there's also a reason beyond the enjoyment. In the name of what?

'I enjoy it, and I also think it's an honourable profession. In the eighties there was a feeling that the discovery of oil and gas was going to be the making of this country and we thought it would be *good* for our country. Like a soldier, we perhaps look for the danger, and there's a price to pay. But it's also great for pulling the girls. . . .'

5

The Stunt Worker

'Fight the good fight with all thy might,' we would sing at school assembly. Had any pupil thought of taking this literally, the wrath of the headmistress would have outdone that of any deity. Little girls didn't engage in any such sort of behaviour. Fighting was what boys did (along with becoming judges, bishops, firefighters, chief constables, airline pilots, editors of national newspapers and head of household on all official forms. This was the 1950s.) Even in girls' fiction, a plucky individual might only occasionally wield a broom handle or perhaps a bucket of water. However, if you read adventure stories for boys or went to the cinema, the world seemed full of chaps who regularly biffed each other manfully, then shook their heads, rubbed their jaws and strode off. And that was the significant part. Pain and damage didn't figure.

Later in life, especially in the seventies, I found that one of the grubbier aspects of journalism was observing various kinds of small-scale conflict: protest marches which encountered opposition, strikers' picket lines and race riots. It was a savage awakening to the world of the real fight, where very few walk away feeling nobly vindicated. First, there are no rules. Second, just about everyone runs the risk of lasting damage, even in the smallest skirmish.

During the miners' strike in 1985, I saw more false teeth on the move than a dentist sees in a decade. Two bands of men, police and pitmen, both filled with determination, used to collide outside pitheads usually just before breakfast time. Whatever the rights and wrongs of the situation, the ensuing rumpus had aspects which bore no resemblance to Saturday morning adventure films. In the scrum, you spotted men with hands to their mouths. Not that they had they been landed fair and square with a mighty left hook. The reality was that men lost their footing over bumpy ground, for the pushing and shoving disorientated them and even a minor bump against the shoulder, knee or elbow of the opposing team caused nasty surprises in the dental area. False teeth cracked, lips were split, and the odd real tooth moved a tenth of an inch and delivered excruciating pain. And should the false set go flying then finding them became an immediate priority in the mêlée. Teeth are personal, necessary and take time to replace. The same goes for spectacles: it was interesting how many pairs appeared to be perched under blue helmets. Hang on, lads – what happens if they get dislodged in a hearty charge? Then you join the people searching for their teeth. You couldn't get a sharper descent from the heroic image of man-to-man combat to the undignified scrabble for NHS supplies.

On picket lines during bitter industrial disputes there was also the hazard of getting mixed up in traffic. Factory delivery lorries and management cars got stuck in gateways, engulfed by angry people. Getting stabbed is one thing; getting stabbed by a car aerial is quite another. Placards get waved and then dropped in the fracas; they are frequently made from lengths of rough wood, so it stands to reason that long, ugly splinters might embed themselves into nearby legs and arms. And people shout a lot in real fights – there's none of this take-it-on-the-chin grim concentration of the Hollywood star. As a result, you are winded more easily and drained of energy just as a knot of hefty protesters stagger backwards into you. (Remember, some have lost their glasses.)

In a race riot you would be advised to keep clear unless you are committed to a cause. And as the aim of that cause is sociological change, there is unlikely to be a clear material objective. The town hall might be threatened with torching, but it's much more likely that there will be a very diffuse show of frustration and anger which will settle on the nearest object. Having twice seen the placid inhabitants of pubs tumbling out of the windows of lounge bars as their watering hole became the hapless target of a careering mob, I have assumed that distance is the best defence. However, you need to be nimble, and that creature of the silver screen or the thinking hero of the novel who dashes like a streak of lightning to safety – well, is that you? Remember, too, that the majority of rioters are young – and they *can* move.

I speak of these matters as one who has learned by experience, having time and again headed into the heart of the storm with a trusty TV crew to record the heat of the action, only to stagger out with unexpected injuries. I have fallen over, been squashed, winded, stood on, hit in the face with a potato – ah, and lost a shoe, another reason to be found crawling around amongst the legs of the enraged: broken glass is a feature of many violent encounters, and bare feet are the surest way to A & E.

And for those who set out to stand their ground, prove their point, demonstrate their commitment and protest in all sincerity, or to keep the peace and maintain law and order, there is real pain: sprained ankles, black eyes, broken noses and jaws (and, of course, those teeth, home-grown or acquired), cracked ribs and crocked backs, scrapes and scratches, bleeding feet and deep bruising. Not to mention the hurt to their pride. And it's likely that not one punch landed where it was intended. This is not how it looks in the movies, the comics or the TV action series, when the protagonists walk away with head held high, dusting themselves off. And is that why we think we're all invincible – entranced by Superman and Superwoman?

Naturally, ancient sagas and fairy tales all have their superhuman heroes and heroines. But there is an argument that the advent of cinema created a much more accessible world of fantasy than oral tales or print. People who looked like us – flesh-and-blood actors – faced extraordinary dangers, and . . . somehow . . . nearly always survived unscathed. Even when they didn't, you knew it was just a movie, and they were alive and well at the red carpet premiere. These illusions appear courtesy of stunt men and women. It's work which sounds curiously lightweight – serving the entertainment industry apparently by using tricks and clever camera angles. But look closer, and it soon emerges that stunt work is a barrier of expertise designed to prevent a large section of the acting profession from spending a lot of time in hospital or, indeed, heading for an early grave. And it also produces those amazing images of car crashes, humans flying through the air, on fire and hurtling from cliffs, which lead us to believe that we could be Superpeople.

'What we do isn't a science – you can't bottle it. "Where's the car going to end up?" the director says. Experience says it could go . . . here. But I remember turning a car over once in the TV series *Tales of the Unexpected* – and it was fucking unexpected, I can tell you – as a man with his wife's body in the back of this BMW. He's killed her, but doesn't know that the body's there – someone else has put it there. Then he has this accident and the police find it and get him. And it was in winter, on a section of the M25. And I hit the special ramp and went up, and the idea was the car was going to flip over and roll down a bank. But it went up . . . and just before it went up it hit this frozen molehill, and the car then cartwheeled – bang, bang, bang, down to the bottom of the bank. I was catatonic, I'd had so many impacts. The director swore. Then he said, "This bloke's supposed to have *lived* through this . . ." And I somehow got out and thought: a molehill. That's all it takes. You have to be able to quantify risk as much as you can, then eliminate risk as much as you can.'

This is Jim Dowdall, one of the UK's elite stunt men. He is in a long line of specialised risk-takers who first made their appearance as the early silent movies vied to thrill their audiences – and retain an actor whose features were still recognisable after falling from his horse and being dragged under a stagecoach before participating in a saloon bar brawl, because many of the first popular films were Westerns featuring tough guys on the frontier. It's true that many of the early stars, especially comedians such as Buster Keaton and Charlie Chaplin did their own stunt work. Then there's Harold Lloyd dangling from a clock face high up a tower in *Safety Last!*, made in 1923. It's a memorable image, especially as Lloyd was hanging on by his right hand which only had three fingers, and is much used to demonstrate his nerve in the face of danger. Up to a point, according to Jim Dowdall:

'Harold Lloyd did *some* of his own stunts, but he had a stunt double – and in those days it was kept absolutely secret. The guy was told he would lose his job, never work again, if he told. Harvey Parry used to do quite a lot for him. And when you see Lloyd hanging off the clock face, the whole thing was erected on the roof of a building just two storeys high and they shot it from a rostrum. So what you think is a tremendous height is actually just one building and there's a mattress underneath – clever, but that's what illusion's all about.'

So even in the era of the silent movie, all was not quite what it seemed. Harvey Parry was an amateur boxing and diving champion who found that his skills earned more money in the studios. Ormer Locklear was a 'barnstormer', who in 1910 started to pilot a flimsy plane at county fairs, 'loop de looping', going into a spin and wing-walking. Film producers couldn't wait to add the new-fangled craze of aviation to their plots. And soon after World War I Locklear was giving audiences the impression that a hero should be able to climb out of the cockpit midair, descend a ladder to a speeding car, biff the villain and then swing back up into the plane. A spiralling dive by Locklear from 5000 feet at night, illuminated by searchlights, provided the climax to *The Skywayman* in 1920. Audiences might well have gasped, for Locklear didn't survive the dive – he crashed into an oilfield.

It was very early in the history of the film business that stars began to prefer a stunt double undertook the 'action stuff', especially when it involved horses – which gave Yakima Canutt his big chance. I first heard his name in one of the late Alastair Cooke's radio programmes, *Letter from America*. He paid tribute to Canutt after hearing of his death in 1998, calling him 'the greatest stunt man in the history of movies'. A ranch hand and rider in Wild West shows, Enos Edward Canutt – he acquired 'Yakima' from the small town in Washington State where he made his name as a rodeo champion – not only rode superbly, but fell off spectacularly as well. He also got dragged along by horses, leaped up on to them at speed, and famously, in John Ford's *Stagecoach*, jumped from his own horse across to a six-horse team, appeared to be shot and then fell underneath them and the stagecoach. Canutt is also regarded as the man who brought the bar-room brawl to perfection on screen, using choreographed movement and clever camera angles. John Wayne had much to thank him for. Alistair Cooke recalled that, before Canutt was forty, X-rays showed that he had broken nearly every bone in his body. He worked on hundreds of films, but, as is frequently the case with this role in the film industry, probably very few people noticed his name in the credits. Most people, however, can remember Clark Gable driving a buckboard while Atlanta burns in *Gone with the Wind* – except that it wasn't Gable, but Canutt.

The allure of stunt work might seem obscure except to the insurance industry, anxious not to have megastars recovering from car crashes while a vast and expensive cast and crew stand around waiting to shoot the next scene. From the start, there have been fatalities. And injury seems to be accepted as inevitable. So what brought Jim Dowdall into the business?

'I was never going to be a scholar – I only got one O-level – but I'd been Sussex schoolboys gymnastics champion and I'd won the victor ludorum at school and athletics this, that and the other. I first joined Bertram Mills Circus as a "beastman" – looking after the big cats.

'After that I had a series of jobs – sold motorcycles, learned all about bikes, took 'em to bits. Washed cars for Kenning's car hire firm for six months – it taught me to park with literally two inches' clearance, then get out of the window. That gave me spatial awareness for stunt work. When people say they have a menial job, I always say there's something you may get from it to use later in life.

'I'd always been a big film fan. As a kid I went to sixpenny Saturday morning movies – flicking cards across the screen, that kind of stuff. I felt I was an under-achiever, and here you could see these guys all dressed in white, being the hero. Wonderful . . . very over-romanticised. My half-sister worked as a picture researcher for Purnell's *History of the Second World War* and, because my other love is military history, through her I managed to meet an old man who owned a private company which supplied everything military for the film industry from a flick knife to an 88mm howitzer. He was extraordinary – at the age of fourteen he'd blown out one eye when dismantling a shell in 1918, having picked it up on the battlefield.

'And so in 1966, through this connection, I got a job as a film armourer and went off to work on all sorts of action films – *The Dirty Dozen, Where Eagles Dare* – and spent four or five months with Clint Eastwood. He was one of my major heroes, and we used to go off and ride motorcycles together! He'd bought three Nortons, one for himself, one for James Garner and one for Steve McQueen, but he wanted to do some miles on them, because he knew that when they got them back they'd just open them up and they needed running in first. What an opportunity!

'I was picking up experience all the way along. The stunt guys were fellas I definitely felt an empathy with, because of the physical thing and the military stuff. Here were these guys falling off buildings and vehicles – and I thought, that's a piece of cake. I was a getting eight quid a week at the time . . . and they were getting that a *day*! But there were no openings in the stunt business, because in those days four men controlled it and they were all ex-wartime soldiers. If you weren't of that era, they considered you a young upstart. So I left after three years, when I was twenty-one, mini-cabbed for a bit and then joined the Parachute Regiment.

'I was champion recruit in the Paras, so I thought maybe there was a career for me here. This was in the early seventies, and there was Northern Ireland for action – but that was about it. And you had as much chance for promotion as flying to the moon. Then I cracked three vertebrae in a jump, so in 1972 I left the Paras and went back to mini-cabbing. However, I still thought I'd like to get into the stunt business, so to get my Equity card I joined an agency called Havoc – "specialists in hazards" – and started to get a few little jobs. They did TV's *The New Avengers*.'

There was much derring-do in this cult series, with Patrick Macnee and Joanna Lumley facing up to the world's bad guys on a rather measly production budget. Skidding cars and martial arts were integral to the plots, so there was much for Jim to do, laying the basis for a long and successful career.

At least he didn't have to double in a wig for Joanna Lumley, who was game for doing many of her own stunts. Though for a woman who has no head for heights, a mile-long trip hanging on to a ladder dangling from a helicopter encouraged her to give way to a stuntwoman for other exploits. And thirty years later, there's still a steady demand for stunt women to fall off roofs and have spectacular car crashes.

As with many jobs, there's no obvious way into stunt work – as Jim Dowdall's CV has demonstrated. Chorus line hoofing doesn't seem a likely apprenticeship for jumping off a cliff. However, Sarah Franzl doesn't seem fazed. She is one of a growing number of stunt women in a business which for many years happily tolerated stunt men as doubles for actresses.

'I wanted to go on the stage. I always wanted to be dancer, so I trained – very strict ballet work – and then got into West End and TV shows. As a dancer you're aware of your body – so now when I'm doing high falls and what have you I'm very conscious of what I'm doing. If I'm doing stair falls, I know where I want to be – I can tell a director, "This is what's going to happen. How and where do you want me to land?"

'I got to a stage where I felt I'd done everything as a dancer, and it was natural to progress. I just wanted to do *more*. And back in the eighties I met someone called Alf Joint who'd been in the business for years.' Joint, known for the 430-foot plunge over the Reichenbach Falls for a Sherlock Holmes series, told her, 'You should consider the stunt business.' She hadn't thought about doing so, but 'it appealed and it was a challenge'.

Although there are a number of courses available which promise training in various skills, there is still no recognised professional 'stunt training school' in the UK. However, there is an agreed requirement that young hopefuls have an Equity card so that they can take stage direction, and they must reach a certain proficiency in several activities before they are allowed on the Stunt Register, which permits them to apply for work.

'The first step is to become proficient in six different sports, and there were a couple of things on the list I really fancied – sky-diving and sub-aqua. My father flies – he has a racing glider and is into sports – and my mum was very supportive. I did sub-aqua, sky-diving, swimming, weight-lifting, horse-riding and skiing. You do three years as a probationary member on the Register and then you need to have done enough work so that you can be upgraded to intermediate member. After that you can work on your own.

'My first work was on something called *Stanley's Dragon*, for the BBC. It was a little driving job, just skidding around and a bit of mad stuff – nothing much, really. I think you get a taste for it, but you have to practise, talk to other people and take advice. I went off with a couple of friends in the business and we hired some cars and knocked the hell out of them on an airfield – you just build up your skills.

'The first time I was in a car knock-down on a film – *Pulaski*, in 1986, which was actually *about* a stunt man – I broke my pelvis. But it didn't put me off – it made me more determined. I thought, I'm really going to crack this. I hadn't actually done anything wrong, it's just that circumstances can make it more dangerous – you know, if it's at night, or you can't see properly, or you've got a hat or a scarf on.'

Getting a taste for a 'car knock-down' indicates the singularity of some of the work. And cars figure prominently in the minds of directors when it comes to exciting events. Most of us have grown used to the sight of a vehicle lurching into the air, almost flying and perhaps turning a somersault – and, of course, to the sight of the hero walking away after it's bounced to a stop. But then, anyone who has been in the slightest skid will surely remember just how out-of-control a ton of car can seem. So what is it about screen chases and prangs? Can't it all be done with computer simulation these days? Apparently not. Jim Dowdall is a veteran of what Americans describe graphically as 'totalling' a vehicle: 'If you're going to crash that car, crash that motorcycle, you're going to have to do it for real.

'You need skill, good preparation specialists – stunt engineers, people who know how to build the roll cages for a car, take the petrol out and so on. We turn a car over by one of three methods. First you can use a normal ramp, drive up it and literally steer into the crash. Then there's a pipe ramp, which is like a steel drainpipe which goes up to four or five feet from the ground, greased, and has a little kicker ramp at the end. You're riding up on the metal parts of the car, not the wheels, then the kicker ramp knocks the nose up and the car flies through the air. The third method is a cannon, where in the passenger seat you have the equivalent of a cannon barrel which points down into the car. It's got a piston inside it with a cylinder of nitrogen, pressurised at 800 pounds per square inch, six inches from your bum. When you throw the car sideways, you fire it and it makes the car flip. But because of the pressure of the 800 lb psi, the violence when you turn the car, you have to have neck braces on. In a perfect world you have cables attached to your helmet to stop the whiplash, but your brain does get smacked about. . . .'

Considering that CGI – computer-generated imaging – is now a marvellous tool for those directors wishing to put their faith in IT rather than in hot flames or the crunch of real metal, it must seem infinitely preferable when measuring risk. However the computers haven't taken over completely yet.

'I think experience teaches one that there *are* ways of giving the effect for real. On the Bond films, before CGI was getting a grip on things, we prided ourselves that *everything* was done for real. So we would rehearse for weeks. For the car chase on the ice with the Jaguar and the Aston that we did for *Die Another Day*, they spent a million and a quarter just *converting* the cars. They were made four-wheel drive, the engines were taken out, they had new front axles and a Land Rover gear box, and then we tried them out on the ice with three different lengths of stud on the tyres. The thin ones didn't do anything, the long ones made them stick like shit to a blanket and they wouldn't swerve at all, but the intermediate ones would allow you to have some grip and still slide them. And then you've got that beautiful balletic thing on ice. Now, you could do an awful lot of that with CGI, but it wouldn't have that *texture*. There's a grittiness about the real thing.'

And a lot of injuries. The roll call of fatalities gives pause for thought, though the regulated British stunt scene fares better than the much bigger American industry. But despite all the preparations and painstaking precautions, the professional does not, like the fictional hero, always walk away unscathed. Human error, mechanical failure, the unexpected: not one can be ruled out. Stunt work offers a varied and grim list of deaths. Even the weather can intervene – high winds and ice, heat and humidity can all knock careful calculations awry by a fatal smidgeon. Yet it's all in a day's work for Sarah Franzl, and it's mildly comforting to know that she recognises there may be problems.

'I did a *Murder She Wrote*, and Jim, who was stunt coordinator, asked me to do a 140-foot fall on a wire – it's called a "descender". So you're fixed to a wire and you jump off the building and fall in real time. If it's a fall over 40 feet you usually put in some safety element – an airbag or something. Just before you reach the ground there's a braking system, and about two foot off the ground it stops you.

'In this particular job it was a girl who commits suicide, and she does it over a glass roof. This was one of the highest falls ever done by a woman in the UK, but over glass it was visually not great. I was happy to do the job, but knowing that there was a huge glass roof beneath me. . . . It's a huge strain on the body as well – the braking happens so suddenly that it's like somebody hitting you with a baseball bat in the stomach. It *literally* knocks the stuffing out of you!

'It was awful, because it transpired that someone really had committed suicide from this office block in north London. I was just about to jump and they'd got me over the rails – it was really windy, and two colleagues were holding me and I was just about to go – when a guy on the top floor below us opened a window and looked up and shouted, "My God, what are you doing?" And I shouted back, "We're filming." He went on to tell me about what had happened – which is just what you don't need to hear. I was concentrating on saying, "Please, please close the window", because if you jump and there's something in the way it could be very nasty indeed.

'The bizarre thing about this sort of job is that you go up in the lift, knowing you're not going to come down in it – I always think it's so funny. A quicker way down than getting the lift . . .!'

Some actors want to do their own stunts, though their greatest obstacle is usually the insurance company. And even when they *are* allowed to perform, people like Jim Dowdall have rehearsed it for them.

'As stunt coordinator, anything that's "*action*" falls into your lap. You then decide at what point you take the actor out of the frame and replace him with the double. If you are working with, say, Tom Cruise, you can spend three months rehearsing with the stunt man, who gets battered to shit, and then Cruise comes in and every single safety element has been ironed out. He can do it nice and easily in a car that's been injection-moulded out of plastic, rubber and so on. But you can't eliminate all the risk – you can launch a man 60 or 70 feet in the air on a wire, and he's plummeting to the ground on a controlled piece of kit, but if the wire breaks, or the hydraulics pack up, or a bearing goes bang, he's "clappers on end".

'Some actors don't want to do *anything*. Richard Burton wouldn't stand on a chair. In *Where Eagles Dare*, his character has to stand on a chair to throw a rope out of the window. But his stunt double, Joe Powell, had to stand on the chair for him. Burton was the most unphysical actor I think I've ever worked with. There's a scene in the film where he had to shoot the radio operator with a pistol. I was the armourer, and showed him three shots – one, two, three – with the gun. So he goes – bang . . . "Bloody thing doesn't work." I say, "You have to let your finger go, and then pull it again. It won't work if you just squeeze it. You have to go 'bang, bang, bang.' " And he says, "No, it's the gun." So I take the gun, reload it and give it to him again. Bang. "Bloody gun." Eventually we did it with just one round – it was easier. Sometimes the job's like pushing snow uphill with a hot spoon! But not with all actors. When we did *Flash Gordon* with Timothy Dalton I got him swinging on ropes, doing this, that and the other, and I just did the hairy stuff, like falling off into space and hanging on to knives – but he was good. However, actors as a race . . . most of them can't think and chew gum simultaneously. They are terrific at emoting, but they are not physical.'

Sarah Franzl takes a gentler view. 'Actors? Well, experienced actors don't want to do their own stunts – it's the inexperienced ones, I find. And on a big production, the insurance just doesn't cover.' But just like Jim Dowdall, she finds some members of the acting profession very unphysical.

'Sometimes actors won't even *run*. Years ago I doubled Melanie Griffith, in a film with Michael Douglas shot in Berlin. When we went to the cast screening, I realised all I had done was run through the streets of Berlin at night. I spent five weeks running. She didn't want to.

'When I worked on *Mamma Mia* with Pierce Brosnan I was doubling Meryl Streep, and even did a shot just standing on the side of a rock face – which she was actually very up for doing. But all the line-ups are with me, all the tests with the wires, so that if it goes wrong it goes wrong with me and not with the actress.

'Some of the actors watch us working, some don't. Meryl Streep watched. But it's very funny, because I spend my time watching *them* – their movements and so on. On *Titanic* I doubled Kate Winslet, and the director, James Cameron, was so particular that he would notice everything. So for hours and hours I watched so that I could walk exactly like her and I knew all her movements.'

All of us, though, have certain phobias, and it's not surprising that actors should find something lurking in the script which is their stuff of nightmares. And surely the stunt professionals have their own dislikes? Maybe heights and fights are OK, but what about fire and water? No problems with the former, at least, for Sarah.

'I'm happy with fire. Although I did once double an MP's wife – Neil Hamilton's wife, Christine – on a Harry Hill show when we did a full fire job. That means you're a human torch – you're completely alight, with flames four or five feet above your head. And this for a comedy show! Unfortunately it was a windy day. They put a lot of this inflammable glue on you, and obviously you become very, very hot. You wear a mask, so that your face can burn for a long time. You hold your breath, and as they put you out you still can't inhale because of the fumes. We have certain signals – because you can't talk, and even lifting your arm isn't a clear signal in a fire. So if you want to be put out – if for any reason you're burning before you should – you hit the deck, because that's a very clear signal. So I hit the deck, because it was getting really hot, and they put me out and took the mask off. But because it was windy I reignited, and of course I didn't now have any protection for my face and my hair. And your hair's always a huge worry, because it goes so quickly. In the end, two of my colleagues had to jump on top of me – and they weren't dressed for it. All for a comedy show.'

She laughs a lot, while I'm squeaking in horror. But Jim Dowdall reckons that the fire stunts are much safer today than when he came into the business.

'We've got some good kit now. When I started, you'd wrap asbestos where the fire was going to be and hope for the best. Now we have silicone arms you can put your own arms inside. We have silicone masks which go over your head, to which you can affix a wig if you want. We have fire-suits which are very thin that we dip into a barrier of cream. You soak it all in a fridge and it's all very unpleasant when you put it on, then the costume goes on top. But it gives you fourteen, sixteen seconds longer on fire than thirty years ago. But fire is very unforgiving. The difference between major burns and getting away with it is only two or three seconds.

It depends on the weather. If it's wet, then damp gets inside the clothes and it turns to steam, and that'll give you first-degree burns much more quickly than on a warm summer day. But on a sunny day you can't see the flames. If you're filming during the day you've got to find a shady area, or wait until evening – but with the evening comes more damp. So you're constantly balancing what you're going to do. But fire doesn't worry me – I've done a lot of fire jobs over the years.'

There's no doubt that, in a major action film, there's a great desire for bigger and better feats of derring-do. And directors may be prepared to push the boundaries, while the stunt crew don't like to say no.

'It's a professional approach,' says Sarah, 'because on some jobs you know you're going to get a whack. There have been times when I absolutely know that I may not come out of it unscathed. On *Titanic*, James Cameron pushed us to our limits. There's a shot where the ship's going down, and the heroine's running down the corridor with a wall of water behind her. And they'd done it a couple of times, and tipped a lot of water into the tank, and the director said, "No, it's not enough. Got to be bigger. I want literally a wall of water behind her." So they've got to dump in a lot of water at the same time. They had four containers full and a fifth on top and they hydraulically lifted the gates together, so there was so much water that it formed a wall.

'I stood at the end of the corridor and asked how many tanks they were going to open. They said, "Only three." I said that was OK. I had to run a fair few yards, and when you're running you lose a certain amount of breath – and you've then got to hold your breath at the end, for two or three minutes, while the water disperses. But I reckoned three was OK. However, when the nod went to the special effects guys all five tanks came down.

'In the shot, there's a little metal barrier which we were running towards and where we fight to get out. And this time there was a *real* wall of water. It caught up with me just as I hit the metal gate, and I didn't feel that I had enough breath left. The force of water was so colossal that it actually ripped me through the gate and I ended up breaking my foot.'

'Did they get the shot?' I enquire.

Much laughter follows: 'They did – but I went straight into the ambulance and you know what? The water had ripped off every piece of costume, even the thin wetsuit underneath. James Cameron came into the ambulance with the stunt co-ordinator and said, "Are you OK?" I said, "I *think* so." And he said, "Have you got it in you to do another one?" And I said, "Er, no."

'The odd thing is, the answer to the question "What's the hardest thing to do?" is "To say no." But you must know the limitations of the shot, because there are certain directors who want more more more – and they don't care.'

Broken feet, whiplash, burns, crushed bones: there must be a moment in the preparation when you work out what might happen to you. Jim Dowdall remembers a very early jump.

'You can calculate, to a certain extent, depending on what you've got down below you. When I was a young lad and had just come out of the Paras I did a jump of about 14 feet, as if from a first-floor window, on to concrete. I recce'd it and said, "Yeah – I can do that, do a break fall." The director said, "No – we want you to land *thump* in front of the camera and then we see you leg it away from the police in the next shot." So all of a sudden, all the kinetics of the stunt which I've already agreed to do have changed. And I remember the continuity girl coming up to me when I landed and saying, "You'll suffer for that when you're older. We could *feel* you landing." Now my knees are knackered – and I put it all down to that one jump.

'It's slightly the school of hard knocks, and of listening to the guys who've done it before. And watching lots and lots of films and finding out how it was done – because there are lots and lots of tricks of the trade. Yes, we are to a certain extent illusionists, but at the end of the day you've got to say, "I'm going to turn the car over, and it's going to be on fire. I've taken all the precautions I can, but the weirdest things happen."

'I'm in pain every day of my life. I don't say that in any dramatic kind of way. I've got five impacted vertebrae, three from the Paras and two from landing on my head in *Superman* in 1976, and those have caused enormous trouble. I cut my finger off in a mobile crash and didn't even know I'd done it, because you're so hyped up, full of adrenalin.'

Jim acknowledges that there may be a few 'adrenalin junkies' in the business who 'don't do fear'. However, he insists that most of his colleagues are more intrigued by the need to overcome problems: how to control a car crash, how to emerge unscathed from a ball of fire.

'There's an element of showmanship of course, and a little bit of aggression, but overall, it's the ability to be in control – at least they're not firing *live* bullets at you! And these days, the pay is much better and there's extra for particularly skilled or dangerous work.' Even so, his wife insists that he ring her immediately after he has completed a 'big' crash or a 'difficult' fire job.

'She once came to watch me slide an articulated lorry down a runway, which was tricky. Afterwards, bless her, she said: "You did it three times, so I guess you know what you're doing . . ."' And his teenage daughter adored her birthday treat: in full diving gear with three school friends, sitting eighteen feet underwater in the tank used in James Bond films.

The impression comes over that it's a guy's world, as Sarah explains, in which the men do the fighting and the women do the suffering: 'Women are often the victims – I end up dying a lot. I've done a few of the Lynda La Plante films for television and they have some pretty grisly killings. I've been hanged, I've been drowned, I've been shot, I've been stabbed . . . you name it, I've died that way. I've been in Cardiff the last couple of days, hanging upside down. Awful. And then there are rape scenes – which aren't great and can be very emotional. Some scripts can be really quite upsetting to film. I was involved with *United 93*, directed by Paul Greengrass – about the hi-jacked flight that went down on the same day as the World Trade Center. I doubled one of the air hostesses, who had her throat cut. It was shot in real time, so the take lasted exactly the same length of time that the flight took. There was an incredible amount of detail, and it was one of the most upsetting things I've done.

'And just falling down stairs is more difficult for women, because you often have a skirt on – the men can wear lots of padding. The costume department also conspires against you because they don't always think of the practicalities. You think it's great to jump on the back of a motorbike and wheelie down behind the hero? Not when you've got a long white dress on, and the guy's going mental because he thinks it's going to get caught in the wheels.

'Generally, in this business, it's definitely harder as a woman. For years there were very, very few women doing this work, and it's still highly chauvinistic. Though things have changed considerably now, and you see far more camerawomen and the odd clapper-loader, a few women directors and the occasional sound-lady – but only in the last ten years.'

One of the advantages of the film industry is that exotic locations and interesting (or at least famous) people are part of the package. And sophisticated technology can give both greater safety and a better stunt. However, the element of danger is embedded in the work. The very purpose of many stunts is to deliver activity which deserves the warning: Don't try this at home! Injuries are a given, and on occasion some stunts fail to defy death. So do you need to be fearless? Jim Dowdall gives his view:

'Adrenalin is what gives you the edge on your judgement. In my mind, there's a very great difference between adrenalin and fear. They're often thought of as going hand in hand. But fear is much harder to control. It will produce adrenalin, and if you can *control* fear to give you adrenalin to a level which will give you the edge, then it's beneficial. But when you trip over that point and your own bodily fear takes over, when you get the red veil thing and go, "I don't want to look – I know I'm going to get hit . . . aaarghh", that's when you hurt yourself.'

For Sarah Franzl, it has been a way to demonstrate that women can make it into what has always been a very male world, and she is the only woman to have sat on the committee which approves new entrants into the profession. Otherwise, she goes out to work like any other divorced mother with a young teenage daughter.

' "What are you doing today, Mum?" she'll ask. And I'll say, "Being hanged, beaten or whatever." And she's been along to see the odd film I'm in – but obviously some of it isn't appropriate for her to see. I think she's proud of me – I do the Harry Potter films, and she and her friends love them. I was Harry's mum in the first one, and Tonks, and I look after some of the girls on the set from the safety point of view. They're lovely pictures to work on. I'm a mum who goes off to have Wand Rehearsals and I get Spell coaching!'

In the name of what?

'Maybe in the name of women. Years ago the guys used to do it all – even doubling Sophia Loren. And it was so obvious. But it's great now that women are coming through, because the world is changing.'

And for Jim Dowdall: 'My father killed himself when I was eight – he was an alcoholic, and I've never drunk in my life. And my mother said to me, "You'll never come to anything, my boy, because you never got your four A-levels and whatever . . . so you'll never come to anything." And I kind of resolved in myself that, if I ever was going to come to anything, I was going to be doing things that I was good at, not things about which other people said, "Well, you might *possibly* be able to do that." And this business has proved that – touch wood – over the years.

'My dad was at Arnhem, as a war correspondent, and when I was a lad he gave me a cap badge that had been given to him by one of the boys at the end of the battle. He said, "Never lose this. And if you see a man from Arnhem, shake him by the hand." And I never forgot that. I wanted to join the Paras because my dad had said what an incredible bunch of blokes they were, and when I joined and got through, put on the badge that Dad had given me, I felt this enormous pride at being part of something.

'The stunt business is a little bit the same. You put your life into somebody else's hands sometimes, and they put theirs into yours.

There's the companionship and closeness you have with people. You think, I'm going to be on fire for eleven seconds, and if I've got a problem I'll give them a certain sign meaning I'm in trouble, and it's down to *them* then. Now that produces the nearest thing to what I imagine the ancient Greeks had . . . the will to defend to the last.'

6

The Terrorist

What's the most dangerous thing that's ever happened to you?

People love lists, the Top Ten of everything. However, I've never been able to compile a One Two Three of Dangerous Happenings, because 'being in great danger' is a very individual judgement. And danger is endlessly comparative: what's being shot at at close range by a drunk compared to having a knife held to your throat by a slightly psychotic drunk? How does random tank shelling every fifty seconds rank with facing a man with a rocket propelled grenade launcher targeted directly at you? How about mortars landing round your vehicle versus machine gun fire directly on your vehicle?

I ought to know, but I don't – and I've been in all those Happenings. They're all bloody terrifying and at the time all seem to claim Number One in the Dangerous Chart. However, with hindsight, they're all rather different and impossible to put into a league table.

On a less personal level, there's nevertheless a vast industry which specialises in risk assessment, from corporate takeovers to conker-playing. There's a serious and reasonable intention attached to much of the work: genuine concerns for safety, the improvement of rotten working conditions, sensible foresight about likely future problems, plus the inevitable demands of the insurance companies and the whiff of American-style 'compensation culture'. At the silly end of the scale come the diktats of the 'risk jobsworths', often only slightly embellished by the tabloid press: no daisy-chain making for small children (the dirt, the germs, the possible infections); no home-baked cakes to be taken to school (all that *E-coli* lurking on kitchen tables at home); permission needed to use knitting needles in hospital A&E waiting areas (you want to add to the casualties?). Such decisions diminish personal decision-making and common-sense on-the-spot risk assessment, that useful and built-in part of our brains which tells us when we are in a fight-or-flight situation. In the business world, however, risk assessment is a complicated and serious process. Theories of risk have been developed and expensive professional advice is on offer. One theory states interestingly that 'the risks that scare people and the risks that kill them are very different'. And the Black Horse, his rider carrying scales, brings both kinds of risk: death through famine, a very likely danger which kills thousands; and, arising from the desperation of famine, death through unfair trade and crime, a danger which scares in much greater proportion than it kills. Perhaps the greatest scare today is terrorism . . . Who brings it, and why?

Some years ago I was several days into reporting the trial of a mass murderer at the Old Bailey when I found myself in the position of ticket tout. Camped on the pavement outside was the usual crowd of anorak-wearing, coffee-slurping media, joined by the rather less appealing (if this is possible) bunch of weird hangers-on who turn up to play Madame Defarge at criminal proceedings. These are the folk who gather to shout at prison vans and lunge at blanket-covered shapes heading for court. From both groups there were wheedling overtures for access to No. 1 Court.

Time was when even the humblest magistrates' court had a press bench of scribbling hacks, whose reports in local papers told you things about your neighbours you would never have guessed. Even the public seats usually contained some curious onlookers. Nowadays, much of the law is administered by officials without anyone present to represent the community, unless a celebrity name is on the charge sheet. However, the high drama of the Bailey is still very popular theatre. And the press benches are not particularly roomy. Therefore, passes are issued for great public interest cases, which is why I found myself in the possession of a pass for the trial of Dennis Neilson. It soon became clear that others had a desire to borrow it – but not to sit through the intricacies of legal argument, nor even to hear the grim details of Neilson's murder of a dozen or so young men.

'What's he look like?'

'Boring. A very boring minor civil servant.' My standard answer was greeted with disbelief, and increased efforts to obtain the pass.

'Surely not – I mean he's . . .'

Yes, Dennis murdered frequently, horrendously, and did unspeakable things with a cooking pot. But he would never have drawn a second look had he not been seated in the dock.

What was at work on the pavement outside was something very ancient and compelling, something more than curiosity. It was the old belief that the character is apparent in the face – that he would '*look* like a murderer'. It is a belief that has surfaced time and again, from the philosophers of ancient Greece to the computer gurus of the US National Security Agency predicting that they can 'spot a likely terrorist'.

'Profiling' is the new tool in America's so-called 'war on terror'. The researchers enthuse about one method which is trying to predict and locate terrorists with systems such as 'brain fingerprinting'. This involves 'memory and encoding-related multifaceted electroencephalographic responses'. Then there are the geeks at the University of Buffalo who are developing systems which aim to track your face and voice and movements to 'test against numerical behavioural indicators to provide a numerical score of the likelihood that an individual may be about to commit a terrorist act'. That deep lurking feeling that we can see the crime in the face won't go away – despite that fact that experience tells us it's fanciful.

What does Anthony McIntyre look like? A writer and college lecturer, with a PhD in history. For that is what he is – a tall, heavily built man with a small beard and lively eyes. He is physically confident and talks at a great rate, an articulate torrent backed by a breathtakingly detailed memory, especially of names and dates, often correcting himself in order to be pinpoint accurate when giving a precise account of what led him to be branded a dangerous terrorist.

'I was born in South Belfast – West Belfast is an area I migrated to when I came out of prison. The first home I lived in, from babyhood, was just off the Lower Ormeau Road. And we were the first Catholic family into Baggot Street. That meant that everyone else there was Protestant – because there weren't Jews or Mormons or anything else, just Protestants and Catholics. But I was too young – one, two – to have any memory of this, and my mother would later tell me about the "X" being daubed on our doors, around the twelfth [July, a Protestant celebration]. This was long prior to when the Troubles started, and it was because we were the only Catholic family.'

We are talking in the kitchen of his home in the Ballymurphy area of West Belfast, which these days seems like a shrine to recent history. Round the corner among a row of scruffy dwellings, their gardens full of rubbish, is a semi-detached house with mildly pretentious pillars and a portico round the front door. It is blackened and gutted, with the words 'Murderers Out' daubed on the wall in three-foot-high letters. This is part of Belfast which seems to have declared UDI from the glass and glitz of the reborn city centre.

But McIntyre's house is neat and family-friendly, with toys everywhere and a front room full of books. And no graffiti on his walls. For he's very much his own man, and has a long history of living dangerously to prove it.

'I was born in 1957. There wasn't violence used against us then – and my memory of the Protestant neighbours is that they were very fine; But we must have known what "X" meant – it must have been daunting, nevertheless. So I *knew* there was a difference from when I was very young. I remember my mother telling me about Protestants and Catholics – she wasn't sectarian – and I think I'd asked her one time, "Why does Drew not go to the same school as me?" And "Why does Drew go to Sunday school and I don't go?" But Drew McDonald's father was a B Special, though I didn't know this at the time, or if I did I didn't know the significance of it.'

The B Specials, abolished in 1970, were special to Northern Ireland: a division of the Royal Ulster Constabulary, entirely Protestant, which had its roots in the partition of Ireland and had gained a reputation for prejudicial behaviour towards Catholics. This was just one of the many differences between the Province and the rest of the United Kingdom which those of us who reported the Troubles had to learn about. And as he grew up, young Anthony found himself learning the hard way about such differences.

'When I was into my teen years, I remember staying with my grandmother in Glenmacken Street. I remember getting beaten up by Protestant kids and being called a Taig and a Fenian. It seemed to me that there was a visceral hatred and that's the only way I can describe it, because these kids were so young yet displayed such hatred and intolerance – and I didn't really know the difference. And I knew from that point on that I could be beaten up simply for being a Catholic.'

The memory comes back sharply, and he says this with quite an intake of breath as if it's unpleasant to recall. As his house bears testament, he has young children of his own these days. And one look at the graffiti outside in his street attests to a cleaving to some to those differences.

'On another occasion I was walking up the railway lines with a friend, David Young. David was a Protestant who lived in Baggot Street along with us, and he was one of my best friends. We got stopped by a crowd from Sandy Row – I don't think we'd reached teen age – and asked what our religion was. I said Catholic and David said Protestant, and I got beaten up and he didn't. The two of us had done nothing wrong. I sort of knew that Catholics got attacked for some reason, and I grew up thinking: Catholics are getting attacked and Protestants are not.

'It was a constant feature of life at school. I was attacked by workmen at school, and beaten on a bus. Simply because I was at a Catholic school. Another time me and a friend got thrown into the river – and I got out and gathered a gang in the Markets and helped rescue him. If we went down Sandy Row we were liable to get attacked, and we were chased time out of number. It seemed to me that I could walk through the Falls Road [a Catholic area] and never get stopped, even though no one knew who I was. And I was *always* stopped in a Protestant area when I was a child. And that was without even wearing school uniform. . . .'

Again he sounds genuinely baffled by such attitudes. 'It wasn't simply about religion. It was that you came from one group of people and religion was the *label*. I could not have told you the difference between the God of Protestantism and the God of Catholicism. And since then I've grown to share the belief that, as somebody once said, you know God's on your side when he hates the same people as you do. And I began to develop the hatred of those who attacked me and the community they came from as well.'

He is thoughtful, examining the roots of his subsequent behaviour, and wonders if it was a childhood which introduced him to danger. 'I've read the likes of Jimmy Boyle and Glasgow gangsters and people growing up in Dublin, and at the moment I'm reading Saddam Hussein's biography and you see *his* childhood . . . gangs, bullying, victimisers and victims. I think it's probably the same the world over. Perhaps if you read *Flashman* . . .!'

In other respects it was a normal enough childhood – a stable family, school and friends – but marred from earliest days by that rather puzzling series of being stopped, shouted at or thumped just for being who you were, with no real explanation other than that you were 'Catholic'. And these events were also territorial: there were areas which were hostile, even to a boy who hadn't much clue about religion.

'In 1969, when the Troubles broke out, I remember coming home with a newspaper and I said to my father, "When do you think they'll bring the guns out?" And he says, "It won't be long now." And I says, "They already have. There's already four people shot dead or something."

'And he jumped up, amazed. He'd seen it before – he knew Belfast was a town of violence. And *I* thought it was exciting. We went over on 15 or 16 August – it was the night after the burnings – and we went to the Falls Road in West Belfast and saw the burnt houses. And the memory's still in my mind of the peculiar, awful smell of a burning house doused in water. And I sensed around that time that the B Specials were a bad crowd and that the UVF [the Loyalist paramilitary Ulster Volunteer Force] were bad and that for some reason, Catholics, who just happened to be Catholics, were getting the rough end of the stick.

'For example, I lived in the Ormeau Road, and what gave me a sense of community identity was that I, a Catholic on the Ormeau Road, could get kicked or booted for the same reasons that a Catholic in West Belfast could, or a Catholic in Derry could. And I suppose from that time I knew that the IRA was something I would have *loved* to be involved in, even though I was very young. I had grown up watching Orange Parades [by the Protestant Orange order] march up the Ormeau Road and I usually joined in, but they always told us about *their* King William and *we* were supposed to have some great King Michael – but nobody ever seemed to know much about him. And then we were told about the UVF after the Gusty Spence killing in 1966 of Peter Ward, a Catholic barman on the Shankill Road, and how the IRA would stop him and so on. . . .'

As he gained his teens the clouds were gathering, but most of the events were filtered through overheard conversations, newspaper headlines, and snatches of hot gossip about the mysterious UVF and IRA. The politics were distant, but the events were on the streets and seemed to relate to how even a teenager experienced day-to-day life.

'In early 1970 I saw an old film with James Cagney, *Shake Hands with the Devil* – it was about the IRA and I was *fascinated* with it. It concerned the Treaty side [the Anglo-Irish Treaty of 1921, by which the counties of southern Ireland which today constitute Eire became a British Dominion] and the Anti-Treaty side, and I was with the Anti-Treaty side in my own mind – undeveloped, uncluttered by any political theory. So from that point on, I knew that I probably wanted to join the IRA and wanted to fight. I was a teenager – it was exciting, it was romantic, it was an adventure. It's like cowboy movies: people get shot and *don't* die. . . .'

It was a short while to his first taste of danger, with the streets erupting around him. 'We used to riot. I remember going up one evening to the Falls Road and Leeson Street and throwing stones at the British army. I was thirteen, turning fourteen. We were *all* rioting in the Falls, and one day I was standing in a shop and a bomb blew the windows in behind us.'

'Danger? death? It was like sickness: it happened to someone else. But the rioting was the first time I came close to danger. I remember on 9 August 1971 the British army, in MacDonald Street in the Falls Road, telling us they were doing a "countdown" – sixty seconds – and if anybody appeared on the streets after sixty seconds they would begin to shoot us dead. And us going through the countdown, thinking: this is *really* dangerous. But you feel young . . . and you also know that the real sense of fear, of trepidation comes when you're looking at guns, and they're only yards away and they're pointing these rifles at you. And you're hearing from all over the city of people being shot dead. At that point you knew that it was dangerous.'

I wondered if that was the point when a young teenager felt like going home and thinking hard about what he was doing.

'Noooo. I was out the next day, doing the same in the Markets area and looking for places to riot – Lenadoon and the Falls. We walked the whole way up there, about six miles, and we *enjoyed* it.

'A real sense of danger came in September that year. There was a man shot in the head: a gunman called at his door – just creased him, didn't kill him. And I and somebody else chased the gunman round the streets. He threw something away which I thought was a gun and I jumped on it, but it was a baton. And I continued to pursue him – but I was really frightened. Really afraid that if he turned round I would have nothing, just his police baton. And I thought: he could kill me here. I wanted to rugby-tackle him, and at the same time I was afraid to get too close to him.'

Not having learned the politics of what was going on, but frequently in amongst the action, did he ever ask himself if he knew why he was getting involved? And if he did know, did it give him added determination?

'I don't know if it did. You weave all this into the purpose that you set yourself. Then you begin to legitimise it. It goes back to the old question: do people fall down on their knees and pray because they believe in God, or do they believe in God because they fall down on their knees and pray? I've often thought about it. I mean, did we believe in Republicanism because we fought on the streets, or did we fight on the streets because we believed in Republicanism? What was the order of things?

'Now at that age – fourteen, fifteen, sixteen – you may think you know an awful lot, but in fact you know very little. You haven't even matured as a human being physically, never mind having reached the point of maturation mentally, when you can deliberate on all these matters. And even today, you can't deliberate on these matters with any degree of certainty. I mean, at fourteen or fifteen the world's very black and white. At my age now, it's very grey. I would not say that the whole thing was changed, that my actions or my purpose changed greatly as a result of becoming more aware. I think I was more aware of events than of processes. The events made me more determined to do that which I was determined to do.

'I didn't notice life becoming more dangerous. It certainly was dangerous to the extent that my home wasn't safe. There were a number of searches on my home. I remember when I was fourteen, in February '72, I got hauled into the back of an army Saracen – a 'Pig' – and my friend Frankie Rae was thrown on top of me. We got brought to Musgrave Street where we were beaten by the police. It seemed strange to me that we were being beaten at fourteen – it was the sort of thing they did to adults! I knew then that things could get dangerous. We were coming out of the barracks afterwards and everybody was talking about the fourteen-year-olds that had been arrested, and the school was concerned about it – but it was more exciting. It was a sense of adventure more than a sense of danger.

'Then the sectarian murders started. We were slightly below the age for targeting, but we knew that people of our age would still get killed and that it would be by a drive-by shooting. There used to be this famous – or infamous – Cortina that would go round shooting Catholics. But then in March '72 Patrick Pearse McCrory was shot dead in Ravenhill Avenue. I knew Patrick – he was only eighteen, but to us he looked like a mature adult, a tough guy. And we sensed that people were vulnerable, that they were not immortal and they didn't come back – like they were going to act in the next film after they'd been shot in the previous one.

'But I didn't sense that my own life was in danger and that death was waiting round the corner. I didn't sense that the actions I was taking were going to lead to any serious situation for me. I always felt that, come the day, I would be the inflicter of pain rather than the recipient.'

McIntyre gets up to make another cup of coffee and puts some scraps on to the kitchen window sill for a couple of hopeful-looking cats who have been staring in for the last five minutes. Then we return to the teenager hooked on excitement – who didn't appear to make a conscious decision to get even more involved.

'I just thought it was a natural progression. I ended up where I knew I would always have ended up, which was in the ranks of the IRA. I joined at sixteen, after having been through Young Fianna activity, which involved carrying guns and doing robberies and learning to fire a Thompson gun and being look-out and all the usual sort of stuff. . . . And at sixteen I became what was called the operations officer for the IRA in the Lower Ormeau Road – the Road's about twenty-six streets, so it's not a great title . . . And I sensed very quickly that, although there may have been fifteen, twenty people within the IRA in that area, very few of them really wanted to take the risks – and I found that I *was* quite prepared to take them. And I enjoyed taking them, because this would give me more time to shoot and such activities.'

Did his parents know?

'Oh, they knew – and they weren't too happy. They knew it was dangerous, and the house was getting raided at this stage. Once it was raided five times in two weeks, because they were looking for me. And the British had said that I was to be shot on sight. This is what they were saying: "Tell the gunman that we're going to shoot him." And they would send messages to me through the people they were arresting, you know: "When you see McIntyre, tell him we're going to shoot him dead." But I didn't feel too concerned about it.'

All this is rattled off as if it were just teenage pranks – but this was a sixteen-year-old who was armed. And who now, when I ask about the first time he endangered someone else, can't quite remember – because there were so many 'operations' and he remembers that he was in danger too.

'Oh, every time when you went out to fire at British soldiers you were in danger. I remember the first time I opened fire on the British army. And people were saying, "There's one hit . . . there's one hit." I was quite pleased with that. But when the TV news was on they didn't mention anything, so I think people made these things up. But throwing petrol bombs and stuff didn't seem to be so potentially lethal.'

How does a teenager react to being sought by the security forces? Did McIntyre give it much thought?

'When I joined the IRA and ended up on the run, my life was completely consumed . . . I'd stopped work and the searches were hot and heavy for me. They searched every house in the area – first time they'd done that. It felt really close. I didn't think of anywhere that was all that safe, unless I was out of the city altogether and was in Dundalk [in the Republic], and even then I was getting hassled by the Garda. And when I look back on it, well . . . most sixteen-year-olds don't go through this, though *I* thought it was run-of-the-mill. Arrests, harassment – the number of times I was arrested was phenomenal, all through '73, and I was very arrogant when I was arrested. I sort of felt, "I'm going to be caught." But it didn't really occur to me that I was going to be killed, unless they caught me on an operation. We had elaborate plans for dealing with the British army: we would always open fire on them from one side of the Ormeau Road and immediately cross the road a couple of streets up, knowing that they would not be searching this side. It worked every time. And we were pretty confident – but I knew, I just knew I couldn't carry on being on the run.

'There was another moment, in '74, when the IRA said they were off to kill a British army spy and they wanted me to be the driver. And I said, "I can't drive – but I'll learn." So we hi-jacked a car that day, myself and a fifteen-year-old lad called John Morgan who in '82 turned Supergrass. We raced it up and down the Ormeau Road, learning to drive – a period of about four or five hours and self-taught . . . terrible, terrible.

'We went to the Markets in the car and, funnily enough, the man charged with the murder of Robert McCartney, Terence Davison, was also in the car, and he said, "Let me drive it" – and he was trying to learn, too, but he crashed the car into a wall. The British army surrounded us and Davison said to me, "I'm sorry Tony, I've got you caught." They put us up against a wall and I thought, I'm going to run from this – he's caught himself, and I'm bolting. I gave a false name and address, and when they asked us what we were doing I said, "Learning to drive – my brother's a taxi driver and lent it to us and he's crashed it.' And they seemed sympathetic. Then they got a call on their radios and they all began to run down the street to pick up someone else. And I thought: *great* – they don't know what I look like.

'I was involved in a lot of operations. I won't go into detail, but people ended up dying, and the one I was convicted for – and I was imprisoned from April '74 until November '75 – was a pretty routine operation, pretty easy to put together. Most people knew that when Loyalists attacked there would be a retaliation, so you'd be sitting waiting.

'That week I had been out every night, trying to get operations together to make sure we got killings. And the Friday night of the operation that I was arrested for I says, "That's me off tonight, someone else can be doing it." There had been a bomb planted in the Markets that morning by the Loyalists, so the IRA asked us to put an operation together in retaliation. It was to take out the UVF doorman in a bar in the Donegal Pass.

'And then we had trouble persuading the locals to let us have one of their cars, and I had to get aggressive with one man in our local bar and show him my gun and say "Give us a car or . . . your wife and child . . . we'll shoot you first." And on the spur of the moment I took the decision: "I'll go with you, do the operation." Gloves on, car, into Donegal Pass, got the target. And all the time thinking on my feet. We pulled up at the bar and went to see if there were any of the local UVF in it. And there were three elderly men sitting in front of us. And I said, "Don't, don't" – they would have been dead if we'd opened fire. So we left that bar and, funnily enough, on the way round we'd seen a man called Norman Rooney, a member of the UVF.

'We'd been planning to shoot Norman for quite some time. I had put in considerable time trying to shoot him in his own home in Charlotte Street. We used to observe his movements and to walk past his mother at the front door when she was "doing a D" – women in working-class areas used to sit outside the door with a cloth in their hands and reach out and clean a D-shaped area. So I said to myself: We just have to put the door in. We can do it and run for it. We can walk down and, if she's there, the door's gonna be open. Straight on past her, shoot him, and back out into the Markets. So easy an operation. The only thing was timing. And lo and behold, Norman appears out of the blue while we're driving round armed to the teeth. And I says: "Aah – there's Norman. It's Christmas time! Let's move round and take him out."

'As we were doing a full circle of the block to cut Norman off before he could get to his house, we passed the very bar we'd initially targeted and there was the UVF doorman that we wanted. So I just said, "Stop the car. That's him." We shot him dead and drove off into the Markets. And I had the presence of mind, because people were coming out from everywhere, to say, "Don't go down that street – the crowds are there and we're gonna have to start shooting and we're gonna run out of ammunition and they'll lynch us. Take a right." And we took the right and then I remember saying, "Don't go up the Ormeau – take a left." And the guy says, "We're coming to the lights. What'll we do? There's a British army sanger [sandbagged position]." And I said, "Straight through the lights. If we stop and he realises it's us he'll shoot us dead. Don't stop – just go straight through."

'I remember all these things, and that I was in absolute control and very lucid and not panicking as we made good our escape. But I suppose there were very few people who would have done it, so they knew who they were looking for. And they arrested us. Me first. And it was all a farce. They said, "Your prints are on the window". It had been a split-second decision of mine, thinking it was wiser to take the gloves off, so that if we were walking down the street no one would see us with gloves on, whereas if we were spotted *with* gloves we'd be stopped for going on an operation. But the police told me my fingerprints *were* on the car . . . and they'd been found some time after I'd been charged, so I've always wondered about the fingerprints.'

The whole episode comes tumbling out at breakneck speed, with precise dates and details, like a running commentary on a vivid teenage scene, but without any relish – or regret. It's a dispassionate caption to a violent strip cartoon of daily life in the Troubles. A teenage lad given over wholly to the IRA, the streets alive with rioting, British soldiers, crowds and bombs. The automatic sense of Them and Us. The quasi-military posturing of the IRA, the colleagues who went on to further violence, the enthralling details of 'operations'. All carried out in your own back yard – literally. The indifference to, even ignorance of, consequences. Starting to go out to kill at sixteen – with many of your school friends and neighbours alongside. And prison made no difference.

'When I got out in '75, I went back to it almost immediately. Planning, discussing, attending meetings – my whole life revolved round the IRA. I had grown up a bit, but the culture – the institution maybe more than the politics – is what motivates people. You know, the *esprit de corps*, all of that. And I think that people are committed to each other. And in a sense it was a bit like a cult – the cult of the IRA. We were all sort of infatuated.'

In February 1976 McIntyre was convicted of shooting a member of the UVF. This time he got life.

'When I went into prison in 1976, I had my "political" status [not having to wear uniform or do prison work]. I got sentenced to the cages in Long Kesh, and life imprisonment, which was twenty-five years. And it was only when I attempted to escape on 29 June '78 that I lost political status and they put me in cellular confinement in the H-blocks. So I went "on the blanket" on 12 July '78 [wrapped only in a blanket, rather than wearing prison clothing], and it was a very tense, a very brutal, a very violent period.'

Having come from extreme violence on the streets, McIntyre went into a world that had its own violent rules. 'We always say that prison is cool, because it helps keep prison officers off the streets. I never thought it was a violence that would kill someone, although I was surprised by the viciousness of it on occasion – from the prison staff. I remember being taken out for a forced wash and literally being rammed into the grilles and kicked and dragged over ground. And I was sort of the opinion that these guys don't really care and they'll do what they're allowed to do, and if they're allowed to kill us they'll kill us. I didn't really feel that the NIO [Northern Ireland Office] would say, "Murder them." But one of the problems was that when some of them got drunk, there was always a fear that one of them would overstep the mark.'

That a dangerous atmosphere existed in a jail such as the Maze should be no surprise. The divisions that caused the trouble outside were present inside. The prison was just another stage on which to continue the fight. And there were various determined organisations inside the walls trying to run the place other than the official authorities.

'The IRA was an authoritarian organisation – but I never felt under threat from other prisoners. I always felt comfortable with them. No. No. One of the great things about prison life with the IRA was the absence of bullying. The IRA didn't allow it, put a stop to it. You always got the individual – but they didn't get too far.'

However, one of the ways not to survive prison was to volunteer to go on hunger strike, yet another escalation in the war of attrition fought within prison walls; first the blanket protest then the dirty protest (no personal hygiene) and finally no food. In a closed society, a vortex of power-play, there was always the possibility that you might face the decision to be a great danger to yourself.

'I volunteered to go on the first hunger strike – but there was a ban on prisoners like myself who were in for what were called sectarian killings. They wanted people who were in for killing soldiers. They had this pretence that the IRA didn't kill Protestants, so we were barred from taking part. I wanted to go on it, and I was very, very disappointed. And in '81, on the second hunger strike, I went back to the OC, Brendan McFarlane, and again he said I would be on it if only for the fact that I was a "sectarian". I suppose there was a mixture of . . . relief and . . . disappointment. I'm trying to think back to what it felt at the time. It's a relief *looking back* on it – a strange mixture of emotions. But strangely enough, you try and weigh up the benefits of dying, and one of the benefits of dying was that you wouldn't have to do the life sentence. I remember saying to myself . . . mmm, is that a death wish? That you'll not have to spend the rest of your days in jail, and you can have a go at hurting the Brits? And in the hunger strikes, we had seen people die and we were determined. Even though we knew and we argued that we needed to call an end to it, we still wanted to inflict one last hurrah and hurt the British.

'I don't think martyrdom appealed to me that greatly. The IRA was not a particularly religious organisation, though there was religion in the jail – but mainly because there was little else to do. But I didn't take part in it. At funerals for IRA volunteers there was a lot of the rosary and stuff, but there were disputes about this and people didn't like it. During the 1981 hunger strike there were women saying the rosary and we were being compared to Christ-like figures and such, and this didn't gel with our image of us. And as for the martyrdom, for those of us who were in there it didn't appeal. Because we tended to feel there's no heroes in a foxhole. Martyrdom is for people who live amazing lives. I mean, for us it's dirt and blood and shit-covered walls. I suppose, looking back, I always tended to think that I looked ahead. Henry Heaney was a guy that died in jail in 1978 and he said to me in 1974, "Don't worry – it's not a graveyard." I always thought of life *after* hunger strikes, *after* protest. I don't think that I was in dying mode.'

It's curious to hear of the attitudes inside the prison when I was always outside, among the crowds of protestors who took to the streets almost every week in support of the hunger strikers. And there were often religious overtones among many of the supporters, who earnestly believed that something very virtuous – even grimly romantic – was under way, something which reached back into Irish history. The tradition of fasting, possibly to death, as a means of obtaining redress is ancient in Ireland – though this had little resonance across the Irish Sea, resulting in sharply differing reactions to the strike. However, within the Maze there was discipline, grim determination and a rigid hierarchy of who actually qualified to starve themselves to death.

Seventeen years were passed in prison. At the age of twenty-seven, McIntyre took his first O-level. Then he studied for a degree, passing with first-class honours, and he now holds a PhD. Life after prison has been very different – but he doesn't feel free from danger. In 1998, when Sinn Fein approved the Good Friday agreement, he severed his lifelong connection with the Republican movement. He is a dissenter, although one who has no desire whatsoever for a return to the violence of the Troubles; rather, he believes that Sinn Fein have sold out. He is critical of the men from Sinn Fein and the IRA who wear suits and negotiate with the British government. This was not what the deaths, the violence, the prison protests and the hunger strikes were for. He feels a deep sense of betrayal, after years in prison for what he thought these men too believed in.

What was it all for? An agreement with the British?

He feels that his views – which he hasn't hesitated to publicise – may well spell danger for him and his family. 'I think if you're in a situation like mine where you're a dissenter . . . people like me tend to see danger even when it's not there. I have felt at times that they might shoot me. The IRA might shoot me – or the Sinn Fein leadership. I have been told by a close journalist friend, Ed Maloney, that he's convinced that the leadership have probably said, "Why didn't we shoot McIntyre and Maloney ten years ago?"

'I have a family and I've felt quite tense at times, and I still feel tense on this estate. The thing that compares most to my life when I go out the door on this estate is a wing-shift in prison. When we were on the blanket we got moved from wing to wing. Now a wing-shift is when you're outside your cell, and it's when the likelihood of beatings and attacks increases. Very, very rarely did I get beaten on wing-shift and Butcher Hughes, a fellow blanket man, used to say, "Look, it satisfies the malign intentions and aggressive intent of the screws, but just get it into your mind that anything you sustain on a wing-shift is something you get like when running for a bus." He was right.

'The point I'm trying to make is that when I'm out on this estate it's the *tension* of the wing-shift, rather than what is actually happening. It's the *order* of battle, rather than the battle. And when we talk about the order of battle, the most horrifying thing on the blanket was when we got the order to attack the screws, because they were going to force-wash us. And the boys on the wing started cheering and I was lying down with flu and I said to the guy next door, "Right, we'll attack them. And if we get hemmed in, that means that every time they want to wear us down they'll come in and we'll have to attack them. Now you and me and a few others will probably sit to the very end of it, however many times they beat us, but the vast majority here won't. Remember, resistance and the strength to endure is of a finite nature, and you have to remember that they will wear down our resistance. And our job is to spread out our resistance and keep this protest going."

'Oh, it was awful, I thought I was going to get killed, thought I was going to die – the flu was horrible too. Now the flu passed, and then the order came, "Don't be fighting the screws." But it's the *order* of battle: it's the same when I'm out on the streets here. I feel tense . . . but I *can't* feel tense, because you know that these people have been winded up to hit me because of my views. My house has been picketed, there've been mobs outside my front door. My oldest child was inside her mother's womb when the first mob arrived with their placards and their wee gangs and howling. And the second night they came I was at a conference on free speech in Cookstown, and my wife was six months pregnant and they came and shouted at her and howled at her, led by the present Sinn Fein councillor, and then I was attacked in the street. But it's a strange situation, because I've been in bars at times, surrounded by Sinn Fein, like the wildebeest in the house of the lions, and had an argument and that's been it – no trouble. So sometimes I feel that the trepidation is an awareness of what *could* happen, rather than an awareness of what is likely to happen. . . .'

He rattles on, an edge to his voice, no longer a young blood out on the streets caught up in excitement and risk but a man in his fifties, still full of commitment to his beliefs but now conscious of the consequences. His young children are playing in the next room and he calls to them to keep the noise down – a reminder of his present responsibilities. And with his background, he is more than aware that some men have not put away their guns. Although I wondered, after all he had been through – and survived, if he was an optimist?

'No, for they say in Northern Ireland that a pessimist is never proved wrong. I'm a pessimist. . . .' He laughs heartily and then sits and muses.

There's a slight chill as we sit in the kitchen, his two young children still making a happy racket next door, a friend arriving for a chat, a noise at the window as a stray cat wowls for food. It's bright sunshine outside, the toys are scattered in the front garden, and some of the neighbours are definitely houseproud (though I doubt they 'do a D' on the doorstep these days). But within sight are slogans and daubed walls, memorials and flags. The order of battle survives in many ways.

So he spent years of his life committed to violence – and then in prison. In the name of what?

'In the name of a belief – a belief in Irish Republicanism that I've had serious doubts about for many years since.'

7

The Armed Robber

Fear of crime is often greater than the prevalence of crime itself. These days government and police statistics tend to be seen as public relations exercises, bearing no relation to the anecdote you just heard in the chip shop from your neighbour's sister whose friend heard that a mate of his had seen somebody stabbed outside the betting shop last night – or was it Friday?

Crime has always been good for gossip. Even in a world of electronic news and internet chatter, what you hear over the garden fence or in the bus queue makes an impact which statistics cannot, however colourful or vague the details. Perhaps it's our fear of crime that makes us love detective novels and films about gangsters, never mind the blood-spattered offerings on prime-time television which would convince a visiting Martian that bullet-ridden corpses are an everyday sight for decent citizens. We know that crime causes misery, but we also detect a dark, glittery glamour in some law-breaking corners. A dangerous glamour. Crime rides the Black Horse of danger, though perhaps it's mildly ironic that it should be represented by the scales of justice. . . .

'Among the mourners at the funeral in London's East End was Mr Frank Fraser. . . .' This apparently innocuous line of script was heading for the newsreader's desk in the BBC television newsroom. It was scrutinised by a senior duty editor, a man famed for his meticulousness in matters of accuracy and grammar, before being grabbed by the reporter who had actually been to the funeral.

'Who altered my words?' he growled. 'No one's heard of Frank Fraser.'

'Then why is he in the report?' enquired the duty editor.

''Cos he's Mad Frankie Fraser, that's why.'

'I don't know if we can call him that on the BBC. . . .'

The ensuing argument ran into more difficulties when it emerged that another gentleman who was getting a mention was Jack the Hat McVitie. And the matter was not resolved by suggesting that '*Mister* Mad Frankie Fraser' might be more the BBC 'house style'.

The BBC didn't really *do* gangsters. One look at the reporters' room would confirm that there was a dearth of shifty-looking hacks in grubby macs who spent their off-duty hours rubbing shoulders with gangland heavies in dodgy pubs. No one could claim familiarity with a safe-cracker or knew how to get hold of a 'sawn-off' (and in any case you'd have to explain that this meant a modified shotgun). Television news has a tradition of rather well-scrubbed and moderately un-criminal journalists who would probably have been instantly exposed in dodgy pubs with the words: 'You're the poncy lad from off the telly, aren't you?'

I once sat in such a pub (in a suitably grubby mac) with one of the doyens of the old Fleet Street, who knew everyone in what used to be referred to as 'the underworld' of crime. After an ordinary-looking bloke sitting in the corner had finished his drink and walked out, I was told that he'd 'done for' several people. You will realise that I too had no talent for this kind of journalism when I tell you that my instinct was to pursue him for an interview.

All large cities go through phases of 'gangland' violence, and in post-war Britain until the late sixties there was an upsurge, especially in London. The twins Ronnie and Reggie Kray became household names for all the wrong reasons and they were rivalled by the Richardson Gang. Although they kept close to their roots in the East End and south London, their tentacles stretched out across the city and into other parts of the country. Even in the north-east, where I was a student in the sixties, there were home-grown smaller versions of protection rackets and clubland corruption – and not a little wariness that a 'London mob' might try and muscle in on local crime. I realised that you can live in quite a small place without ever encountering – in fact, remain in complete ignorance of – the undercurrent of violent and organised crime which can seep into 'respectable' communities.

Print reporters were much more adept at burrowing into the 'underworld's' undergrowth, and most of the murders and armed robberies that I encountered were at the trials we reported for television. The nearest I came to poking my nose into 'the heavy stuff' followed the notorious Brinks Mat gold bullion robbery in 1983. The theft of more than £25 million worth of gold from a warehouse near Heathrow airport spawned numerous convictions and involved me in an odd chase around Tenerife with sundry suspect persons and a fight with a gang of transvestites. I never quite got the hang of this kind of reporting. The only time I felt my 'street cred' acknowledged was when Kenny Noye, who is at present serving a life sentence for murdering a motorist, used to shout 'Hello, Kate' from the dock during an earlier murder trial for shooting a policeman. Although I expect he only regarded me as 'that poncy bird from off the telly'.

Whether you accept that there's such a job as 'professional criminal' probably depends on your background and moral outlook, rather than an assessment of what practical steps are needed to warrant such a description. But if, in the course of conversation, someone refers seriously to the rest of society as 'straight-goers', you get a hint of a different outlook on life. And if this life involves acquiring lots of money, attracting the opposite sex and having a high old time – it stands to reason that it may gain quite a devoted following. Why everyone doesn't feel quite the same about crime can be ascribed mainly to moral objections – but there's another factor too: rather a lot of danger. Some lines of work involve danger just because certain people wish to appear 'dangerous': any business using terms such as 'putting the frighteners' on somebody should come into this category. Such behaviour leads to real danger and even death (often not referred to directly by those in this line of work – 'little accident', 'rubbing out' and 'pushing up the daisies' being preferred options). And this avoidance of plain speaking extends to the job itself.

'I used to tell my bird's mother that I was in banking. She was a posh bird and I didn't want to embarrass her.'

Bobby Cummines was merely being economical with the truth. He *was* in banking, in a way. He was a bank robber. A dapper and courteous man, nimble and engaging, Cummines has now hung up his sawn-off, so to speak. He has spent most of his life breaking the law and serving time for it, although, once inside, the company he kept was in line with his activities outside – he is an ex-cellmate of Reggie Kray. And he began early:

'I was the youngest of eight and I lived in King's Cross in north London, which was rife with prostitution, gang warfare and all that. And as you grew up, in the schools it was about fighting – it was about how far you was prepared to go. My family weren't really violent people, though one of my uncles was an illegal bookmaker and some of the others were a bit dodgy – but not like the criminality I was later involved in. We owned a building firm, with fourteen lorries and scaffolding and all that, and in our own area we was quite wealthy, I suppose. But my dad was cash in hand, didn't take no notice of book-keeping, and before we knew what was happening the taxman come in and took away our home and we was bankrupt. Then we moved to council accommodation – one minute you got everything, next minute nothing. And there was a rule in our community: you can rob who you like – jewellers' shops, banks and things – but you don't rob your own. You'd break into warehouses, but you didn't break into working-class people's houses. So people left their doors open.'

He talks fast and articulately, conjuring up an Artful Dodger, alert and intelligent. And yet the threat of danger enters the story very quickly.

'The first bit of violence happened when I was getting ready to go to my secondary school, and I come from an Irish background and we tend to stick together. So, fighting on a Sunday afternoon.

Stand up, fists up, have your fight, but afterwards everybody was
best friends – and you went home with cuts and bruises and Dad
was happy as long as you'd put up a good show.

'We had a bully in school – Jimmy Brennan. He was a big Irish
kid from Connemara, a redneck, and I was a very small kid. He
used to go around nicking the kids' marbles out the gutters. We
used to get on all right, go to the same church youth club, the
Penny Club. But he had this girl he liked – and I got on all right
with her and he didn't like that. In the playground he started his
tricks – and we was only kids, eleven or so – and I thought, if you
come on me I'm going to fight you. And I've never had fear of
people – I've always been willing to take them on. He tried it, we
had a bust-up and I come off worse. I went home, saw my dad, and
he said, "Been fighting? Don't look as if you come off too good.
. . ." And a friend – who had the hots for my sister – said to me,
"Bobby, with a bully, what you've got to do is to hurt them so hard
that no one wants to fight you again. So don't fight fair."

'"What do you mean?"

'"Get yourself a lump of wood," he said. "And hit him with
that."

'I thought about it. I was quite a devious kid anyway – I used to
plan how to break into warehouses and that sort of stuff. So I got
my school duffel bag, then got my sister's rounders bat – we didn't
use knives in them days – and popped it into the bag. I knew Jimmy
used to wait for the girls by the bike sheds, and I thought: that's
where I'm going to give it to him. I'd planned it in my head – just
like when I done banks later – and I knew it would work. I got up
really early that morning, with this really, really weird feeling. I felt
I'd got the power back. I thought: this is the leveller. No one can
touch me now. And with that bat in my hand I would have fought
anyone. I thought: you may be a big roughneck, but I can take you
down with this.

'So I trotted up and I did him across the shins and I beat him to a
pulp, basically. All his ribs. But I didn't touch his face. It was just
like a bit of work – and it wasn't the violence for me: it was the
terror. I could see it in his eyes. I said to him, "If you ever come

near me again, I'll put you in hospital for such a long time." He was out of school for a couple of weeks, but kept the golden rule, never grassed up. We become best mates after that. Everything was good. I'd learned that violence had a voice.'

This kind of early learning experience is what Bobby Cummines now counsels against. He is immensely concerned that young people should know how they can go off the rails and what might happen to them. Even so, he looks back on his own progression from toughening-up young schoolboy to tough young teenager with no regrets; he fitted in with his milieu, and there was nothing around him to indicate that he should choose another path.

'I started boxing and was Islington boys' bantamweight champion for four years. I bunked off school often, but as long as I won cups for the headmaster he was all right about it. You didn't win money – you got tea services! My mum had loads of them – gave them away to all her friends. But she never came and saw me box, because she didn't believe in violence . . . Then a couple of older people said to me that I could earn good money "using my hands". All to do with people owing people money – you're terribly manipulated when you're a kid. They said, "People owe money and they're not paying – but if you collect their money, for every hundred quid you get we'll give you ten quid." I thought: yeah, that's a good proposition! What I didn't realise was that they were getting fifty quid, and I was the mug along the food chain.

'So I started doing that and used a baseball bat, then went collecting with a bayonet – and then someone stabbed me with a carpet knife and ripped me. So at the age of sixteen I got a sawn-off shotgun. I let off a couple of times when people was going for me, and that's when I realised I was going to be giving it back. I was one of the youngest what ever got done for possession of a sawn-off.

'It was a progression. From very small violence – a baseball bat, a scrum – it became a business. It wasn't *personal*, this was *business*. No different to an army really – if you've got a tank, I'm going to get a nuclear weapon. Up the ante all the time. When you're whacking someone, whether it's a knee- or a head-job, or whatever, you've got to study that person. The effect I had on people was like throwing a pebble in a stream – the ripple effect. You wanted to do it so well that people thought: I'm not going to mess with that guy. But then there were those who wanted your job, and you had to be wary, because you could get set up yourself.'

The descriptions are chatty, matter-of-fact. The pictures they conjure up are not immediately conceivable if you have led a quiet life. But the details tumble out with the ring of truth: a parallel existence to respectable business, with its own methods of career progression and recognition, and its own code of practice.

'The rules of the game was these. You wasn't allowed to do innocent members of the public. You wasn't allowed to do journalists. And you wasn't allowed to do coppers, 'cos it causes too much aggravation. If you do one of them, all the Old Bill will come in and *everyone*'s rackets will stop. Oh, and you couldn't do anyone if they was with their wife or their children, because you wouldn't want that done to you. There ain't them rules now – it's gone out the window with drugs coming in.'

There's a pause for reflection on a lost world full of arcane etiquette, with honour among thieves. But understanding that this world was in any way wrong doesn't seem to have percolated: 'We all knew each other as I gradually got into it. And I got really angry when someone first called me a gangster! A guy said to the girl I was with, "Did you know you was living with a gangster?" So I dragged him out the pub and took him up the side street and stuck a gun in his mouth and said, "Don't you ever say bad things about me to anyone. You're bang out of order. All I ever do is earn money. Don't you ever call me a gangster." You see, I didn't like the stigma. I was a businessman, collecting debts. It was later on I went on to rob banks and all that.'

So he was a young man 'in business', operating in a world that had its own territorial markings, its own way of closing a deal. It was a world in which you progressed through increasing levels of violence, bolstering your reputation by intensifying the danger to those around you and to yourself.

'I operated in north London. When we was working rackets, doing organised crime and that, we was young and had nice clothes from the boutiques that had just opened and ate in the new Indian restaurants – I'd go and see the Archway and Highgate boys and say to them, "We've got new shops opened – and they need their windows put through." So they'd go and smash all their windows. There'd be uproar and we'd go round and tell the shop owners, "We can stop all this happening. We'll sort it out – if you give us a little piece of the action." Then we'd go up Archway and on to Hampstead and do their windows the same. So the Archway guys got their cut too. A little earner thing, with the understanding that I wouldn't go on their patch and they wouldn't come on mine. But like everyone, they got greedy. And I got a message one day that they was going to come and get me and feed me to the dogs, and I thought I'd better put a stop to this. Went up the Archway – there was about ten of them, and they used knives. I was on my own, but they'd never seen a gun before – and they ran. So we expanded our patch.

'One guy said to me at that time, "You're either mad, or you're very brave." I said, "Do you want to try it on with either one? 'Cos either one's very dangerous. . . ." It's that *power* . . . When we started doing the "heavy gang" – that's anything to do with firearms, armed robbery, banks and so on (not drug dealing then – like sex offenders, they was low-life) – you met others in the same line of business, from other areas. And then when you done your jail – brilliant, 'cos now you're networking. You know guys in Manchester, in Glasgow, in Birmingham, so now you could really go to work.'

He pauses to muse on today's criminal scene. He disapproves of the huge profits to be made through dealing in drugs, the easy way addicts can be pulled into the distribution system, and the addiction itself. That odd streak of gangland Puritanism shows itself: drugs were something that old-time hardened gangsters rarely, if ever, touched themselves. He laments the passing of the old-style 'heavy' business.

'Heavy's now drug-dealing, 'cos armed robbery got hard, because of cameras and intelligence-led policing. The rewards in drugs was a lot more. Also, you was sending out people who weren't going to shop you, because they needed the gear, and all you had to do was mind the business. I'll never forget when drugs come in. We were at the heavy game, our rackets, shooting each other, and we had problems with the Turkish mafia which come in, up in Finsbury Park, who dealt in cannabis and prostitution and gambling houses. And we'd had to sort them out for creeping into our patch. They was very good with knives, but they was wary of guns, so we sorted them out. Then the Chinese Triads arrived: it used to be the tongs. I went up to Soho, to Gerrard Street, and met Mr Fu, and he took me into a restaurant basement and there were all these guys playing mah jong – and they were betting cars and restaurants. I'd known him in jail, when he was doing a ten [year sentence], and he'd said, "When you get out, come and see me – good business." I was young and I was violent, so they probably thought they could use me. . . .'

He didn't need to go into drugs anyway, because the protection business was doing fine. A country growing a little more affluent – new shops, new restaurants – offered lots of opportunities. But the level of danger needed to be maintained.

'I was in my early twenties. I always had a gun with me. I slept with one under the pillow, I had the pump-action under the bed and I had one in the toilet. Any room where I went, I would always have a shooter there, because *I'd* once shot a guy through the letter box, so I was very aware of how vulnerable I was.

'I was in a crowd, the centre of attention, but on my own. I didn't trust no one. Any one of them could be carrying a gun, and any one of them could do me. And as I got more involved and my reputation grew for the heavy game, I wouldn't drink alcohol, I wouldn't take dope – I wouldn't have anyone near me who took it, because they'd be a weak link. So although it was glamorous and you had the nice clothes and that I never enjoyed it, because I was always on my own.

'When someone come to me and said, "Bobby, we want you to whack this geezer," usually because this person was causing aggravation between two firms, they didn't want to do it them-selves, and they didn't want the other firm to do it either because that would cause gang warfare. So they'd get me, the outsider, in to sort it. What you'd do, you'd do him in the leg. Or once we went to the pub, took this guy out into the car, and then I dragged him over next to the railway line, knelt him down, put a gun to his head, fired into the ditch and said, "Next time I visit you, it'll be in the back of your head. Now behave yourself." And then we took him back to the pub, back to his seat where his drink still was. Never had a problem with him again.

'I did feel I was in danger. When you go out with a gun, you must realise that when people come looking for you *they'll* come with a gun. The name of the game was to whack them first, before they got you. But I always knew that one day it would be my turn. If someone comes at me with a gun, doesn't matter who they are I'm going to take them out, 'cos when you got there with a gun you were like a god – you had the power of life and death in your hands. If I pull that trigger, you're dead. If I don't pull that trigger, I'll let you live. People talk about cocaine rushes and all that – no, no, it's a different ballgame. When you're there, you can decide whether this person *exists* or not. So even in the criminal world, once you've whacked someone, once you've shot someone, people know you're a serious person and they don't mess with you.

'It's just a complete sense of . . . *being*. It's almost like you believe you're invincible. When you was going out to do violence, at the beginning, you always thought it would never happen to you. You were that good, that sharp, and you could put it down. Until it happens to *you*. And then when you're laying there, with a bullet in you – well, you think, *this* makes your eyes water. It ceases to be fun.'

Bobby Cummines is laughing uproariously at this point. He sees how he got himself shot, how he got caught, how he came to spend so much time behind bars. And he was aware at the time that it wouldn't go on for ever – you just had to make certain that your procedures were as watertight as you could make them. Weak links would break you.

'When you look at armed robberies, you've got to look at the people you're working with: are they weak, are they strong? We had one armed robbery went down, and this guy froze on me. I've got the pump-action, and I could see the other guys were getting the money out – and this guy's freezing. So I stuck a gun at his head and said, "If you don't move now, you're fucking temporary now." And he moved.

'We got in the car and I was laying down with a crash helmet on, so that if anything pulled us up I could get up and do the business – take the radiator out or whatever. And I smelled . . . shit. "Someone tread in dogshit?" I asked. And the driver said no, it was the guy who'd frozen. And I said, "Stop the car",' cos we were on London Bridge and it went through my head – and this is where the organised crime and violence come in – that this guy knows all. We could get thirty years. And I was going to shoot him and throw him over the bridge. And the rest said, "Bobby, no, no, no." But I said, "He's got to go, because if he's done that now, if the Old Bill get hold of him, thirty years we're looking at." I said to all of them, "If you're going out doing this for a living, it comes to a state where if you eat the meal you pick up the bill. You don't get away with nothing in this world." And I knew that one day in my life I would either be lifed off [to prison] or I would be dead.'

Cummines, though, never underestimates the thinking which drove his life. There was a logic, a way of life, a set of rules. You went along with it – and there were others involved – and it was separate from much of the rest of society.

'I didn't understand straight-goers. I'd never mixed with them. People who worked for a living . . . they was just part of the crowd in Oxford Street. I didn't know what they got up to. They were quite odd, you know. I mean, if I wanted money I just pulled up a security guard – when I saw a guy with that bag walking across the pavement, that was *my* wage packet. I was earning more than the prime minister. It was kicks, chicks and champagne. And when we went to places and they said, "Oh, the club's full, the restaurant's full," straightaway we got a seat. One girl I was with – beautiful, but not the brightest spark in the box – said to her mum, "It's really good, Mum. You know, we go to these places and when they're full they give us a seat – and they *give* you money!" She never understood it.'

And there was a community which knew what Cummines and his colleagues were doing. A community to which he felt obligations, where certain aspects of his conduct mattered. 'In my community, the elderly people said to me, "Bobby – it's all a little bit dodgy?" That's how they put it, bless 'em. Every Sunday we used to go into the Anchor Arms, and I'd buy all the elderly people in the pub their meat from a mate who had a butcher's. And a bag of fruit and veg, on both Saturday and Sunday. And I paid for anything they drank – they only drank Guinness and maybe a little whisky, and none of them took liberties. Or we take the local kids and give them a nice day out, and give them all free ice-creams when the van comes round. People said, "He's very kind and all that." Though I remember a judge saying, "With what he does for a living he can afford to be generous."

'You had responsibilities. For example, if a girl's husband was doing jail, and she had kids and was struggling to pay the rent. And there's a rule that if the man's in jail you don't go round there yourself, because someone might talk maliciously. You send a woman round with the money, so the girl didn't know who it come from. The old man inside knew it had come from us – but it was sorted. You looked after your own. And if we found people doing the "market game", or bag-snatching, or rolling drunks, terrorising working-class people, we took them in the van and beat them with a baseball bat.

'You see, people didn't want to go to the police – didn't want to be seen as coppers' narks. So it was easier to sit in the pub and they'd say to my dad, or one of my brothers: "We're really having problems." Like one of the Turkish geezers that I did. He'd got a girl on heroin, and tried to force her on the streets. Her dad owned a fish and chip shop – ordinary, hard-working people – and one of their friends came to me and said, "We'll pay to have it done." They were old-fashioned, had all their money rolled up in biscuit tins, and they said they were really frightened. "So can you stop it?" I'm looking at him – and the dad's got an apron on, smothered in fat, and mum's an ordinary person. And we'd just done a bank, so we were all right. And I thought, if that was my daughter – and they were scumbags anyway, selling the heroin. Later the guys took the piss out of me, because there was a certain set amount of money you would charge for this, but I'd said, "Keep your money – and I'll stop the problem. But if any of us ever come into your shop then we get fish and chips free."

'This Turk used to have a little lock-up garage where he kept a couple of cars, so I got a four-ten [double-barrelled shotgun] – a nice piece, the size of a pirate's pistol, a bit like a blunderbuss, cut down so that it would slip into my coat – and we drew up outside the lock-up. My driver asked me what we were going to do – just frighten him or what? The guy was under a car, fixing it, so I just walked in and shot him straight through the leg. I then went into the office next door, stuck the gun to his brother's head and said, "Leave this borough within twenty-four hours or we're burying both of you."

'That was the only time my driver froze on me. I said, "Drive away." He said, "You've just shot him." I said "Drive away. And don't break the speed limit." You see, he thought I'd blown away the Turk's legs. But what we'd done, see, was loaded the butt with block salt. They call it a "stinger". It rips you up and stings like mad – then it heals up. The salt melts in the heated flesh. So there's no residue – and they've got nothing they can do the forensic on. I stung him, they was gone in twenty-fours hours, and we got fish and chips for life.'

The catalogue of violence spills out, and with it comes the sense of being in charge – if only of a small patch of a big city; the sense of being able to order people about, to have things done your way – in your own small world. Being King Rat in the Cellar. And exclusively through violence, giving the impression – and meaning it – that you were dangerous and would never hesitate to show it.

'I mean, we didn't always shoot to kill. Mostly it would be to injure, unless it was a contract – that's different. A bad armed robber is one who does violence during a robbery. You've got to be able to control the crowd. You go in and – bang, one in the ceiling to show them it works, then on the floor, kiss that Axminster or I'll blow your fucking head off. You control it, and you have to do it in three minutes without hurting anyone. The guy who shoots people is a mess – you don't want to work with him. Because if you hurt people, then the scream is bigger. And you're looking at a bigger sentence. It's the same when you go to meet someone who's been stepping out of their pram. You go to meet them – you don't go in screaming with guns. You sit down, like we are now, and ask in a nice quiet voice, "You all right? I've come to see you. You've been a bit naughty. Now, does your mum like visiting hospitals? Because if you carry on like you have, she'll be visiting you in the Intensive Care Unit and the next thing you know, you're heading for a plastic tube up your nose in there." And that's the sort of thing that's got to be done – gentlemanly. So they've got their warning. Then you walk away, and hopefully it'll solve the problem.

'Another way I used to do it – you have a bullet, you shake hands, he gets it and you say, "Remember me, and if you keep messing about, that's what they'll be digging out of your head." And then you walk away.

'Violence is the last resort. The object is getting the message over, the psychology behind it. Once you've built up a reputation that you'll really do it on someone, then you don't *need* the violence. You only need it when you're growing up. I can always tell a man of violence. They never do it socially. They don't go round fighting, bashing people: you don't embarrass yourself socially. People who do violence for a living are very respectful. Because they *want* respect. You got to show them what it is. Even to this day, I open doors for people, I give up seats on a train – I was brought up that way. I'm not a rude person. I did violence for a living. I didn't do bad manners for a living.'

On one occasion, his gang got a tip-off from a man whom they paid £2000. They recce'd the building and confirmed the security van delivery. Having planned and prepared, Cummines was in position in the back of a van near the bank, wearing a crash helmet and carrying a sawn-off shotgun. At the last minute, he looked out of the window and saw another van across the road 'with a bloke looking out, wearing a crash helmet. I saw one of my gang members walking down the pavement towards the security van. The door of the van opposite opened and a similar man walked down the pavement. We'd paid two grand for the tip-off and so had another gang . . . one of the few instances of a double-booked robbery, I suppose. We was both so surprised, we missed getting the security van.'

There is no way that Cummines is nostalgic about what he did, though he obviously regrets the passing of a way of life which he thought had some 'proper' values and a code of behaviour that excluded the general public from much of the action. And as he talks, there's a growing emphasis on the downside of a dangerous existence: the recognition that it wasn't going to last for ever and that there was very likely to be some sort of reckoning.

'We done some terrible things. We weren't always nice guys. We used cut-throat razors on each other and so on – but always between each other and not on the public. If you were going after a security van or to a bank or trying to get both – double the amount of money! – and you were on the pavement and you got a "have-a-go hero", then, bang, you're looking at thirty years inside. You're gonna whack 'em, shoot 'em in the leg – and that person is the equivalent of putting us away for thirty years. You've also got to have in your mind, and I always said this to anyone who joined the firm, that you've got to be prepared to get shot – 'cos that *will* happen to you. Or you've got to be prepared to do thirty years. Or it might come to that time when you weren't prepared to be banged up for the rest of your life in a stinking cell, laying on a bed that two hundred people slept on before they slashed their wrists and pissed in it or whatever – so when you know it's coming, know they're on to you, you go and have your nice lunch, your nice bottle of champagne, your nice bottle of brandy, and you put your gun in your own mouth and pull the trigger. Because, when you come down to it, you can't go out and do it to people unless you're prepared to do it to yourself.'

Cummines did long stretches in prison, once with a twelve-year sentence. But he had tasted jail early, and it didn't put him off his chosen career.

'In the old days they had detention centres – turning out superthugs. I did some of that. Then, when I was nineteen, I did the Young Offenders' Institution. And I was a "starred" prisoner, because I was doing a long sentence and would eventually go to another, adult prison. For manslaughter. But it's a terrifying experience for a young guy. You hear all these weird stories. But I wasn't afraid of going in. Everyone I knew had been in prison and I knew a lot of people inside. So it was like when you was in a club at night, when you was in prison – you was just in the *other* club. You all knew each other. And before you got there, you'd do remand and they knew you was coming. And you was part of the firm. So you'd have your teabags waiting, all your goodies there, your tobacco to do your trading with, because you would prepare for prison when you were outside. You'd get a couple of hundred quid, see the wife of someone inside and say, "I want him to get me tobacco" and so on. You didn't have to smuggle money out of prison – you'd paid it outside so's you got credit inside. That's how it works.

'Life inside depends on the sort of villain you are. If you're someone who goes around to elderly people's houses and cheats them for putting roof tiles up, then you're low-life. The bottom. Then there's muggers – know why they're called that? It comes from the American Mafia. The wise guys rob banks. The mugs rob people on the streets – so there's more brains in a wooden cuckoo clock than in a mugger. All part of the hierarchy. Then the fraudsters, who tend to stick with other fraudsters. And as you go up the hierarchy, armed robbers and such, you'd have dinner together. There's not a lot of class barriers. Sex offenders – they live on a different unit, because we'd burn their face off or kill 'em. Because we've got wives and children, sisters and brothers outside, and we can't protect them while we're inside. What we *can* do – if they come near us – is take them out, so they can never do it again. And that's why when Jimmy Costello done the Yorkshire Ripper in Parkhurst with a coffee jar, he was well looked after, because he'd sent a message out: "You touch ours and we'll touch yours." Child molesters, rapists, oddballs like that are called nonces – 'cos with robbery, drug-dealing, fraud, there's a *sense* to the crime: need, greed or power. Sex offences – there's *no* sense to the crime. No sense – nonce.'

But even though he lived at the top of the prisoners' hierarchy, meeting and plotting with the other full-time criminals in his game, there was no feeling that he had left the danger outside. On the contrary, prison, he insists, was full of risks.

'Oh, yeah. I was tooled up twenty-four/seven. I had a six-inch nail hammered into a stiletto. When I was in Parkhurst, we got a guy to nick a pair of garden shears. Reggie Cray had one half, and I had the other. We paid a tenner for it. And that used to be under my bed. I had it wrapped in the towel if I was going to the shower room, or under the grey overcoat – smugglers' coats, we use to call them – whenever I left the cell.

'You don't trust anyone. Not even the prison officers. You're on your own in there, if you're a "face". They're pissed off with you because, for example, one of my girlfriends was a model. And they're looking at you and thinking: you flash git. And they wind you up a bit more, saying, "Yeah, but I'm going home to my wife", or "I'm going down the pub", and I think: well . . . I've got a bottle of whisky in my cell, if I want to drink it. 'Cos they're all corrupt. Twenty-five quid it used to cost me. And a lot of the boys got cannabis the same way.

'Everyone carried a tool. Because you don't know if there's an enemy from the past going to be there, or you're wheeling and dealing. Then you might be a bit tasty, have a good "rep" – reputation. So you have a young guy who's got no clue and thinks: if I do him, then I've got the "rep". You look at these young guys and think, you do that to me, and I'll put it straight through your neck and you'll be crippled from the waist down, for life, 'cos I'll cut your spinal cord. Violence is very cold-blooded. You know you're going to do it. That's why I say to the young guys today, "Even these replica guns, get rid of them. Get them off the street. Don't carry weapons." Because if you do, you don't know the guy sitting next to you. He might be a professional at violence, and he knows, if he stabs you in the neck – like the Jamaican gangsters, the

Yardies, do – you'll be dead from the waist down. Or he might be sitting there with a loaded gun, and pop you right in the head. Violence is a serious business.

'Life is very, very cheap now. In "the good old days", you couldn't get hold of weapons. And you had to be trained. When I was thirteen I was taken with the sawn-off to Oxfordshire, and learned how to use shotguns. I was shooting squirrels. We used to get five bob a tail. I didn't realise what I was being groomed for – I was very young and they were very clever. They groomed you into violence like a paedophile grooms you into sex – exactly the same. It's glamorised – they make you feel good about it, then all of a sudden your reality is other people's nightmares. And that's your life. It's so easy to get into it. Bloody hard to get out.

'Nowadays there's no rules like there was then. Now it's drugs, cartels and foreign countries. It's a different sort of power. The only armed robbers that are still doing banks are those who aren't very bright. The others are now the minders for the drug cartels, who have mercenaries and hit men and all sorts of people. And there's different hierarchy in prison as well. Then, to use a gun, there was disciplines that we all knew. Even in the worst places you didn't shoot members of the public, and so on. Now everyone's fair game. And people get killed in crossfire, because these guys don't know about guns. When I was young, first time I had a gun in my hand we was over in Holland and I was shown how you use it, how you hold it properly. And I learned about the difference with an automatic, which can jam, so if you're going to whack someone you use a revolver, because they don't spit out and leave something behind. If you wanted to cut someone, and you wanted the scar to be a bad one, you'd run the razor through garlic first so the wound puffs up and is harder to stitch. With the IRA in prison, if you were going to do someone you'd get a nail and soak it in human excrement. Then you'd stab them and they might get toxaemia. If you want to whack a guy and he's in the cell and got a weapon and is very clued up, and you can't actually get to him, you can get the lights – the fluorescent tubes – and grind them up and put ground glass in his sugar. There are many ways – but you had to be *trained* in all these things before you ever had a gun. They'd send you out with someone who'd done it for a long time, to watch him.

'You was there as a kind of apprenticeship. And then you'd go out with a gun, and someone was with you. And when they know that you're *safe* with it – sounds weird, I know, because they didn't want innocent members of the public being blown away and stuff like that, and when you went to knee-cap someone they didn't want you putting it in their head – then they said, "OK." So there was rules.

'But now, in south London, you can buy guns in pubs. Guys who get them like this aren't trained, they don't know the weapons, and young kids get caught in the crossfire. And you can get a replica gun now, change the block, rebore it – don't even need a gunsmith to do it. Thirty-eight quid and you've got a shooter. It used to be professionals doing the business. You can go to Glasgow now and have someone stabbed with a hypodermic infected with HIV, or you can have someone shot, for a couple of grand. When *we* did it, all them years ago, we used to collect ten grand – a lot of money in them days: people who worked for my dad used to earn twelve to fifteen quid a week. Now they talk about respect all the time – but they don't know what it is. People have got it mixed up with fear. But anyone can terrorise someone. Respect is caring about your community or the gang you're working with. It just makes you feel you're a human being.'

Listening to an armed robber complaining about modern crime is a case of pot calling kettle blacker. On the other hand, if you believe that there's a little spark of virtue hidden in every human being, then it's possible that it merely sparkles in a distorted manner in some people. And there's no doubting Cummines' sincerity when he frets about today's street scene. He objects to a disordered, random criminal world, in which there are no guarantees of safety, however bizarrely concocted.

'Life's more dangerous for young kids these days – and their parents don't know what respect is either. There's a missing generation between today and us in the sixties. We respected elderly people, women and kids. Now, you pick up the paper, there are people in Brixton putting a knife to a mum and baby, taking their jewellery. We would have shot such people in the back of the head. Popped 'em and left 'em in the dustbin where they belong. Such things were never heard of around us. Robbing banks and such was all right, but doing those sort of things would have meant you weren't brought up properly.'

A lifetime of crime does not always produce reflection and analysis. However, Cummines and his contemporaries found themselves being overtaken by changes in society. Spending long periods shut away in prison in the seventies and eighties, they were bypassed by a young generation outside who were not interested in inheriting their hierarchical gangland regime. It began to dawn on those inside that they had become somewhat old-fashioned. Cummines, though, took some time to realise that he might possibly join the 'straight-goers'.

'I looked around and saw the bubble bursting – slowly. I saw Reggie Kray shuffling along the prison landing in his slippers – an old guy. He sent my mum flowers when she was dying of leukaemia – the respect thing. I went into his cell and he said, "Bobby, when you get out you'll have this bit of London." He had the little map out. And I thought: I've had that anyway. And now there's fifteen-year-old kids out there who, if you was out there tomorrow giving it large, would blow your fucking head off. 'Cos they don't care. And I felt really sad for him, 'cos I thought: *you* would not survive out there. They don't care who you are.'

The other realisation was that the criminal justice system, for all its flaws, is weighted against those who carry guns. Cummines puts it simply: 'When you had the robbery squad in those days, if I shoot one of them, I get life. If they shoot me, they get a medal. It's a cheaper way of justice. That's also why I gave up armed robbery.'

He gave up. It took him a long time to arrive at his Damascene conversion, but he finally got there. It was not a brilliant career move in the first instance, coming out of prison and having to take menial jobs. Social status as a shelf-stacker at Tesco's in Maidstone did not compare well to swaggering round his patch in north

London. He had a succession of jobs, trying to better himself every time, but met redundancy and prejudice because of his record ('Any employer would run a mile, wouldn't they?'). But by now he had decided to join the rest of society, whatever the difficulties.

'I went into higher education. I got a university degree. Plus, I married the prison librarian and now have a little girl. And I don't want her to grow up in the world I grew up in.' Having found out the hard way how ex-cons are treated, he applied all the energy and organisational skills which used to be focused on bank jobs into sorting out a better deal for ex-prisoners. He is now the chief executive of Unlock, a national association for ex-offenders which has been successful in getting the conventional tools of stability into their hands: insurance, mortgages and employment. He is practical and knows what detail is all about – bank robberies needed planning and information. Today's society is complex for anyone coming out of prison with a poor education and no familiarity with 'straight-going' conventions. He was also instrumental in getting the vote for prisoners: if you don't get a chance to vote, you have another grievance about how society is run and are less likely to be convinced you are part of it. He understands social exclusion – both as a criminal and as an ex-criminal. And he is messianic about getting young people off a life of crime. He writes, lectures, advises and regularly descends on youth who are showing signs of heading off the straight and narrow. All the while, he reminds himself that he will never return to his former life.

'There's young bucks out there now carrying guns. I can go into a pub and I know they're carrying, because you never lose that instinct. Like know their like. But even though the instinct is still there in the back of my mind that if they threaten me I'll take them out, everything round me now is so precious – my life has changed so much. I now see the beauty of this world and I really love people. I get a buzz out of making a change. In prison, I saw all these old geezers planning what they were going to do when they got out, a little bit of this and that – and I thought: you haven't got another prison sentence in you, have you?

'That's when I thought: I'm still alive, they ain't killed me, I've still got a few years left – and I want what ordinary people have got. I wanted to be normal, and my money couldn't buy it, my guns couldn't buy it. I just wanted to be a nobody. And it's really nice when you can be in that crowd in Oxford Street and no one knows who you are. And you just smile when people are rude or bump into you – you don't think, I'm going to take your fucking head off. No. You just look and smile. You don't live that life no more.

'I don't have violence or danger in my life now. I've got a beautiful life. And I love my naughty kids – that's why I'm down in the schools, telling them the truth: "Listen, when you get shot, it's not like in the films. You don't get up." Because we've got to get the kids today out of the glamorisation of crime. There is no glamour. It's just pain and misery. Because the biggest victim of crime is the criminal.'

He did what he did in the name of what?

'Greed.'

And what he does now? In the name of what?

'Decency.'

8

The Hostage Negotiator

The risk of being taken hostage might horrify a good number of people, but it's not likely to happen to them – most of us are not rich enough or important enough to attract that sort of attention. The threat of great danger and possible death is nearly always attached to it. However, there's usually little the hostage can do about the situation. That responsibility passes to someone charged with solving the problem, and it's very much a case of a life being put in their hands – a dangerous position to be in.

In the mid-eighties, at the height of the violence engulfing Beirut, where, without warning, gunmen popped up in shopping arcades and tanks trundled over pavement café tables, the scene was further complicated by a series of kidnappings. Journalists, long-time foreign residents and sundry visitors found themselves the unhappy guests of various factions who issued an array of demands, coupled with all-too-believable threats. Governments found themselves dragged into controversy as they pondered the ethics of paying a ransom rather than calling the kidnappers' bluff. There was no international consensus. Recriminations bounced around embassies as it became clear that negotiation was absolutely out of the question (the British stance), something to be done secretly and efficiently (the French), or secretly and inefficiently (the Americans embroiling themselves in the Iran-Contra arms-for-freedom deal).

However, the largest number of people held hostage were local. Without the publicity attached to the foreign captives, whole streets occasionally vanished for a day or two. A block of flats would echo over the weekend to the sound of unfed dogs and miffed cats. It wasn't thought particularly heinous – just one of the inconveniences of a very mixed community with differing views on how to resolve differences. For the Lebanese, kidnapping was part and parcel of the way both criminals and militias conducted themselves – partly as a fund-raising operation, partly as a show of power. The victim's friends and relatives took the simplest approach to the whole affair: let's talk now and do a deal. On the whole, these local affairs didn't make it into the press. But once foreigners were involved, the journalists were on the case.

I was always struck by two things: the wholesale mendacity of many involved (on all sides) and the faint surprise shown by some kidnappers that holding someone against their will should be deemed outrageous. More than once, particularly in the Middle East, I heard aggrieved voices stating that the hostage had been well fed and was unharmed, so what was the fuss about? The notion that individual freedom should be held as an inalienable right was puzzling to them. One argument went that a hostage who suffered no physical damage was in a better position than the people the kidnappers were trying to draw attention to. On the other hand, it was argued that depriving someone of their freedom cancelled out any pleas for better treatment of the kidnappers' cause. Not that morality usually made much of an appearance during the fraught period when demands and threats filled the air.

Mornings when a kidnapping story broke were mornings when I wished I had stayed in bed for a month – or for as long as it took for the grubby game to play itself out. At such times, journalists find themselves enmeshed in a murky web of information, hints, manoeuvring and manipulation. And at the centre is one horrible fact: danger to the hostage, which even a journalist may unwillingly cause. You can find yourself being used as a channel of communication, either publicly via press conferences and announcements, or covertly via messages embedded in interviews or statements. A tip-off or a briefing from an insider may not be the useful titbit to freshen up the next news bulletin, but rather a misjudged revelation which precipitates more trouble. The authorities are as devious as the kidnappers: this is a mad game of poker, and no one is going to reveal their strategy. Relatives lie, the police are economical with the truth and the kidnappers lie even more. And should a journalist uncover such behaviour, it matters not that it's a fact, for the greater fact is that the hostage is still in danger and any little change in the scenario could lead to disaster.

In an ideal world, a journalist's prime source in a kidnap situation would be the family or close friends. It's rare that you get a sniff of them. So you tend to come across more tenuously related people, those in the outer circle who may be keen to catch a little of the limelight: 'I don't know him that well, but I *do* know . . .' And it sometimes turns out they are not an ally of the hostage. I had an earful of damaging gossip in Beirut from one such relative, who thankfully betrayed his true relationship with the hostage by announcing that he richly deserved what was happening to him. On another occasion, in Italy, a family member rabbited on in such detail about the hostage's behaviour prior to his disappearance that I was left in no doubt about why the locals might be exacting revenge. None of this can be put in the public domain, however, before the case is resolved. These days, press reports reach the most obscure cellar and mountain hideaway, and 24-hour news dribbles unconfirmed incoming snippets on to screens everywhere before any wider picture is gained. And a journalist has to be aware of creating more danger for the victim, possibly lethal.

Perhaps the very worst aspect is one which you would welcome in other stories: getting to see the players at first hand. But stealing off to visit hostages is not a particularly honourable move. Admittedly, you may return to confirm they are still alive and in one piece. On the other hand, to return to freedom – having left them – is a deeply disturbing matter. And there's a nagging feeling that being polite to hostage-takers is at best creepy, and at worst disreputable behaviour.

Having disliked being drawn into the web of deception and intrigue that surrounds kidnapping, even as a mere reporter, I was curious to know why people should involve themselves for a living. Going into a situation where a life is at stake, and dealing with distraught people on one side and very ill-intentioned folks on the other, is not what most of us would choose to do. However, advising on kidnap is a well-established business these days, even though those who offer their services take on not just an assignment but a great deal of the responsibility for the victim's fate. There are two kinds of danger involved: the organisation of what may well be a hair-raising final act to a successful deal brokered with violent people, and the risk that it may all go wrong and the victim will die. So who takes on this kind of role? Someone who has familiarity with life-and-death situations.

'One of the things I really did find interesting when advising on a kidnap was that we'd go in front of big corporations, multinationals, where the CEO was responsible for 150,000 employees all over the world. It could be a business which involved great engineering feats, offshore operations, physical risks and so on, and they could make decisions about profit and loss, employee cutbacks and that sort of thing. These were businessmen with formidable reputations for toughness, yet none of them were comfortable with, and some bloody awful at, making decisions which involved the possible injury or death of a named person.'

Arish Turle worked as a kidnap adviser for many years for the British specialists Control Risks. At the heart of the job lay the ability to recognise that decisions had to be made about life and death, and that you had to introduce a rational process to stabilise the situation. Not easy, when both the hostages' families and their employers were usually unprepared and understandably less than capable of rational behaviour when it was most needed.

'It was quite an education for me, early on, to go into board rooms. I was nervous, because these were senior executives – knighthoods, big able people – faced with "If you don't pay, then the wife of this executive or that employee or whoever may end up a bloody corpse on a road." But even the most eminent businessman confronted with a demand for a ransom against the threat of indefinite incarceration, or even mutilation or execution of a hostage, will find it's a lonely decision. And I learned to recognise the way they transferred responsibility – almost imperceptibly – from the board room or the family to the adviser.

'Others just made instinctive decisions: I remember one chairman of a very, very big British company, a household name, saying, "I'm not going to pay these bastards. Let's put 5 million into an account and hire our own people to go after them – let's fund a police operation to do it for us." All that sort of thing.'

It is at this point that reason and a cool risk assessment are needed. While the natural instinct is to run round in circles, the analyst, experienced in the way things are likely to develop and also knowing that the company will have the resources to make things happen, is considering all the options. 'I'm not saying that the adviser always knows the answer, but if you're doing your job properly and you've won their trust, and you have the experience, the technical resources, the legal, financial and diplomatic advice and all that, they *will* turn to you.'

A career in the military gave Turle some background for life-threatening dilemmas, although it was only by chance that he had come across hostage situations. 'After the Olympic Games massacre in Munich, the then prime minister ordered the SAS to provide a counter-hostage capability. I was involved in the planning and training, and it was the first time I'd had to think about hostage incidents. At that time we were exclusively orientated towards politically driven hostage-taking by armed terrorists, with the eventual requirement of a military or commando-type operation to recover the hostage. It was probably the first time that any of us had ever worked with the police in this country, and the training was linked with the Met negotiating in an environment of a politically or terrorist-driven kidnap. That was in 1973, and from that point I began to have an interest and an involvement in such negotiations.'

It came in useful. In 1980, a group of dissident Iranians burst into their country's London embassy, taking members of the staff, a British diplomatic policeman and two BBC journalists hostage. Quite a chunk of central London ground to a halt as the building was isolated and surrounded by a large number of police and a horde of journalists, including me.

Not for the first time did I feel I was in a grey area when it came to divulging information. As the two BBC journalists were both my colleagues and friends, there were all kinds of gossipy morsels that would have fleshed out the rather bare facts about the ensuing siege. But suggesting how they might react to their situation, describing personal qualities or recalling how they had behaved during other news stories, just might have tipped the balance inside the building. We knew that the kidnappers would probably have access to news – which they did – and initially we had little idea of the atmosphere or tension. So we chose to be circumspect.

I learned considerably more when I was taken to the house next door to the embassy some days later, at a time when the hostage-takers were demanding that a TV crew should come in and interview them. I was willing to go in, but had firm ideas about the conditions of such a venture in order to avoid being manipulated by either the police or the Iranians. A lot is at stake at such moments and much can go wrong. The police might insist on your being wired for sound or demand that they substitute one of your crew with their own man. The hostage-takers might add you to their collection. Or the opportunity for a fracas might arise, in which you found yourself part of a bid for freedom or the unwitting pawn in a contrived murder plot. And lots of other variations on a dangerous theme.

However, the interesting part of my brief visit was to see the listening equipment clamped to the walls and glimpse the police negotiating team in action. Tension and tempers were high. The stakes had been raised next door, and I was seeing the reaction in people who had been working intensely for days. The outcome envisaged by the police concentrated on the success of negotiation; that envisaged by the SAS team standing by – coincidentally comprising many of the men who had served in the 1973 team – involved bloodshed. This added to the tension, as Arish Turle recalls.

'The police understandably want a negotiated settlement, leading to the arrest of the perpetrators, and then the normal criminal justice system. Inevitably, the soldiers' viewpoint was: well, if we're asked to risk our lives in an actual assault, we *will* want to shoot our way in – and you can worry about the niceties afterwards. When we were training, the emphasis on forensic and evidence during the post-incident debrief certainly grated to begin with. . . . Of course, where the two sides got on well together, neither had difficulty negotiating their differences. Whereas those police who resented military involvement – and vice versa – did create barriers from the outset.'

In any kidnap or hostage-taking, there are these fundamental differences. For years after the SAS successfully stormed the embassy, live on television with yours truly commentating while lying flat in the road outside, the reaction of many people who had seen the coverage was that all such incidents should be dealt with in the military manner. However, those who analyse the problem, especially from the military angle, are wary. Their training makes them accept that they are in a lethal situation, and they attempt to work out just what may happen and whether there's a better way of dealing with it. Even so, at the inquest which followed the siege it was clear that not everyone thought on those lines.

'I think part of it must be that lawyers, even the police, have no notion of what being in danger is really like. During an inquest, they tend to give the impression of not understanding the tension and pressure of an assault action and what a soldier has gone through. They concentrate on, "How many bullets did you fire? Why did you fire? Who did you fire at? Which gun did you use? If you were the hostage-taker and you had three notional rooms and everyone went into them, who would you fire at?", or "Why did you fire twice? Once would have been enough" – and that creates tension at times. It's understandable that they do this, but I do think it's impossibly hard, even when you're on a training exercise, to replicate the adrenalin that you generate on actual operations. Even an hour later, when you've all had a cup of coffee and a smoke, you're not the same person and you're not thinking in the same way as you would have been during the assault. Training is supposed to – and in most cases it does – hold back your extreme, perhaps "undisciplined" reactions. But on the other hand, if you're expected to bust your way through a window or a door and run the risk of getting killed in doing that, you're not going to hesitate. If there is a person in there and you think they will shoot almost as soon as they've seen someone, then clearly the objective of the training is that you get faster and faster and better and better at making an incredibly quick judgement: Is it a hostage or is it a neutral or is it a terrorist? And maybe mistakes are made.'

The Iranian embassy siege pointed up the differences in approach, and conscious efforts were made to bring a more sophisticated response across the board. Some years earlier, serving in Northern Ireland, Turle had gained more experience in working between the military and the police – something which proved useful in negotiations later.

'It educated me in police and paramilitary and military areas of overlap or tension. In 1969, while I was serving with the Greenjackets, we'd been sent to Northern Ireland in a "peacekeeping role". We were issued with 1947 Indian army training manuals . . . so we turned up with barbed wire and banners which said "Halt" (some of the banners were from Aden and in Arabic!).

'After going to staff college I went back to the SAS, and got involved in setting up and training a special intelligence unit for Northern Ireland. And I spent my last two years there, before leaving the army, liaising between the military, the police and the government intelligence services. Then, towards the end of 1976, I got a call from a friend who'd also been in the Greenjackets and the SAS, and who'd started work in a new venture involving Lloyd's of London and the insurance industry that sounded interesting. A young insurance broker called Julian Radcliffe, had had the idea of starting a security consulting business focused on kidnap and ransom ("K & R") risks and the threat from terrorism to multinational companies. The kidnappers were mainly left-wing extremists or involved with organised crime. In the mid-1970s the multinationals were paying huge premiums to insure themselves against K & R – and Lloyd's had over 70 per cent of the market. The ransoms they were paying to the kidnappers, mainly in Latin America and continental Europe, were huge as well.

'Companies then – and families – were pretty unprepared as to how to respond to a kidnap threat. And there'd been little thought about the three main drivers to such a response: morality (you need to be able to justify the decisions you take and the reasons for doing so); commercial considerations (what will be the costs, the disruption and the legal implications, and what will happen to your reputation?); and public order (will the actions you take reduce a future threat or encourage the crime to be repeated?).

'So, with the majority of K & R insurance being handled in London, Julian persuaded a leading underwriter to offer a policy where a percentage of the premium would offset the cost of a security audit and would include a plan against the eventuality of a kidnap, and agreement to pay for an adviser. And this was the start of Control Risks.

'The SAS had provided me with counter-terrorist training which included security planning, bodyguard training and VIP protection. We'd been on teams in many parts of the world. Julian had recognised that the multinational companies had a need, Lloyd's had a product and the SAS had the training and experience.

'When Julian rang me and asked if I'd like to come and talk to them, I said, "What's in it?" He said, "You'd get a car and you'd work nine to five and wear a suit. And you could buy your own house and commute." I thought that sounded a pretty good job. Normal office hours and commuting from your own home where you could put down roots was very appealing after constant tours of duty overseas and eleven houses in nine years of married life in the military. He forgot to tell me that you worked fourteen hours a day and most of your clients were in South America – and I wasn't bright enough to ask!'

The 'Security Consulting Business', now a recognised and vast multinational industry, was in its infancy then. No one was quite sure what the rules were – and there are many murky areas still today. However, in South America in particular, kidnapping was rife. Grabbing diplomats and foreign company executives was common, and the demands varied.

'The most common was money (almost always US dollars). Even if there was a political component, there was always money. Then there were political demands, which varied from a change of regime to the release of prisoners or the delivery of food. One ransom demand was for notebooks and pens and schoolbooks to educate the underprivileged – but it was accompanied by a certain amount of gold. And there were demands for companies to pull out of areas they were operating in.'

'Multinationals at that time did not have a security department set up to focus on counter-terrorism – it was often just an adjunct to health and safety. In Britain, the blue chip companies would usually have a retired police officer of many years' service who would advise them on pilfering and crime prevention, and if you ever needed help probably knew the chief constable. But few, if any, knew much about the local environment in those foreign countries where kidnapping was rife.'

But even though British companies and the Foreign Office found themselves entangled in such crimes, there was a certain reluctance to countenance the involvement of specialist kidnap advisers. 'Many, though not all, police were very hostile, and so was Margaret Thatcher's government. They argued that insurance was an incentive to the crime, in the belief that people who were insured would be more able – and therefore more willing – to pay a ransom. They claimed that this would prejudice police operations, because it would truncate the time that people were willing to wait before they paid the money. But that was a completely false argument, and in the early days a great deal of our time was spent in arguing and providing statistics to prove that it wasn't the case. Our argument was: if you've taken out insurance, you've already indicated an awareness of the risk. The success of our business was built on the basis that people who bought an insurance policy were offered a percentage discount on the premium if they would take advice in three areas: First, information about the nature and level of risk in different countries and how it manifests itself, and why they might be potential targets. Secondly, prevention – we needed to conduct surveys and identify the measures needed to reduce the risk. And thirdly, a contingency plan: if there was an incident, they would have a known basis on which to respond.'

It was one thing to justify the security company's existence, but what about the personal role?

'At first I was beset by doubt personally – and perhaps all my colleagues felt the same. I wondered if I should be doing this, for the moral reason that I'd be bargaining with someone's life. Even if it's not me making the decision, I've probably influenced those who are. And if I get it wrong, and the person is killed or doesn't get released, should I be doing it? The second thing is that something in one's upbringing tells you that it's a crime, and the only way to try and stop that crime is for it not to be seen to be successful by imitators or others. So to what extent should you help people pay a ransom? And to what extent should you put the hostage at risk in order to assist law enforcement by helping, or at least not obstructing, their operation? And the third point is the commercial one: am I really worth it to this company if they pay me a fee? Can I justify it? I think there *are* answers to all of those, and I think the answers unquestionably outweigh the scepticism about the business.'

So, having got into this curious business, does a kidnap adviser have any template for action? Or is every case different?

'Nearly every kidnap has a pattern – a predictable graph. The organised gangs will aim to abduct the hostage and disappear without any witnesses. Sometimes that means killing the body-guards – but they'll aim to get a guy on his own. They'll have spent a lot of time and money finding out where he'll be vulnerable and, ideally, alone. There's the classic case where the guy will have security everywhere he goes, except Monday night when he slips out to see the girlfriend he has in the flat round the corner . . . and the gang pick him up there. Their aim is to pick you up with no witnesses, and with no police hue and cry. Then they wait.

'And they're waiting, not because they don't know what to do, but because they're putting deliberate psychological pressure on. They're also debriefing the hostage about what he's worth and how the company's doing. Sometimes they'll even show him his own company's annual reports! They're working out who to contact. The popular theory is that they ring the wife – they probably won't. They'll talk to the hostage and *then* they'll make a judgement. They want to speak to someone whose identity they don't think the police will guess and who they hope can be intimidated into complying with their demands. And you can wait three weeks, four weeks, before you hear anything. Probably it's a phone call. Maybe a letter. Or a call to say: "There's an interesting package in your dustbin." And then the phone goes dead. This is to not to the wife or the husband or the chief executive, but to someone the hostage has described as "a friend I think you can trust".

'In the meantime, if we're involved, as soon as a kidnap is reported we'll have put together a team and briefed them all. Often it's the family who are the weak link because of the extreme emotional pressure on the decision-takers. They are one of the indirect victims, right from the start to the final outcome. All the indirect victims – the family, the employer – share a goal: the hostage's safe release. But the means to achieve this and the risks involved aren't evenly shared. Let's say your husband's kidnapped and a senior executive comes to see you and says, "We'll do everything we can." You are then the focus of that company's attention for as long as it takes. The chairman rings you up every Monday to ask if you're all right. An adviser comes to talk to you, to help with family arrangements – a trip to Venice this week, perhaps. You're likely to get very generous treatment – and you tend to get used to it. And when your husband comes out the pendulum swings away – unless the company listens to our advisers. All the focus is on him, and the wife is suddenly left on her own and gets very upset. So you have to predict issues and help manage people who are deeply, but very differently, affected right through the whole affair.'

Having watched videos where long lists of grievances are put forward to justify a kidnap and listened to political rants from 'friends of kidnappers' about the virtuous aim of their actions, I have never been fully persuaded that depriving people of their personal freedom can be seen as wholly justifiable. However, I wondered if there were any thoughts in Turle's mind that kidnapping is morally ambiguous – that it isn't, as some people claim, the greatest of crimes.

'I think when you come into direct contact with the indirect victims – let alone the hostage who faces mental torture on top of a possibly lonely death – and you see the devastation it causes to their emotions, then I'm not sure if you'd describe it as a *great* crime, but as a devilish, devious, cruel crime. It's one that relies to a great extent on the effect it has on people's emotions, through its longevity and uncertainty. Whereas a murder – minutes? A kidnap can go for weeks or months, or even longer, and it's the apparent indefinite uncertainty that destroys people. And it also has quite a long-term effect. I think it's a *nasty* crime, and should be looked at as GBH or murder. And I don't see any justification in the argument that only one person suffers, as opposed to the hundreds on whose behalf, perhaps, the kidnappers may claim their demands are being made. There's unlikely to be a direct link between your victim and the activities that the kidnappers are protesting against. And the kidnappers are behaving in a way that is equally cruel or vindictive or uncaring about other people's welfare. I'm not sure it's an excuse that has strength in moral terms.'

There's no doubt that Turle has first-hand experience of just how nasty some kidnappers can get. He's seen the effect of violence on both victims and their families. But what about him? Is the adviser called in to handle negotiations also at risk?

'There's always the *threat* of danger to the adviser. It's rarely an actuality, but it would be foolish to ignore it, especially during a prolonged incarceration. But the hostage is always under the threat of death, even if statistics show that it's a rare occurrence. The pressure from a kidnap is as much the uncertainty of the outcome and how long it takes as the threat of violence – in that if the kidnappers do kill their hostage, or let him die, they've lost their only negotiable asset. And the loss of the asset is not just the failure to get the ransom. They'll also have invested a substantial amount of time and money – so even the kidnappers have got financial pressures which have some bearing on their behaviour.

'In a kidnap situation you can rationalise the probable behaviour of a gang which is controlled by people who are capable of a logical train of thought – perhaps they have previous experience and have the ability to work things out. Once you're pretty confident that that's the opponent you're up against, you're under much less pressure – though not altogether, because there's still uncertainty about the hostage's health. That may deteriorate, regardless of how much the kidnappers try to look after him.

'But if there's any degree of clash between individuals, a lack of control, ill discipline, the unpredictability factor creates additional tension in any debate about what the response should be. The threat of death is usually made at some point, sometimes only as a reminder, but it's always "If we are attacked by the police, we will kill him." And "We're confident the police aren't going to find him" and "This is going to go on for ever." Some gangs have chopped off a finger or an ear – but it happens infrequently, probably because they know that if you injure someone then that's damaged goods, and maybe the person's health may deteriorate and not be able to sustain incarceration before the ransom's paid.

'I've known instances of hostage-takers going to incredible lengths to look after their hostage – even in one case providing a very pretty girl on Friday nights! And when the hostage came out, he said to me, "If I tell you this, you won't tell the wife, will you?" In another case, the hostage had a regular medical examination from a qualified doctor. I've been involved in cases where the hostage got the medication he needed, was asked what menus he wanted, what wine he preferred, what books. So there are as many cases of kidnappers nurturing their hostage as there are of violating them. There's always intimidation, of course – "If we are raided, we will kill you." One wicked group, a political organisation, used to wire the hostage up to explosives and keep him in a coffin. And if the lid was lifted off by someone who didn't know where the catch was, he'd be blown up. So you can go through the whole spectrum of bad and good behaviour. There was one case in Italy where mother and son were kidnapped and they cut off the son's ear in front of the mother, took a photograph and sent a copy to the family. That came as a terrible shock to the family, not least because the police had earlier said that they knew who the gang was and such behaviour was not likely.'

Arish Turle speaks with immense calmness and very precise attention to detail, considering his words carefully and covering all options. Not surprising when he has spent days and weeks with families at the end of their tether and corporate *grands fromages* utterly out of their depth, all yelling, 'What are we going to do?' every ten minutes and actually meaning, 'What are *you* going to do?' There is a great deal of steel behind the patience, but a never-wavering attention to the actual plight of any hostage. His eye never goes off that ball.

'I think that most people involved who have any sense of responsibility never go and talk to people on the basis of "Don't worry, it'll be all right – I know what's going to happen." But they *can* say, with quite a legitimate degree of confidence, "This is the behavioural pattern which will probably be the basis of the next few weeks." And certainly, one of the strengths of a professionally managed security company is a comprehensive database of carefully analysed previous cases. On some occasions we could certainly tell by the tactics employed, and even the voice of the negotiator, the identity of the gang and the probable outcome.'

I had assumed that a kidnap adviser was the voice on the phone to the gang, but this is not usually so. Perhaps I've seen too many movies where just about everyone grabs the phone and delivers an emotional plea.

'The negotiator has to have fluency in the language – and if you're an English-speaking adviser you probably don't have the linguistic skills needed. You're probably looking for a local dialect, and you need a voice and personality that come across as belonging to someone the gang believe they can deal with – someone who has a manner which makes them feel, "We know this guy is working for the family or the company, but he's probably sympathetic to us – to the extent that he's not trying to trick us." So the selection of the negotiator is not necessarily (and this is where, in my view, the British police used to make a mistake) someone who's been trained in a classroom and has all the buzzwords and is familiar with the police jargon. In my view, that can be dangerous. You don't want a member of the family, either, because the emotion will get to them. Nor do you want a close friend of the hostage, for the same reason. The classic background, is, frankly, a lawyer. I've dealt with dozens and dozens of cases, and the choice in most cases has been a lawyer. He can let slip that he's acted for people in court charged with crimes, so he's already got empathy with the kidnappers' spokesman.

'A good negotiator has to work to a very strict script, even to the extent that when you record a conversation (most contacts are by telephone, and all kidnappers suspect they are being recorded) you make a transcript in minute detail, using a stopwatch to measure pauses between words. You're looking for hesitations, pauses, inflections in the voice and choice of words. I learned a great deal about how much you can interpret when someone issues a threat – that they are reading from a script, in the same way that your negotiator is – and it's all part of negotiation. It's the adviser who interprets correctly and who constructs the response properly who will have the greatest influence.

'So I've been a professional adviser, but not the voice for direct communication with the kidnappers. In my role I'm advising the family or the corporate entity: my advice concerns the composition and deliberation of the crisis management team, the selection, briefing and training of their negotiator, the tactics to use, the way to liaise with the police, the interface with the rest of the company, the public profile and the link to the media. It's essential to have a plan which anticipates the influence and involvement of the media, as they can significantly influence the negotiation, knowingly or unknowingly, for better or worse.'

And the media are probably existing on pretty thin gruel. The length of time that kidnappers are prepared to hang on to their man is in direct conflict with editors' patience. If you're going to keep a story going, it needs fresh fuel every day. Unlike the situation with a mystery disappearance or a murder hunt, it would be unwise to snatch speculation out of the air or hire a PR team to grab a new rabbit out of the hat before every bulletin and fresh edition. Who knows what's going on – and when the danger is at its gravest? Only the insiders know.

'It's when a threat is made. Have they got the willingness and the intention to carry it out? Because, if or when a finger comes through the post – and this is all about danger to the hostage – it's not *your* finger. Equally it may not be the hostage's finger but one cut from a corpse. The crisis management team's probably based in a comfortable hotel. None of you around the table has lost any blood or got hurt, but your hostage has been tied up or kept in a cave underground somewhere, maybe for months and months and months, and he's probably being physically threatened or enduring the dread of being abandoned. And he's living every day with the fear that the nice guy who's looking after him, and with whom he has a bit of a relationship, will be taken away and others will come in and cut him or beat him up or kill him . . . or just leave him to starve. And if there's more than one hostage, the great fear is that they'll kill one because they've still got another – and the price goes up. But it doesn't happen very often. So the most dangerous point is when a threat is made, and I think the *moral* pressure on the adviser is at its highest then. Everyone turns to you and says, "Will they do it?" And that's when you really do feel lonely. That's when a responsible adviser consults with his colleagues and goes back to the control room, as it were – he looks at the research again to find out how many times the threat has been made and what the outcome was and so on.

'Inevitably you are making judgements based on your intuition, and comparing the present case with previous ones. But it's quite surprising how accurate you can be. We worked on one European case, and when we went through it we said, "That's not a local gang – they're South Americans. They probably come from these two countries and it's not going to be a 24-hour kidnap. You must be prepared for months." And a very senior local police officer said, "That's completely untrue. There's no evidence for that at all. This is a local criminal gang – it'll all be solved in a week." And that didn't help our relationship in the beginning, so I said, "You may be right, but I think all the plans should be on the basis of a prolonged one . . . and let's hope you're right." In the event it went on for months and it did prove to be a gang from the countries we had earlier identified.

'In every case I worked on, the police were involved to a greater or lesser extent. In European capitals, 100 per cent. The Italian government at one time tried to ban negotiating ransoms. But it was a crassly stupid law, because what do you do if you're a multi-millionaire or a business associate of the family or the hostage? You get on a train and go to another country, and you negotiate from there. We always got the parameters within which we were allowed to negotiate, as well as the intended objective, established with a government official. The ideal objective is for the police to find and rescue the hostage, and before mounting an assault to sit down with the negotiators and the family to spell out both the sophistication of the operation as well as the possible risk: "We know where they are – but we don't think we can raid it without getting the hostage killed", or "We think we can get in – so do we have your permission to go in?" Some police are purists and say, "We're never going to ask permission." The thinking police realise that if you go in to rescue the hostage and kill him during the raid, you're very likely to run the risk of not getting cooperation in future kidnaps.

'So the police have restraints which affect their judgements, and if they're not going to attempt a rescue you try to put into place a sophisticated surveillance operation which waits for the hostage to be released. There's little point picking up the people who've come to collect the ransom – they're not Mr Big. I remember on one occasion the kidnappers arrived to collect the ransom wearing suits instead of the usual jeans and T-shirts. They explained that it was such a lot of money in cash that they needed to be well dressed in order to deposit it in a bank without causing suspicion! Anyway, there are all sorts of things that can happen – like the police helicopter running out of fuel, a covert police car crashing, or the time when the place where the ransom was to be handed over was completely lit up, thanks to the TV camera lights being already set up following a police tip-off; it's all happened. These things are funny afterwards – but not before the hostage is released.'

'The Hollywood image of the simultaneous exchange of a hostage for a suitcase full of money in a deserted car park isn't reality. Both sides are fearful because they're at their most vulnerable. The ransom is paid, but the hostage isn't released until the gang believe the money is safely under their control. Even so, there's sometimes an element of honour among thieves, with proof of life provided before payment and those who deliver the money remaining unharmed. A couple of days later – or maybe a week – the hostage is released, clean shaven, wearing clean clothes, with money for a taxi in his pocket and an address to go to, all as requested when the deal was struck. On the other hand, it can happen that the hostage isn't released and a second payment is demanded.'

In any event, once it's all over the public may learn little of what has happened unless the hostage decides to tell his story. But there is another kind of kidnapping which gets the full glare of publicity, and where money plays little if any part: the gesture made by the terrorist or religious group which outrages decency and treats a human life as a mere object to be thrown away for the 'cause'. Not content with a gruesome execution, these days kidnappers often supply videos of an individual's awful fate. In these cases, meaningful negotiation often seems out of the question, with kidnappers' demands often aimed at governments, who may express concern but rarely make concessions. Is there a way of dealing with this kind of threat?

'If you're dealing with a determined political group, whose modus operandi includes terrorism or extreme violence – perhaps driven by religious beliefs – I think your risk-assessment leads you to persuade your client to accept greater police involvement. Because you have to tell them that the probability is the gang don't intend to release the hostage anyway. The negotiation aims therefore not so much to conclude with a handover, but to prolong the time in the hope that the police can find the hideout and mount a rescue operation. . . . and it's much more worrying. In a politically motivated kidnap, the hostage target may well have been identified as a sacrifice and, if so, it was always the intention of the gang that he should be killed. Their aim is to make a point, rather than to collect money. The kidnappers still want a bit of time, because it's generating publicity – they're in the news. So you're playing along with that and advising that the risk from the police getting more overtly involved is desirable – because both your client and the police know that, however great these risks are, it's the best chance to avoid a planned execution.'

Having shepherded the business colleagues and the family through the negotiating time, the crunch point arrives. My own experiences of this moment have been rather bizarre. Several weeks in Tripoli with no indication that a hostage story we were following might ever have an end suddenly turned into a flurry of night-time dashes hither and thither across the city with a bunch of men – only one of whom I vaguely recognised – followed by a lot of shouting on an ill-lit piece of waste ground. A few minutes later I was having to calm down two British citizens who had been held for spurious reasons for many weeks. The biggest hurdle was trying to reassure them that a journalist was competent enough to look after them and prevent more nasty surprises from happening to them.

Again in Tripoli, four British hostages, the Archbishop of Canterbury's envoy, several go-betweens who didn't give their names, a clutch of sinister military men and the colonel who runs the place conspired to cause twenty-four hours of mayhem before freedom was assured. My sharpest memory is of negotiating the second hand-over attempt (the first had been botched) when the only weapon in my armoury was to threaten that 'Mrs Thatcher will be *very* angry if this goes wrong' – and realising that the Libyans were impressed by this . . . In a constant state of worry, I realised that I'm not suited to this kind of thing. When it comes to the crunch point. I'm not Arish Turle.

'It could be a five-day kidnap, it could be an eighteen-month kidnap, but you're always trying to head for an agreement – which you'll get eventually, you get agreement. As a very rough estimate, 10 per cent of the original demand probably gets the hostage released. You'd probably brief your corporate executives on that basis. It's up to them – and again they'll look at you and say, "What would *you* do?" But it's they who have to make the decision. I'll give them the options, and they always include pay now or pay later, but in each there are risks.

'Eventually the phone call will come to say, "Have you agreed?" They say they'll contact you again. It could be a letter, an advert in the paper, or another phone call: "Have the money ready, and a driver. We want a photograph of the driver, the name of the driver, the description of the car" and so on. They just want to be sure that the driver and the vehicle with the money will be recognisable.

'I've done two as a driver – and nerves are taut on both sides: "Go to such-and-such place and wait for a call." A series of cars or buses or trains or even a helicopter, over a number of routes and lasting a period of hours, usually at night, are all designed to avoid surveillance or entrapment. Any mistake or suspicious act and the gang may abort the payment, with potentially fatal retaliation against the hostage: "There are four suitcases – transfer the money into them. You've got two minutes to do it, or the deal is off and the hostage will be harmed."

'One of these events went on for about six hours, with four or five car changes, until eventually the delivery car was ambushed in a very dangerous slum area of town. Armed men surrounded the car, smashing their guns against the bodywork, demanding to know where the money was, all shouting. The driver rightly followed his script, despite the intimidation, and asked for the agreed proof that the hostage was alive. At this moment you're at your most vulnerable – when you hand the money over, you then have to wait for the kidnappers to release the hostage. You don't know if they're going to keep their side of the bargain. So all you can try and do is make certain that he was alive at the time the ransom was delivered – that morning's paper with a signature on it would be proof, or the answer to a question which only the hostage could have known about.'

In this instance, negotiations had been going on over many months, and a sense of understanding had developed between the two sides that payment meant payment and release meant release. This kind of 'understanding' seeks to reduce risk – but it can't eliminate it. 'Release' doesn't include the exact timing or the place. And there's risk for the kidnappers as well: 'In this case,' says Arish Turle, 'we had the permission of the police to pay . . . and every note had been photocopied.'

And he did it in the name of what?

'I was paid to do it – it was my job. I think I can do it better than other people. I think I was able to communicate with and to win the trust of those who were decision-makers as well as those who were victims. I felt I was able to make a contribution in what is a very difficult situation. And if I believe I'm good at it – not infallible, but committed to doing my utmost to collect information, analyse it, communicate to people under stress and help them make a judgement, then I'm helping them make the right decisions. Some of this belief comes from my and my colleagues' background – we were in a better position than many businessmen or families because our military training had dealt with decision-making about life and death.

'Perhaps the ultimate test is whether those you tried to help feel comfortable with the decisions *they* made – whatever the outcome. And that people get to know that you can be trusted to deal with danger should they need your help again.'

9

The Prostitute

Two of the most potent forces in the world must be sex and money. Put them together and you have something very dangerous – 'the world's oldest profession'. Prostitution should probably win first place in many countries' risk assessment lists. But it gets omitted on grounds of taste, prejudice and the sheer embarrassment that so much danger and death are to be found on the streets of every town. However, some face their fate with the Black Horse of the Apocalypse with remarkable resilience – and the occasional laugh.

As a reporter, you bump into prostitution quite regularly. Probably the first time I saw it on a grand scale was in Hong Kong, from the useful vantage point of a hotel next to the Hong Kong Topless Pink Pussycat Club. Towards the end of the Vietnam War, the US navy was wont to allow its aircraft carriers to head for the port for a spot of 'R & R'. With a huge grey ship just a dot on the horizon, the narrow alleys of the colony exploded into activity. Up went the prices chalked on the bar boards, up went the skirts from workaday cotton to mini-mini silk and brocade. Whole families could be seen organising themselves for the acceptance of lust and dollars. As several thousand sailors swarmed towards Tiger beer and temptation, the military police patrolled in busy little jeeps, batons at the ready, in the sure knowledge that this invasion would not be entirely peaceful.

In Freetown, Sierra Leone, the large seafront bar frequented by UN officials, foreign military personnel, aid workers and journalists swarmed with thin young women who wore scarlet hotpants or much less. They were personable and they were educated – I met several lawyers and teachers. They were also desperate, since this was the only source of income for a huge number of relatives devastated by civil war, mutilation and economic collapse. They had grown used to foreigners arriving to restore harmony to their country, bringing with them desire and cash. Peacekeepers are far from home and usually richer than those they are protecting, and in Africa AIDS travels in the baggage train of the soldiers. The European military were more circumspect. In the bar in Freetown, many found the overtures confusing: young women who could converse about Shakespeare or the difficulties of a disrupted judicial system didn't quite equate to the conventional tart.

In Britain I spent mornings as a member of the press hanging around magistrates' courts when Persons of Note were having the misfortune of being hauled before the beak: the Celeb on a Charge story, involving minor members of the aristocracy defying traffic regulations and major members of the entertainment profession attempting to defy gravity with a lot of chemical substances up their nose. One day, I sat through twenty-two cases of 'soliciting while walking up and down the pavement' which were cantered past the bench. The women who stood glumly in the dock were all known to the stipendiary on duty, who went through a rapid ritual of identification, charge, anything to say, no, right then, fined. Imprisonment was dished out to several, with mutterings about 'being a public nuisance'. This brisk system appeared to be aimed at delivering a squirt of moral air-freshener at a city's pool of vice.

Outside the court room, a straggle of resigned and dowdy women minded infants and children, sighing when they learned that a mother was getting fourteen days or digging into handbags for loose change to help out with the fine. It was a scene light years from the image of the glossy tart, the knowing siren, the successful whore, the upmarket call girl of independent means. This is the street scene – that part of prostitution where desperation has set in. A reporter sees it repeated wherever there is extreme poverty, although in shanty towns and refugee camps and amid the misery of flood and famine there is often a tendency to gloss over what is the only source of money to women in such dire circumstances. And a war zone is not an active war zone without a brothel. Again, there's a reticence about reporting the less heroic side of conflict. One Bosnian town whose plight was well documented, indeed trumpeted, during the early 1990s owed some of its survival to its local reputation for being the 'biggest little whorehouse in the Balkans'.

One of the abiding themes of a prostitute's life is the surprise experienced when the first lot of money is handed over, because it's so much more than she has ever earned at any other job. Over thirty years ago in Bristol, women told me they had worked in shops and hairdressers' and factories and their monthly wage shrank, in their eyes, to a laughable pittance when they turned their first trick. The excitement, the sense of wonder, when clutching the actual cash is probably hard to explain if you have always been comfortably off. But in modern terms, it's like winning at least a share of the lottery. And just as rich people so often want more, so does the hair-salon trainee whose wages never quite stretch to the end of the week.

'I used to go to the Ritz for tea. It was great. Getting served all the nice things with people calling you madam – in the place where I used to clean the rooms.'

Amanda is laughing happily at the memory. She's thirty-three and a highly likeable black woman who laughs a lot. Warm and friendly, she has a ten-month-old daughter who's her pride and joy. She was born in Hackney in east London and left school at fifteen with almost no qualifications – though she later discovered she was dyslexic. The usual girlish dreams of being an air hostess or actress faded very quickly as she went on a Youth Training Scheme, from one course to another, before falling pregnant at sixteen. By this time she was working at the Ritz Hotel in

London's West End as a housekeeper – a modern euphemism for long hours and low pay for tidying and cleaning up after the world's travellers. She accepted that this was probably all she would ever do. Her mum looked after her baby – and her sister was pregnant too. From the beginning she was aware that the work might hold a few surprises, although she didn't fully understand what went on.

Off she went one evening, in her uniform of little black dress with lace trimmings and black stockings, and having knocked, was told by an Arab guest to come in and clean. As she was leaving, he asked, 'Any extras?'

'You want more pillows?' she enquired brightly.

'I was naïve,' she says now, 'but I cottoned on after a few seconds that he didn't mean pillows and I scuttled out.'

This happened several times, and she also heard the other girls saying, 'But you get plenty of money – and for just two minutes' work.' She says she got a bit scared and started to look for another job.

However, naïveté doesn't disappear overnight. She asked her boyfriend about an advertisement in the local paper which she thought said 'messenger'. He told her, 'It says a massage".' Innocently, she headed for an interview in Walthamstow, where the woman she met told her it was indeed massage. It was a family business, reassuringly entitled 'Professionals', owned by Dad, with Mum on the front desk, daughter and cousin working in the sauna.

OK, she thought. Then Mum said, 'And they might ask for extras.'

Still the penny didn't drop. 'Extras?'

'Well, they might ask for French.'

Amanda was still rather baffled, thinking that French meant a kind of kissing, and with not a clue about oral sex.

'Why not give it a try?' said the daughter. 'You'd make good money.'

She rattles on like a teenager as if she still can't understand how she had arrived at this point and admits, 'I don't know what possessed me – but I did.' She wasn't short of money at the time, nor did she know anyone else who did this. Then, in the next breath, she admits that when she was older she worked out that it went back to childhood: 'A so-called uncle got into that routine, you know? And he gave me money, and as I got older and I wanted trainers and things I'd pop round, blah, blah . . . you know? I think it all started then . . . but I was too young to know what was what.'

There's no sense of a great step having been taken. She was a young girl with limited options who had already been abused and also had a child. Not so much ignorant as unknowing, with a friendly, compliant nature and the ability to make the best of any situation. She's even shy, avoiding direct terminology and narrating her experience as if she's reliving the moment, especially on her first, nervous day at the massage parlour.

'When I came to go to the sauna, two days after the interview, I was so nervous. . . . And you had to wear a sort of uniform, white overalls with, like, kinky underwear underneath. . . . And the men came in. And they flood to you, 'cos you're new. And with the first one I thought, oh, my God! Another girl said, "Don't be nervous – just go upstairs and massage him." And you were told never to ask them what they want, because the police used to come in and if *you'd* asked, then *you* got arrested: it was always for the *men* to approach. So I was giving this massage, and he was on the table saying, "Are you new? Where're you from?" Then he said, "Do you do any extras?" and I thought, here we go." And I was in such a shock I couldn't remember the prices I'd been told.

' "That's £30, then there's that at £40, and for £50 . . ." and I was thinking, "ask for the *least* thing, please." He mentioned the other girl who was downstairs. And I said, "*Both* of us?" Then I thought, she can be with me, so I'll get her. And, thank goodness, it turned out he wanted the domination thing, with the dressing up and that . . . and I was in stitches, peeing myself with laughter, and the other girl kept telling me to stop laughing because it puts them off! But I was killing myself, 'cos he wanted to be dressed up in frilly knickers and such and there's me in boots and things.'

By now Amanda is helpless with laughter, having never quite come to terms with the more esoteric desires which are to be found in the human imagination.

'But once that first one was out the way, I kind of sailed through. Really weird. And at the end of the night I couldn't really believe how much money I'd made. It was a shock. And I hadn't had a thought about what I was doing. It had been so busy, just 'cos I was a new girl – they'd told the clients that on the phone, and so many came in. When I was getting dressed at the end of it I was finding money coming out of my bra, in my make-up bag, in my shoes. We had to give the parlour owner £20 for each of the first three that came in, then £10 for the next five, then it was all ours after that. The lowest charge was £40, and £120 was the highest – for a full hour. It was amazing – I counted up £420 at the end of the night. And I got such a buzz from it: I couldn't wait to come in the next day. I was about twenty then, and I stayed for two years until the boss got a bit heavy. He fell head over heels for me, and it became a bit of a problem with his now ex-wife on reception.'

She looks back on the time as one of affluence. Much of the work involved fulfilling men's fantasies, which she never got tired of giggling about. But there was also a pervasive atmosphere of possible trouble.

'The punters in saunas are totally different from those on the street – quite weird, they were. We had security guards on the door. But I also started working in flats – several of us worked out of one flat, and I had trouble there. One guy attacked me, asking for his money back, and whopped me in the eye. I wasn't having any of that, so I whopped him back. But he was a huge bloke, so I did give him his money back. It was quite frightening. You'd hear horror stories when you worked in the flats, and then the police changed things so that if there were more than two girls working out of a flat it was classed as a brothel, so it got more difficult.

'There was a series on the telly called *Band of Gold*, and there was this character in it who owned a chicken factory and he used to come in with a suitcase with high heels and stockings – we got someone *exactly* like that. He was really creepy, and tried to strangle one of the girls with one of his stockings. Weirdos, they were the main trouble. You know, you get a businessman from the City, all suited and booted, and he'd come in and dress in a tutu and want you to tell him what a lovely girl he is. Quite worrying. I mean, you wonder why? What sort of guy is he? Some of the time I suppose you get on with it because you think if you don't, he's going to go out and find a little girl and do something . . . so we made ourselves think we were protectors, otherwise they might go and take out these fantasies on kids. One time we had a priest come in – totally dampened my faith, I can tell you – and he wanted me to put him over my knee and spank him. That was a bit worrying. But at the time, I was making such money . . .

'I didn't save, though – that was a big mistake I made. When you're new and young, the money floods in. We started living the high life. Going to the Ritz for tea – yeah, back to the hotel where I'd worked. But as easy as the money went, it came back again. We'd go up the West End and blow like £400, and say to each other, "Not to worry. We'll go in tomorrow and make it back." And you don't notice that new girls are coming in, younger, and the punters are getting a bit used to you and the money's slowing down.

'So I became "Dominatin' Diana" – and that brought much more in! I was good at it – and there was no intercourse involved.' Amanda has been reduced to helpless giggles again and much eye-rolling. She isn't contemptuous of her former clients so much as bemused and slightly exasperated by them. But although she concentrates on the side of the business which brought her temporary wealth, she readily admits that danger was never far away.

'I even got a stalker: every sauna I went to, he found me. He'd wait for me when I'd finished work, be outside, call out my name, offer me a lift, and when I said no he followed me in a cab. This is not something you can go to the police about if you're in my business. It felt really creepy, and then I realised it was possibly dangerous. 'Cos when I'd started working, I never thought about danger – I didn't realise that some of the regulars would get obsessive and ask me about my work and about my money and follow me home and always ring up for me in the sauna. But the money was good.

'By this time I had a daughter by my partner and he was very controlling, obsessive – mind you, he thought I was still working at the Ritz! So I was leading a double life, coming home and making sure that I didn't have any of "my bits" in my bag, leaving them in the dustbin before going into the house – a dustbin full of sexy underwear and high-heeled boots and all the stuff for my domination work! Then I'd sneak out in the middle of the night and rescue it. In fact, no one knew what I was doing, not even my mum. She thought I was housekeeping at the Ritz.'

Life was good in the sense that there was money and a ready clientele, from whom, 'on a good day', she earned £700–800. 'I went from hand-me-downs to silk and satin. I remember buying a Prada handbag with gold embroidery for £1000 – I saw it in Bond Street for £4000, but you could get one cheaper from the people who came selling round the saunas.' She loved going to places she'd never dreamed of being able to afford, and having little shopping sprees for scent and clothes and handbags. 'I went to the fanciest places initially, and I had lunch. I wanted to be a lady who ate lunch – and I left ridiculous tips.'

This was in the early years, when she moved from sauna to sauna, relatively indifferent to the work but earning enough to stop her reflecting on it. 'Years passed, and then the drugs started. I was working at a sort of "high-class" sauna – the manager was well known and the clients were singers and songwriters. Famous people, lots of names I could name [she laughs a lot] but I won't. Maybe I'll get 'em one day when I'm broke! But the guys were coming in with the Charlie [cocaine] and bottles of champagne and we'd have a party, all a bit more glamorous. No, this wasn't Walthamstow! I'd moved on, this was your upmarket Camden.

And the boss kept appearing in the *News of the World* – so did we! He got busted in the end . . . But I wasn't *buying* the drugs at that stage – the guys all brought it in. You know, football players and cricket players, loads of money. And the boss started to arrange private parties in their houses, six of us girls seeing a dozen men in a mansion on a regular basis, Millionaires' Row stuff, down Chigwell. Every time you walked in there were lines of coke on the table and other stuff.

'At the time I wasn't a drinker, and I'd only ever smoked a bit of weed [marijuana]. But I loved the champagne and coke, because it kept us in a party mood *and* it blocked what we was doing as well. You got used to it. So I started ringing up and ordering it: £60 a batch – that's to keep you going for a whole night. But you often had two snoots – so that's £120. And I began to feel I can't do what I'm doing without having it, you know? Then my partner found out what I really did – and that caused trouble. He started following me and hanging around outside the sauna. Like a bloody handbag, he was. And he was very abusive.

'Then I sort of slipped from coke on to crack – I mean, I just asked, "What's that?" And the other girls in the sauna said, "Well, it's just a totally different buzz." I didn't know what hit me when I started taking it. I spiralled totally out of control. Then my partner started taking it. And that was it. I became too desperate, I felt too rough to work in the saunas. I couldn't do the eight-hour shift without paying for something to keep me going, getting it off the dealers outside the sauna. So I sort of slipped away from the sauna – but my partner needed the money to keep up with *his* habit.

'Up to that time I'd met quite a few people who tried to help me with a different career. I really wanted to act and I could have got on – but my partner messed it up. I even did some work as an extra and got an Equity card. I loved it, and I done a few bits and bobs, and was even on a James Bond film when it was filming over at Shoreditch. I met people at parties – and I could have done modelling as well. I was offered Pretty Polly tights, but my partner wouldn't let me go, saying it would be a porno-shoot! They even sent a white limo for me, with a man all dressed up and with flowers. And my partner wouldn't let me go. I was gutted.

'Why did I stay with him? I don't know. I didn't know how to get away from him, and he was so good with my daughter. . . . But he used to beat me up all the time. And by then I looked too bad to go back to the saunas. With the coke you lose your looks. You lose a lot of weight. It takes everything from you – looks, dignity. I did used to look glamorous when I first worked in the saunas, but the crack took it all from me. All I cared about was where the money was coming from for the next smoke . . .

'Before I went downhill I was making good money, but it all went on coke and I didn't even have a pound for a bag of chips afterwards. Then came the streets. We girls in the saunas never mixed with the girls on the streets. We knew they were rough and they couldn't work like us. But I found it was *totally* different. I mean, all of us in the saunas were working to keep up a lifestyle – nice things, clothes, even a mortgage. But the street was just drugs.'

To those without much knowledge of prostitution, it may seem odd that there's a hierarchy when you're 'on the game'. The high-class call girl, the private escort, the shop-window model, the saunas which offer various 'services', sometimes indistinguishable from brothels – there are rarely any precise categories, though the law in many countries feels there ought to be. The result is usually a muddle of euphemism, ignorance and odd definitions: 'Are you standing in this street, madam, or walking it?' However, it's generally accepted that street work is the grimmer end of the business. And it's certainly the most dangerous.

Completely dependent on drugs, Amanda found that the price was greater than the £200–300 she had earned in the sauna. She hasn't a trace of self-pity as she describes her condition then – 'a wraith, dreadful' – and pats her now plump thigh. She pauses to work out how she should describe the next step in her life: she is very circumspect with words and avoids using language which she thinks 'isn't proper' and which might offend someone. However, even though she had spent years in the sex business, the prospect of going on the streets appalled her.

'My first time was in Stamford Hill, me and another girl. I remember standing there and being shouted at by other girls: "Get off my patch." I didn't understand. I walked down the road and a car pulled up and I thought oh God! I put my head in, he asked, "Business?" I said, "Yeah." "Jump in." So we went round the back of the flats nearby. It was so . . . different. I know that it was over in two minutes, but it was just . . . shocking. This physical stuff – and *that's* when I needed the drug – I didn't want to even think about what I'd just done. I wanted to forget.

'And I hadn't thought how dangerous it was to get into a stranger's car. Then I got attacked, several times. But it's only when you're off the drug for a bit – in between taking it – that you realise what's been done to you. And they do it – attack you – 'cos that's how they look at street girls. You get beaten up after you've given them sex, and they're trying to take back the money. It got so bad that, even after you'd got hit, you went out to find another punter to pay for the stuff to block out what had just happened. It's crazy.

'I got badly harmed sometimes. Two Polish guys smashed my cheekbone. I used to report it to the police. When I first did that, I just gave a description and didn't wait around. I mean – you're ringing a police station. And I didn't realise that they would go after someone for you. And when it happened again, they were really good. People say you don't get any help from them, but you really do. And they look for men who attack you. But very few girls report it, 'cos they're in such a state.

'I was so much into the drugs that the violence never put me off. I was out there again straightaway. It's really scary, especially if you go back to their house. A Somali-American took me back to his place in Finsbury Park. And when I asked for the money – in advance, as usual – he wouldn't pay me and got out a gun and hit my head with it. And then I had to do it – with a gun to my head. It was horrendous. And he had pictures up on the wall of him in an American police uniform, with his family and kids and everything.

Then he suddenly threw me out. Down the steps. Naked. Then threw my clothes out. So I rang the police, waited for them to come, and the feeling that I got when I saw them coming out the house with him was: how *stupid* are some people? Even so, I didn't answer the calls the police made to me to go to court. I was back on the streets. Not thinking.

'Then you realise there's disease as well. I mean, you always insist on a condom, but you can be threatened and they force you to do it without. And how do you prove to the police it was rape? I mean, what chance? And you're terrified those men are the ones who've got AIDS. And you know, I wasn't really used to doing intercourse. We hardly ever had to in the sauna. Oh, I got paranoid. Oh, God. Sex. . . .

'All the time you hear terrible stories from other girls. We were all sorts – black, white, Asians, Eastern girls. . . . I was on the streets for about four years, mainly in Stamford Hill. Turkish guys and Jews, and they liked us black girls – but often it was just touching and things. Then I moved to wherever there was a drugs house, so that you could get the stuff quicker. And it got rougher. Out every night, and you stopped sleeping and went day and night on the beat. Then you'd realise you'd been up for five days, 'cos the drug keeps you going. Sometimes you could see the girls nodding off while standing on the pavement. What a state we were in! I never wanted to look in the mirror. I didn't dare.

'In the end my kids went to my mum's, and I'd try to keep off the game for a few hours and get washed and get some clean clothes to go round and see them. I'd knock on the door and see my mum's face. She knew, then, that I was on the streets, and she said I'd got to stop taking the stuff. But my partner was stronger, and he was bingeing on drugs.

'I tried to be a mother-hen to some of the other girls on the street, but it all got worse. One girl I knew was stabbed to death. And my partner took me off the streets and used to march me to punters' houses. Which was frightening. But he had a habit to feed and he wanted to make sure I'd earn it for him. Then I got trapped in a car with some guys and I thought they were going to kill me. I OD'd on drugs several times and got arrested. The most dangerous places were crack houses. If you drive women off the streets they end up in crack houses, which are much worse: sodden mattresses, dealers with guns and shooting. Dealers threaten you and want sex – lots of them. And you can hear girls being attacked in the bathroom, being raped, and no one's doing nothing. Crack's an underclass drug and no one cares.'

Amanda is describing what I saw in Miami almost twenty years ago: a drug associated with extremely violent behaviour which tends to isolate its users even from other drug addicts. I interviewed the head of the local hospital's Emergency Room about the long-term effects of crack. 'Couldn't say,' he replied. 'No one's lived long enough for us to tell.' Having been on a raid with the local Vice Squad, I thought I'd got myself on to the set of a horror film (rather than the glamorous TV programme *Miami Vice*, which was based on this unit). A filthy, stinking house, in darkness, with figures on the floor out cold, on a drug high, or, in one case, dead. Followed by a brief gun battle. And as the head of the Vice Squad said to me, 'Just low-life, ma'am, and no one cares what happens to them.' And crack has been around in Britain for some years.

On the streets of London, Amanda had at first been earning about £150 if she worked all night – £30 each time for sex. But that had now gone down to £10, or – especially with dealers – nothing, in exchange for a little bit of crack cocaine. She felt her life was collapsing. 'You'd hear of girls who'd died. You knew the drugs would get you. "Is it me next?". We'd all say that to each other on the streets. But it didn't stop us. We'd cry about those girls for a day, then go in search of another smoke. I was smoking both heroin and crack at the end. Crack makes you moody. Heroin gives you cramps and makes you sick And all the girls on the street – *all of them* – are on drugs.'

Amanda is a warm, kind woman and she looks haunted as she recalls the life she slid into. She is well aware that there's little sympathy for prostitutes. But she is emphatic that the appearance of so much drug-dealing has changed the women's situation. The circle of addiction and turning a trick to pay for it is understood by every dealer and drug runner. They hang around, turn up when the women are at their most vulnerable and are only ever interested in making money. It doesn't seem to be fully appreciated that street prostitution is now driven by drug dependency, and that the fortunes being made by dealers at the top of the tree partly depend on exploiting the women at the bottom. Amanda's final time on the streets was increasingly frightening.

'It's become much more dangerous in the past year or so. There are more dealers and they're fighting among themselves. They beat you up if you don't go back to the same one, because they're in so much competition to sell now. Punters are also on the stuff as well, much more. And they're more likely to attack you. It's all about money. And it's getting out of hand. Punters sometimes rob the *girls* for money for drugs. It's so much more dangerous. . . . And I'm now out of it. When I first started, I thought I'd never get out. But this is what started it – my little angel.'

Her ten-month-old daughter has sat quietly all this time and is smiling serenely. Amanda clearly dotes on her. 'I was still on the drugs when I got pregnant – but with someone different. My old partner had run into serious trouble with some other dealers – he grassed up some Yardies and was told he'd be dead if he came back to this area. Then I met my little angel's daddy. And he knew what I did, but he stepped back and waited for me to make a decision. He said, "Come on, you've got kids and there's more to life than drugs." He'd come looking for me on the streets, and say, "Home, bath, bed."

'One day I literally woke up. The sun was streaming through the curtains and I woke up in a clean bed, with clean clothes on. He walked in with a tray of breakfast and I thought: ohhh. It was something *normal.* Something I hadn't seen or felt in what seemed like a lifetime. And I said, "Thank you." And he said, "Are you ready now?" And I cried and cried, and that was the start. I went into rehab and got help – and there are people who help you.

'I look back on it as a horrible life. The craving for the drug, the money. A nightmare. I could easily be in my grave like so many of them girls. Could have been me next. And it's a miracle what's happened to me. And I want to tell the other girls my story, and help them.'

So why did she follow this life? In the name of what?

'In the end – survival. In the beginning it was the buzz of the money, a different lifestyle. I was a wealthy young girl for a bit. Then, to feed the habit, it became an everyday fight for survival.'

10

War

'War, ma'am, is a risky business.' A simple phrase, but for ever stuck in my memory as it was spoken to me very quietly by a British colonel contemplating the few hours left before the ground assault on Iraq in the first Gulf War. Tough and charming, standing under a desert night sky, he was thinking about his young soldiers and their families at home. Not in a sentimental manner, but hugely conscious that he was responsible for them and that war produces every sort of danger. You can plan, train, drill, practise and exercise for war, but every conflict produces its own special surprises and horrors.

Nor is war confined to a 'battlefield', a neat and easily delineated area in which professionals operate. War is messy, indiscriminate and unfair, spilling over into the lives of ordinary people who usually have no choice in the matter. The Red Horse, his colour left all over the battlefield and beyond, has a rider with a sword. Those who, like him, take up arms do so for myriad reasons. . . .

'As we're wearing crowns, any chance of us sitting on the throne?' The occasion is the annual Christmas party for the men and women of the Not Forgotten Association, held in St James's Palace. We're in the State Apartments, a riot of curlicued gilding and very busy wallpaper. The bright gold almost glares at you, and there's so much of it – on ornate chairs, on huge vases, round the doors and windows, on the enormous sprouting chandeliers – that it would be vulgar were it not royal. And there's a throne at the far end of the three grand rooms being eyed by a very sprightly gathering sitting down to a delicious tea and a glass of mulled wine, having pulled elegant crackers and discovered the obligatory paper crown.

The Not Forgotten are disabled and wounded ex-service personnel. Many sport two rows of medals. One elderly lady wears an impossibly elegant hat and observes politely that one of the special guests, Dame Vera Lynn, is not. The clichés can come out when these folk are gathered, but why not? They *are* indomitable, impressive, modest. There's a single representative of World War I – the irrepressible Henry Allingham, at 110 the country's oldest man, the only remaining survivor of the Battle of Jutland and the last remaining founder member of the Royal Air Force. The noise level moves up as the Prince of Wales and the Duchess of Cornwall move slowly round every table in the three rooms, some of the guests standing to attention when a royal heaves into view.

Those who fought in World War II are friskily eyeing up the young waitresses and appear to have an endless supply of jokes. Many recall in precise detail the units they served in, the names of all their mates, the number of planes shot down, the exact distance of a march. They describe their service with pride but don't bang on about their own efforts. Raise the subject of courage and it will be brushed aside with a shrug: 'Just doing our bit, you know.'

Then there are the younger set, veterans of post-war conflict such as Northern Ireland, the Falklands and the Gulf. Their modern wars evoke less nostalgia, but the injuries represent all the dangers of war eternal – especially among those back from Iraq and Afghanistan. They are survivors, thanks to improved medical techniques, but have had to come to terms with impaired lives. They, unlike most of their elders in this room, were not conscripted or made to do National Service. They volunteered for service life, even though peacetime in post-war Britain has been almost permanently marked by overseas adventures, many of them intensely fought and extremely risky.

Snake-venom collector Bill Haast at home in Florida, with his favourite garden ornament – a King Cobra.

Diver Gie Couwenberg returning from more than three hours inside the hull of the capsized ferry, the *Herald of Free Enterprise*.

Stuntman Jim Dowdall spending a routine day on location, falling through flames, in *Indiana Jones and the Last Crusade*, 1989.

Stuntwoman Sarah Franzl, in a 70 foot back fall for the BBC TV series *Bugs*.

Everyday life for teenagers like young terrorist Anthony McIntyre
in West Belfast in 1972.

The SAS storming the Iranian Embassy in London in 1980 – one kind of
outcome to the work of hostage and kidnap negotiator Arish Turle.

Twenty-four year old WAAF Avis Parsons with her Military Medal.

Detecting the German bombers by radar in the Battle of Britain in 1940.

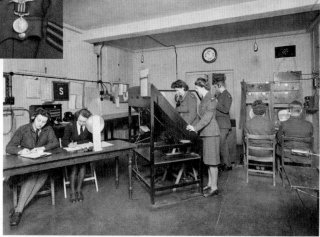

Leeds men volunteer for Korea to honour pact with dead brother

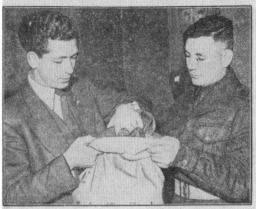

The *Yorkshire Post* October 23rd 1950: Derek Kinne (left, with his younger brother Valentine) decides to join the army after his elder brother dies in Korea.

Stuart Archer, pioneer bomb disposal officer and oldest surviving holder of the George Cross.

Rope, ladder and a lot of digging – how to deal with an unexploded bomb in 1940.

Doing the lonely 'long walk' towards a bomb in Northern Ireland, despite the high-tech 'wheelbarrow' robot.

Ben Remfrey of the Mines Awareness Trust, with the Kenyan Army and Mine Dog Asta.

The Rwandan Army returning from de-mining tea plantations near Ruhengeri.

Conservationist Richard Leakey with twelve tons of elephant tusks - $3 million of ivory – confiscated from Kenyan poachers in 1989 and about to be burned.

Bodyguard Will Scully organising the defence of the Mammy Yoko Hotel
under attack from rebels in Sierra Leone.

A policeman's lot in Northern Ireland during the Troubles –
all in a day's work for Brian McCargo.

Protestor Zhao Ming safely out of China after nearly two year's detention and torture for belonging to the Falun Gong movement.

Falun Gong members being hauled from Tiananmen Square in Beijing by Chinese police in 2000.

Mathura Prasad in Mandawa, India, a survivor in the very dangerous business of food tasting.

A tall, handsome lad from a Guards regiment stands stiffly with his crutches. 'Helmand,' he says briskly, naming the bleak Afghan province where he lost his leg. 'But I can still do a job,' he says determinedly, 'and the army's my life.' His mates in their wheelchairs nod vigorously, still wedded to the military business. They are matter-of-fact about their experiences, still laughing about some of the more bizarre moments, telling unrepeatable jokes about the difference between a goat and a Taliban fighter (don't ask), and rarely grumbling about the lack of equipment and the hardships of an unfriendly and violent land. They speak in spare style about 'contacts', about real firefights and ferocious attacks. They are conscious that most of the population has little grasp of professional fighting and limited understanding of decision-making in dangerous surroundings. They talk comfortably to each other in their own military lingo, and when they do have a niggle it's about us journalists.

'Where are you, then? Why isn't there much in the papers? Our mates die and it's just a line on the news, if anything. Doesn't anybody care what we're doing?' Modern soldiering attracts varied coverage – and the degree of danger in a conflict zone is now much more influential in newsrooms, or rather board rooms, obsessed with health and safety and insurance. Most television coverage of front-line aggression now comes from freelancers, independent of the fretting executives, who take the risks and so relieve the companies of responsibility. And stories on location centre on '24-hour' presenters tucked next to a satellite dish – and the unwieldy dish, 'going live', is unlikely to be near the hub of the action.

Granted, there are hundreds of young hopefuls pouring out of the academic media departments who believe that reporting a war is the ultimate aim. In many cases, this belief goes hand in hand with complete ignorance of the bloodstained reality. Pain, misery, the gross unfairness of who gets killed, mosquitoes and diarrhoea are not part of the imagined scenario. The perception of danger is fuzzy and tinged with Hollywood excitement. However, they soon discover that the major channels worldwide are none too keen to have staff becoming a liability in a minefield. That's what the local freelancers are for – savvy about the situation, speaking the language and often with a little bit of military experience. The preferred option is to go in an official 'facility', where risk can be controlled, ditto the journalism.

So the soldiers wonder about TV stations which trumpet their conflict coverage in slick trailers, with claims of being 'where it happens, when it happens.' The men go months without hearing a word said about the patrols fraught with threat, the roadside explosions, the snipers and the angry crowds. As they access the internet in sleeping quarters regularly hit by mortar fire they find little substantial coverage, except when a politician drops by momentarily for a grinning photo opportunity. No wonder they question whether anybody cares.

They now form a small minority in a population that has little or no direct experience of warfare. Except for the elderly veterans who surround them today, many of whom come over for a chat. For many years there was only the occasional youth who joined their gatherings. Iraq and Afghanistan have changed that, and now there is a small tide of the seriously disabled who don't find it easy to explain to their peer group in civvy street just what the danger was like.

'I do admire them – they chose to join up,' says one white-haired former infantryman with a long row of World War II and Korean medals. He goes on to say that he didn't want to describe the Normandy beaches on D-Day to the young ones, because he felt he'd merely been 'doing his duty'. 'Had to join up – no choice. Did what I was told for five years,' he says. 'Did what we all had to do – we were all in it together.' They sound like clichés, but they're not. Attitudes were different when the whole nation's survival was at stake. Everyone had to 'do their bit'. And life went upside-down for the most peaceable of citizens.

Many of these veterans are now in special accommodation funded by the service charities – at the party I get lots of invitations to come and see them. Mrs Violet Long has come from Rustington in Sussex and says no one's got a nicer view than her in Princess

Marina House – straight over the lawn to the sea. Her room's next to Avis Parsons', she eagerly explains, who can't be here today; but she's rather special, says Mrs Long, and has the Military Medal. Mrs Long, well into her eighties, has become Mrs Parsons' unofficial PA, so frequently is her ninety-year-old friend asked about her wartime experiences.

And, when I do get to visit, I find it is indeed a very fine view of the sea at Rustington as Mrs Parsons and Mrs Long bustle about for the photograph album and scrapbook and military histories on radar. The large books live near the top of the wardrobe, frustrating Avis, who is a fraction over four feet ten inches tall. Settled with a cup of tea, they bring out the photographs – tiny snaps of lots of jolly girls in uniform.

'It was such important work – you had to keep it secret,' says Avis. 'Otherwise, you would have been shot.' Both ladies nod, seriously. And in the ensuing tale, what emerges is the immense sense of pride in having played a vital part in the country's defences, with Avis's own role on the night of a huge air raid consigned to 'doing one's bit'.

'I'd joined the Auxiliary Service six months before war began – made quite a change from getting my living from making curtains and loose covers. I wanted to be involved. I'd left school and been at home since I'd been ill at thirteen, looking after my three sisters and earning my living by sewing. My mother once said, "You'll never amount to anything . . . ."

'I didn't get my uniform immediately – they hadn't made enough of them yet, and when I did it was far too big. But I learned to be a plotter, training first at Leighton Buzzard and then going to Fighter Command at Bentley Priory at Stanmore. We WAAFs had this enormous table, all squared off like a Ludo game. The Officer Commanding was Air Vice Marshal Dowding – he used to peer over the balcony and watch us, but he never smiled. We didn't look back – we were all rather scared of those people.'

Although she found it rather daunting at first, especially living in cramped billets and never having even undressed in front of her sisters before, Avis developed an appetite for technical details which she rattles off today as if about to go on shift. The pressure was intense – no time to think of bombs, for all the young women were focused on delivering information which would get their own side's planes up into the air as soon as possible.

As the war gathered pace, so did the need to release men from technical jobs for front-line duties – and to train more women. The plotters were moved on to the new, secret world of radar and sent to windswept Bawdsey on the Suffolk coast, very much a 'hush-hush' establishment, then on to RAF Poling in Sussex to work on one of the Chain Home Low stations – detecting low-level enemy aircraft coming in over the south coast between Portsmouth and Brighton. At least the living quarters were a change from the wooden huts and converted schools and Bawdsey fishermen's cottages, for the Duchess of Norfolk offered accommodation in nearby Arundel Castle: 'Big rooms, with baskets of logs in the corridor, which we burned as fast as they could cut them down. And we never got bombed, because people said Hitler wanted it for himself when he got here!'

Avis spent her time glued to a console in a dimly lit room, staring at 'blips': 'We looked at a row of little lights going along – when you find an aircraft you get a little V-shape, then you use your Goniometer knob and turn it and it inverts the trace.' Avis dives with glee into the detail of the device, which is all about two pairs of crossed dipoles interpreting the signals from receiving aerials – and loses me. 'You had to keep your wits about you,' she says, noting that I'm looking rather blank. 'You had to get the information out. We didn't think about planes and the people in them – because *we* had to get *our* planes up, and every minute counted.'

The work increased in early 1940 as the Germans seized air-fields on the French side of the Channel and raids came day and night. Nor were the radar operators underground – some were in wooden huts, others in a small brick building. 'We'd watch the screen fill up with blips and know that some town was going to get it.' At the height of the Battle of Britain, when every radar station was working flat out to give warning of approaching bombers, the airfields and the radar stations were pounded continually. They were not difficult targets, with 360-foot receiving aerials rearing into the sky, but it had been expected that bombing raids would concentrate on towns. Avis and her colleagues got no warning of any raid: they *were* the warning.

At Poling, Avis went on duty on a hot August Sunday after a short break on the Isle of Wight, where she'd heard that a sister station at Ventnor had been hit. When she went to the radar hut to relieve another operator they were told that a mass of aircraft were coming in, and the sergeant in the next-door building advised her to take cover. 'I said I couldn't because I'd got too much information coming in to me, and he said, "Well, I can't make you go." I got my tin hat and stuck it on. I'd never worn it before, because it was too big.' She found herself alone, staring at the blips and holding two microphones connecting her to the ops room at Bentley Priory, the nerve centre of the Battle of Britain. She knew that the station on the Isle of Wight had been targeted a few days earlier, and also the airfield not far from Poling at Tangmere. As she started to concentrate on the blips she heard the planes themselves.

'Over my headphones I heard the plotters saying, "Poling, Poling, this plot is right on top of you." I said, "You don't need to tell me – they're almost dropping on my head."' Above her were thirty-one German JU87s busy dropping ninety bombs. 'All our fighters were up – and elsewhere. It screams, does a bomb, when it comes down near you. And the planes sounded hideous too . . . I thought the Germans used to put it on deliberately!' Avis does the ultimate small-boy German bomber impression . . . *neeeeeeaaaw*. 'I don't think I altered my routine. Or raised my voice. Just kept going. I thought about my sisters. I thought, I'm not going to let them down. If I die, I die. So I carried on.

'I wanted to save my country. I was born in World War I, and war seems to have played such a part in our family's life. Father was away in that war, and there was rationing, and Mother used to make shoes out of old felt hats. Then I remember the Cenotaph being unveiled in our town, and a little boy with his father's medals on. And all I thought about that Sunday was that I wouldn't give in to them – over my dead body. I mean, even if we were taken prisoner, which might be possible because we were doing such a secret job. Our instructions were written on rice paper so we could get rid of them easily. Even our parents didn't know what we did – we weren't allowed to tell them. And the Germans never *did* work out how we were spotting them at low level. . . .'

Avis is very determined. She looks thoughtful when I ask her if she had thought much about being in danger.

'I don't think we'd ever thought we'd be a target. And it would have been a silly question to ask us: would we stay? I don't think I thought about danger. I was defending my country.'

The 18th of September came to be known as 'The Hardest Day' in the Battle of Britain. The RAF lost 51 aircraft, with 10 pilots killed or missing. The Luftwaffe had 96 aircraft damaged or destroyed, with 125 pilots and aircrew killed or missing. Extraordinarily, no one was killed at Poling, but Avis emerged from the radar room to see the damage: 'This RAF officer, he had a most beautiful car, a Lagonda, poor man. . . .' She smiles sympathetically. 'Coming out of the radar hut, everyone else turned out to be in the air-raid shelter – they thought I'd been killed. I did have a bit of shrapnel in me – but I'd had my tin hat on, even though it was miles too big.' Debris, unexploded bombs and craters, all around was a sight that people grew accustomed to as they emerged after a raid. Even so, it was shocking that day, and the news that there was a German bomber on the ground nearby, which had bombed an RAF station a few miles away and caused many casualties, sent everyone in hot pursuit.

'I was lifted up to see it, and in the cockpit, there was vomit. I never knew if that pilot had died, but actually to see, for the first time, the aircraft with the swastika. . . . well, I was full of hate at the time. Afterwards I realised that he was only doing what he was told. He was attacking my country and I was defending it. Then I went to church, and prayed to God for my life and that the war would soon be over.'

Four months later, she was heading home to Amersham on leave when someone said, 'Avis, it's just been announced on the wireless on the eight o'clock news that you're being given a medal.'

'It came as a great surprise – it really did. When I got home, a reporter from London rang the doorbell, but I said, "I can't tell you anything whatever." You see, it was a secret job, special, and you couldn't say. You could be shot for it! I went to the Palace with my mother and father. We were all organised into groups and lines in different rooms, so we wouldn't get the wrong medal from the King. I was twenty-four by then, and getting that medal changed my life. Not that I behaved differently – just that I wear it on Battle of Britain Day, and Remembrance Sunday when I go on parade, and I always think: I was just doing my job.'

Avis Parsons, who died in 2008, is one of only six women who were awarded the Military Medal in World War II. In the name of what?

'Defending my country.'

There is, of course, more to war than the battlefield. Even when battle is over, the danger doesn't vanish. As a child, I heard talk of a schoolfriend's father who had 'had a bad time' in the war. He had been fighting in the Far East and had ended up a prisoner of war of the Japanese in Burma. It is often assumed that being a PoW means that life goes quiet – a period of suspended time until hostilities end and repatriation occurs. But from the hushed tones in which adults muttered about my friend's father, I gathered that it was not a time of camaraderie enlivened by daring escape attempts. Not everyone observes the rules, the Geneva Convention. He had gone through hell. And there are others, too, who saw this face of war.

The theme park at Old Tucson in Arizona fulfils a lot of fantasies. For men more than women, I suspect, because I've never heard a woman say she dreams of moseying along past the saloon to twirl a six-gun and drill a hole in a lousy varmint while dressed in fringed leather and high-heeled boots. No, that's what blokes who love Hollywood Westerns do. Women tend to be relegated to wiggle-on roles as bar-room floosies and pert schoolmarms.

Old Tucson fulfils these dreams. For decades this film set in the Sonoran desert has hosted stars and tourists, all acting out the idealised horse-opera which passes for the Old West in the nineteenth century. You can ride in a stagecoach, watch a gunfight, play heroic marshals and cowboys exemplifying a moral code that is simple and attractive: tough, no-nonsense men, upright and self-contained, and given to lines of dialogue extending to 'Yup' and 'Nope'.

Just over the Tucson mountains lies today's version of shoot-'em-up fantasy. Not a saloon or hitching-post in sight, though. Nor are you given tourist access to the huge complex of anonymous buildings. Instead you are directed to a website which seems to embody many of the principles which informed the gunslingers of the old Wild West: 'A commitment to the highest ethical standards . . . diversity . . . integrity and excellence'. But we're not talking slugs of lead. We're talking missiles. For this is Raytheon Missile Systems – the world's largest missile manufacturer. In the way that the Winchester and the Colt 45 became household names via fiction on the streets of Old Tucson, the products dreamed up in modern Tucson are famous via their lethal reality: the Patriot missile, the Tomahawk, the Stinger and the Sidewinder . . . all with that little hint of the Sonoran desert in their name, as they go to work in the world's war zones.

Past the missile factory and south of Tuscon you are into desert very quickly, a place where you can watch coyotes and javelinas rooting in the trash cans in the yard. At dusk, the wild dogs howl gently and the wild pigs truffle short-sightedly near the French windows in Derek Kinne's house. Derek says we're still within the city limits, though it doesn't look much like it to me, as we've negotiated dry river beds and bounced past the cactus in his all-American car – which bears a Union flag numberplate, even though he's been here for almost half a century. On the wall of his living room is a large collection of framed photographs and certificates and invitations – not surprising, for he's just retired from running a successful framing business. However, there's a common theme to his mementoes – a small emblem in the corner of each card: VC GC.

Derek Kinne comes from Leeds and belongs to that small elite, the men and women who have earned the highest British decorations: the Victoria Cross and the George Cross. We are talking about the kind of duel which occurred halfway between the American Old West and the American War on Terror. For Derek's war was in Korea, and neither the modern gizmos of over-the-horizon warfare, nor the code of honour of the gunfight in the corral, were remotely connected to his war.

He joined the army with no thought of being a hero. 'I grew up in Leeds in the 1930s. It was a happy childhood for us kids, but hard, in the Depression. We'd collect wood out of old houses and take it home. My stepfather would chop it, then we'd go out and sell it. He was Italian and used to sell ice-cream, but he didn't speak very much English. Kinne's not Italian – my father was Belgian, my mother Italian, a Casenelli. They'd come to England, but he died after an operation. Then she married my stepfather. When we were little, none of us spoke English – we all spoke Italian.

'And when World War II broke out, we were ostracised. We were forever trying to defend ourselves at school, because we were "Eyties". Most of my family on my mother's side were deported, and some of them were interned on the Isle of Man. My grandfather was a fascist and he was deported back to Italy, taking his youngest son. The other two sons stayed here. Ironically, my third eldest uncle was an interpreter for the British army, and when he got to Italy he met his younger brother – who'd joined the Italian army and was a prisoner of War. So he used to go to the PoW camp and take him out for a drink – two brothers on different sides . . .'

There were 'ice-cream families' all over Britain, many here since before World War I. Debates on integration were rare – no one worried that Italian could be heard from Glasgow to Bristol as long as the ice-cream parlours served up treats for British families. They opened cafés in Nonconformist South Wales, subtly adjusted their cones and wafer sandwiches in Sheffield and New-castle to a more 'British-tasting ice-cream' and started up those familiar restaurants with red-and-white checked tablecloths and

Chianti bottles swathed in straw. But war intruded on this tolerance, and internment came as a great shock to many who thought they were settled and busy and had never reflected on the claims of nationality. 'Collar the lot,' said Winston Churchill about these Italians, when he heard that Mussolini had joined forces with Hitler in 1940.

However, in the Kinne family no one seems to have worried much about which side you joined. Soldiering was a way to see the world, perhaps to learn a trade, and brothers ended up fighting on opposite sides, getting swept up in the massive machinery of mobilisation. And in the late 1940s in Britain Raymond Kinne, two years older than Derek and very close to him, joined up as yet another war was approaching.

'My elder brother joined the army when he was eighteen – just for the chance to travel. He got to India. When he came home on leave we went to Lewis's store in Leeds and thought it would be great if we both bought signet rings – you know, a "Beau Geste" sort of thing. I had "Kinne 1" and "Kinne 2" inscribed on them, and said that if he ever died in action I'd take his place. Just one of those silly things you do as kids.'

In 1950, a British-led Commonwealth Brigade was sent to join the war in Korea. Raymond Kinne, serving with the Argyll and Sutherland Highlanders, saw action. Derek recalls: 'I was working away from home, as a waiter in a hotel at Scotch Corner in north Yorkshire, when I got the message. On a Wednesday in October 1950 I went to the cinema in Darlington on my day off, and someone from the hotel saw me and told me to call home urgently. So I called my uncle and he told me Raymond had been killed in Korea.

'I thumbed a lift back to Scotch Corner, and I'd already made up my mind what I was going to do. Another Italian I knew, Divanni, was a lieutenant in the army and had been killed in a motor-cycle crash in Cyprus – and his family had put a photograph in the newspaper. So I went straight to the local paper to do the same thing. They said they'd write about it, but they didn't think they'd put a photograph in. And as I was leaving, the lad there asked me where I was going, and I said I was off to the recruiting office. He said, "Have you got a photograph of your brother, and would you mind if we took one of you?" And that evening, the paper's headline was "First Leeds man killed in Korea", with a picture of my brother – and one of me, the new recruit.

'I've got a particularly stubborn streak. I make up my mind, and I won't deviate. Don't know where I get it from. It's always been my way.' Impatient to get to the Far East, Derek was accepted under the special Korean Volunteer Scheme – but he had to wait several months before he found himself on board a troopship with reinforcements. There was supposed to be six weeks' basic training in Japan but Derek, desperate for action, wangled his way early into a unit boarding a boat for Pusan. He arrived in Korea six months after Raymond's death, to serve with the 1st Battalion, Royal Northumberland Fusiliers. 'I intended to find my brother's grave. And to get revenge. I wanted to kill. I think that's what made me a very good front-line soldier. I'd been a hopeless "civilian soldier" doing National Service – in eighteen months I'd done 148 days CB [confined to barracks for misdemeanours] and never saw a shot fired in anger!

'I was thrilled to bits to get to Korea. And any patrol there was, I wanted to be on it. I was "Fighting Kinne", really gung-ho. They used to say, "Put Kinne in the front." I was a walking arsenal – if anyone had hit me with a bullet, I'd have just gone up with a big bang.

'I'd thought war was a bit like an Errol Flynn movie, where you'd smile and lay back and die and there'd be no blood and guts – and even in the real thing, I didn't think I'd be killed. I'd thought about being wounded, but when you're that age you think you're invincible – and I never thought I'd be a prisoner of war. Never entered my mind.'

Like many young men who joined up, Derek Kinne had given little thought to the whys and wherefores of the war. It was being fought in a distant and unknown land, and the kind of emotions which had fuelled soldiers and people at home in World War II were much less in evidence. Instead, the Korean peninsula had become the scene of the first confrontation of the Cold War. where two superpowers fought in a third country and the main casualties were its citizens.

'Before I went there I'd mainly read the papers for sport and the cartoons – I liked cricket and football – and when it came to who was fighting and why, all I thought of was, well . . . whoever I got in those rifle sights. All I wanted was revenge for my brother's death. Maybe it was wrong. But to me it was right. I don't carry the hatred now that I had then. I remember even when I was in prison camp, in solitary confinement, I would visualise that there'd be another war, and *I'd* be a guard – and I'd be waiting for this lot to come in front of me . . . that's how naïve I was.'

Korea turned out to be a cold and unforgiving place that winter. Raymond Kinne had been killed in the month when the war seemed on the verge of ending: the UN forces had pushed back the North Korean People's Army and General Douglas MacArthur had spoken of having the troops 'home for Christmas'. However, a catastrophic miscalculation about the intentions of the Chinese Communists brought about an unexpected and violent reversal of the UN operation. What had been considered a victory in the making for the UN forces turned dreadfully sour. The Chinese poured into Korea. What they lacked in sophisticated weaponry, they made up for in sheer numbers and revolutionary fervour. They used unorthodox tactics, sneaking around for stealthy night attacks, then pressing home with a huge wave of men in a tumultuous cacophony of bugles and gongs and gunfire. Action came thick and fast, and so did the chaos and confusion.

Fusilier Derek Kinne arrived as one major battle succeeded another, and headed into a war zone with desperate fighting, heavy casualties and thousands of Korean refugees complicating the picture. In April 1951, the Chinese launched their Spring Offensive with nearly three-quarters of a million soldiers. Derek Kinne was near the Imjin River. Later he wrote: 'First we were winning; then we were losing . . . fire and counter-fire sang over our heads or buried itself in the earth on either side of the road. Men moving in all directions; weapons firing rapidly: my mind could not cope with it all. It was like a film running too fast.'

And then, on 25 April, came the fate he hadn't expected, and one that hadn't happened in the films he'd been fond of seeing in the cinema at home: he was taken prisoner. The citation for his George Cross has an unusual ring to it: it states the Date of Act of Bravery as 25 April 1951–10 August 1953. His fight with the Chinese was only just beginning.

First there was a prolonged and grim march north, during which the Chinese troops' treatment of the Americans and British in their charge indicated that the rules of the Geneva Convention were not uppermost in their minds. Men died of untreated wounds, hunger and cold. When they finally ended up in camp, conditions hardly improved. The physical privations were immense: ill treatment, threatened execution, appalling rations – and torture. But added to this was the obsession of the Chinese with the *thoughts* of their prisoners.

'I'd no idea about what the Chinese would do to us – or what their methods were. They would come out with this stuff to us, and you'd have to study in your room – and it was just rubbish, utter rubbish. The political side of things never interested me. I'd known nothing about propaganda. I was in Korea for just one purpose. And I suppose I was enough of a Christian to say to myself, "I chose this. I've been there and killed them. So I suppose this is my reward." I accepted it as a fact. I'd done it wilfully, and now this was the repercussions, the results of my actions. I was happy in the knowledge that I'd done what I'd set out to do – and there I was, a prisoner.

'But when the politics came in I thought, no, this is wrong. You see, although I wasn't interested in politics, I did know the difference between being free and what the Chinese were talking about.'

The Chinese were looking for both publicity and converts. They were convinced they could 'educate out' any prisoner's belief in democracy, affirming the superiority of Communism and turning men against the countries they had fought for. There were hours, days, months of endless interrogation, propaganda lectures and demands that the prisoners betray each other if any dissent or trouble occurred. Fusilier Kinne was having none of this. He took to non-cooperation like a duck to water, kept up morale among his fellow prisoners and developed a determined appetite for escaping. The prison guards neither understood nor appreciated his efforts.

'The Chinese beat the crap out of me. They said, "We're here to help you." I said, "Where are your doctors?" Guys were starving and dying. They said, "You've got to look at it this way. We're not the doctors of your body, we're the doctors of your mind. We have to cure your mind. *You* must cure your body."'

'Treatment', the Chinese called it, regarding any prisoner's refusal to hate his own country and admire Communist China as a mental aberration which could be lectured out of him. It wasn't brain-washing precisely, but, considering the awful living conditions, it came very close. There was no avoiding the dangers in camp: men died of disease and malnutrition. When they were buried their name-tags were removed by the Chinese so they wouldn't be traced. And resistance to propaganda brought retribution; recalcitrance on the part of anyone was assumed to be part of a Great Plot. So who were the ringleaders, the conspirators?

Some men broke under the pressure, signing 'confessions' or 'peace petitions'. But Derek Kinne did not, attempting escape yet again and then speaking up about the Chinese disdain for the Geneva Convention – no access to the Red Cross, no parcels. He was told, 'We feed you and clothe you – and then the Americans come over and strafe the camp.'

'I said, "It's not marked as a PoW camp, as it should be according to the Geneva Convention."' The Chinese beat him again, accusing him of being 'insincere, hostile', of 'sabotaging compulsory study' and of 'being a reactionary'.

'I tried to commit suicide twice. The first time I'd been brutalised, and they wanted me to confess, so I was writing away about Goldilocks and the three bears – I wrote thirteen and a half pages. They read it, took it to the commander, and they got madder and madder and they yelled and they screamed, and came running at me. I gave one of them a short jab and they jumped on me. And they took me into this room, and hung me up with my hands behind my back and a rope around my neck, and said if you let your foot down you'll kill yourself. Then they left me. I was hurting. And then I thought, this is ridiculous – it's going to be a very slow strangulation. I figured the best thing was to do it right away. So I slammed my leg down and it tightened the noose. They were looking through the cracks in the wall, but I didn't know that. So they came in and took me down.

'I wasn't going to go slowly – I wasn't going to let them decide it. I had a purpose. A lot of guys didn't. I knew an officer who got the GC posthumously – and he did it out of a sense of duty as an officer. I did it out of a sense of duty to my brother – I had to answer to him.'

The months dragged on – and ironically, it was the prisoner-of-war issue which became one of the main sticking points during the peace talks: the complexities of repatriation kept the negotiators at the table for nearly two years. Meanwhile, Derek Kinne and his fellow prisoners were in a bleak valley with almost no contact with the outside world. After a year in captivity he still hadn't given the Chinese an inch, and spent much of his time in isolation – something the Chinese had refined into what the prisoners called the 'wooden boxes'.

'What seemed to be a long, low box stretched from end to end along the back wall, reaching out almost halfway across the room. Separate square grilles of wood formed the wall of the box that faced me and, now, outside some of these, I perceived some objects. Shoes. Surely they were shoes! I thought suddenly of the old days at the hotel at Scotch Corner. The guests' shoes went out each night for cleaning. Who were the guests of the Chinese? . . . Leading the way into the room, the guard NCO stopped by one of the grilles outside of which were no shoes. He pulled it open. The Crab – one of the interrogators – shone his torch into the recess to disclose a narrow little box, hardly five feet high, and ending five or six feet back at the rear wall. There was some old, soiled straw on the dirt floor.'

Spending weeks on end in confined squalor, how did Derek Kinne find the determination to endure? He looks back on it with a simple explanation.

'When an alcoholic joins Alcoholics Anonymous, there are twelve steps. But he has to do every step twenty-four hours of the day. And so with me, and the torture, I decided I'd do it – for the next ten minutes. And then ten would be up, and I'd decide to do it for another ten. I'm stubborn: I'll do it one more time, I won't quit.

'Only about four months ago it came to me – it all came together. I was in this wooden box, and this guard put a bit of barley in my can, and it was 99 per cent water. I protested. I had to stand to attention in the box. Someone in one of the other cells looked out for the shadow of the guard coming, so I could rest a bit of the time. The Crab came and started beating me with his gun – it went off, and it killed him. They put me back in the box. Then they took me to a room and strung me up and beat me. I hollered terribly and fainted.

'Woke up, sun was shining on the wall – on a large nail. If I moved my foot just a bit and could stand on it, I could get some temporary relief. Then I realised that it was hopeless, for I wasn't going to confess, or inform on fellow prisoners. So I got up some momentum to swing my body, hit the nail with my head, blood running. They took me down, and I remember them telling me I was dying, and I remember being really happy about it. And I laid there, shivering. One guard brought in a blanket, but I was still terribly cold. He brought in this can of barley with hot water – it wasn't the regular sort, and it was full of flies, and I took my hand and crushed off all the flies and underneath there were two pieces of paper. It was the newspaper that they pasted on the wall, and we used to tear it off to communicate with each other, using clay and piss and a stick as a pen. And somebody had written on one piece of paper: "Great is truth." And on the other piece was written: "It shall prevail." And at the time I thought: the bastards are not going to get me. I'm not going to die. I'm going to live. And I'm going to tell people what happened. And I pulled in this barley can under the blanket and it was so hot to my hand I could barely touch it. It got beautifully warm under the blanket and I fell fast asleep. And it was so hot that it left marks on my chest. And that night, very late, they came and took me out, gave me a uniform, and then I got sent to a court martial.

'And I've got to thinking about it. If that barley was so hot, the flies couldn't have sat on top of it. Also, it was the wrong time of year for flies to be there. And I hated flies, so I'd always scrape them off – and everyone knew that. That barley didn't come from a PoW – it was from headquarters. So who put the notes in? Why the flies? Why did it stay warm all night? It had to be an angel.'

In October 1952 he was tried by a Chinese military court for trying to escape – again – and for being 'hostile and reactionary'. He was sentenced to twelve months, solitary confinement, increased to eighteen months when he complained at the trial of being denied medical attention.

As a last hurrah, he was awarded another bout of solitary confinement on 2 June 1953: The prisoners had by now begun to get some letters, and the coronation of the new Queen was the main topic at home. An enterprising soldier in the Gloucesters gathered tiny scraps of material and made some red, white and blue rosettes. Wearing a rosette was clearly a 'reactionary' move.

Release came on 10 August. And only just, for he was still protesting about the lack of interviews with the International Red Cross and the Chinese threatened him with non-repatriation.

'I never had the thought of a medal. I never write "GC" after my name. To me, I did what I felt I had to do. I was fortunate that I was given the medal by people who had heard about what happened to me – from what other people said. I did what I did. It wouldn't have made any difference if I hadn't got a medal.'

He didn't fully grasp the significance of the George Cross – in fact, he felt a teeny bit disappointed when told about it, because he knew about the MM, the Military Medal, given to NCOs and other ranks for bravery, and thought it sounded, well, rather more military. But later, when he was invited to meet other holders of the award, it dawned on him that he had joined an elite.

'You know, when I was working at the Great Northern Hotel I went to see the movie *Odette* five times in one week, and I was enthralled with that lady [Odette Hallowes GC, wartime SOE agent]. And it was years before I realised, on one of our Victoria Cross and George Cross Association anniversaries when we went to Odette's house, that I'd walked in that woman's moccasins. We shared something – and it didn't have to be said. Here I was – and I'd got the same medal. That was the first time that it really meant something to me, when I sat there with her.

In the name of what?

There's a long silence. 'I can tell you. Picture a barn facing east and west. You're hanging from a rope . . . and you wake up and you say to yourself, "The fish swim, the birds fly. They're free, why not I?" It's my very private poem about what we are prepared to endure through the world's brutality. You have to find your own way through it. It's never been written down.'

It's evening now, and Derek hears the wild pigs snuffling outside the kitchen door. At night, when he can't sleep because of an old injury to his knee, he plays computer games and e-mails his family and friends, while listening to the ring-tailed cats scrabbling across the roof. He has no hatred of the Chinese. That went out of him long ago, he says, and he's since been to China as a fascinated tourist. He doesn't have nightmares. And he has never quite got over joining the small band of Victoria Cross and George Cross holders.

'I never thought of the danger,' he says. 'I just refused to give in.' And he stuck to that – for two years, three months and sixteen days.

11

The Bomb Disposal Pioneer

One of the more surprising aspects of the first Gulf War was the number of American soldiers who seemed somewhat peeved at the very idea of going to war. There they were, in a bleak desert assembly area in Saudi Arabia, kitted out in the very best that dollars can buy: smart boots, hefty rifles, night sights, goggles, radios that worked and lots of ammunition. No wonder the average British soldier eyed them with envy – and spent many an hour plotting how to relieve these overburdened US forces of surplus equipment.

The peevishness was a mystery. Fear might be a common emotion in an army about to engage the enemy. Or at the other extreme gung-ho enthusiasm. Or myriad feelings set in motion as tanks growl on the starting line and the artillery load up hundreds of shells. But peeved? Slurping down their sugary rations, they gave vent to a kind of minor petulance about having been deployed to hostile foreign parts (many thought Saudi was a sandy bit of Germany), but they firmly denied that they were reluctant to fight. It was that they just hadn't ever *expected* to. Stationed on air-conditioned army bases across the States or in friendly nations overseas, happily engaged in routine work and exercises, often studying for qualifications which they could never afford to pursue outside the military and looking forward to a decent pension, they had somehow missed the suggestion that they might one day have to do something in anger.

But soldiering is fighting, at least in the British tradition. Something different from other jobs. They are the only people trained to kill. The risk to life is not only inherent, but to be robustly embraced. It is true that an army may be deployed on peace-keeping duties or aid distribution, but to quote several commanders during the 1990s, it's more efficient to use professional NGOs, international police or even the boy scouts (the latter highly effective in Rwanda as a hard-working, tough bunch of lads who brought order and everyday decency back to several villages). Compared to volunteers or charities, soldiers cost a fortune. Bring in the military to help in a disaster, and they cost *seven* times more than any commercial outfit.

On the other hand, you bring in the military when warry problems pop up in civilian life. My post-World War II childhood was made more entertaining by the constant discovery of unexploded German ordnance in unlikely places: a 500-pounder lurking under the local Inland Revenue Office, for example, with half the town willing it to detonate immediately; cute little brass 'butterfly' bombs lovingly polished by old ladies until some ex-air raid warden choked on his teatime biscuit when he noticed it on the mantelpiece; or 1000 lb of explosives under the school playing fields, meaning the curtailment of hockey practice and the arrival of men with coils of wire and the possibility of a loud bang. What was clear in all cases was the necessity to call in the professionals, those who dealt with war-things. Dealing with Bombs and Mines is not an approved course at evening classes; nor a university degree. It belongs with the military. It's irrelevant whether they're dealing with their own ordnance or that of an enemy. They take full responsibility for dealing with the hidden or ticking danger. Though in some countries, they're not always around when needed.

As a journalist, being plonked on board a massive US Navy aircraft carrier by a tiny delivery plane in the middle of a major operational period can prove disorientating: with eighty-odd aircraft fuelling and jinking into position, crew dressed in colour-coded overalls waving illuminated batons, bombers taking off with a scream and a roar, there's no time for a quiet look around. The idea is to make your way down below deck fast before you become roadkill at sea. However, no one seems to notice that your route is a veritable obstacle race. Piled everywhere are large objects, usually pointy at one end and with little fins at the other. Some are short and fat, some have stripes, some have lengthy lines of coded print on them. Others are slim and long, with yellow tips and sharp noses. They lie in heaps, as if everything came out of the lethal toy-box all at once, and you have to climb over these bombs and missiles to get to safety.

Getting yourself over a large bomb while carrying TV equipment and without getting entangled in the finny bits is not what my education encompassed. Anything that explodes should keep its distance, in my view. Bombs are nasty, and don't get any nicer upon close inspection. At least when they're in mint condition from the modern munitions plant, waiting for deployment, they're likely to be stable even if you stand on one. It's a different matter if they've already been primed and then dropped but, for whatever reason, have failed to detonate.

On a particularly fraught afternoon with a bunch of excitable local officials, I found myself in a small press group touring the city of Benghazi a week after the American raid on Libya in 1986. We were trying to ascertain the targets of the US bombers, amid claim and counter-claim about President Reagan's intentions and Libyan protestations. As we viewed piles of rubble and holes in the road, it soon emerged that neither side was fussy about precise truths: The Libyans were insisting that the targets had all been civilian, but were sheepish when we pointed out that next to the wreckage of a school was a military barracks, and that a technical college with blasted classrooms had a missile site poking above the perimeter wall. On the other hand, American inability to hit the military installations with any accuracy was equally obvious.

Confronted with facts, the Libyans resorted to a lot of shouting and increased their efforts to damn the Americans. This involved a smart canter over a set of ruins to a small crowd clustered round a couple of young lads. We were ushered through with much enthusiasm, to find ourselves wondering what we were supposed to be looking at. The penny dropped when one boy borrowed a stick from an elderly onlooker and whacked at our feet. There was a resounding clang. A second whack dislodged a large stone and the fuse mechanism of a huge bomb gave off a bell-like tone. Standing on an unexploded bomb is stupid. More so, if someone's decided to hit it.

In the Balkan war of the early nineties, more ordnance flew around than I care to recall. Anything that didn't explode was whisked away by enterprising militia groups for recycling, regardless of the risk. On the occasions when the supposedly more efficient members of the UN or NATO forces came across something suspicious, there was a marked reluctance to pounce on it. That was what the locals did – and if you left it long enough, they would arrive with a wheelbarrow and solve the problem. (These were people whose bomb-making facilities resembled the worst kind of do-it-yourself workshop, where cigarettes, sparks from hammers and cordite being crushed with a rolling-pin added up to a hell's kitchen on earth.)

Sometimes, though, a shell landed in an awkward place. Like 100 feet in front of the BBC 'office' – a former garage workshop under the ramp to a car park in the Post Office building. It had been a noisy afternoon in September 1991, with Serb artillery active and one of their tanks prowling nearer than usual. Amid the all-too-familiar bangs and crumps came a very odd sound – an almighty *boingggg*. Curious, my colleagues peered out and failed to see the reason. A few seconds later came a second *boingggg*. Then another, and another. Straight ahead of them, across a scrap of waste land, was the rear of the PTT building which boasted several storeys of rickety iron fire escape. Down which a large shell was slowly making its way, bouncing from landing to landing. They watched, stupefied. It hit the bottom, which was concrete . . . and nothing happened.

I was in the PTT building, a place abuzz with UN peacekeeping activity – mainly paperwork and laundry, the odd shell being regarded as an intrusion on office routine and easily ignored.

I had heard the clonks on the fire escape and eventually went out to peer down. When I finally dragged a protesting colonel to view the large fat cylinder nestled below him, he looked more puzzled than alarmed. As well he might, since the only bomb disposal team in the whole of Bosnia had been sent back home that morning, there being 'little for it to do'.

Eventually a unit of sweating French Engineers poked the thing with a grappling hook and tumbled it into a box full of sand. They lugged it only a short distance past our office – 100mm tank shells are heavy – before sending it sky-high along with a massive bang, lots of soil and rocks and two unfortunate cars parked 'for safety' next to the PTT.

Perhaps I recall incidents with bombs in Bosnia and Libya, along with air raids in Beirut and Afghanistan, because, unlike my older relatives, I lack the family experience of two world wars. My maternal grandmother, for instance, once hurtled off a train in Northamptonshire to spend time in a ditch while a Zeppelin passed over bearing new-fangled presents from the Kaiser. When I was a child, World War II 'bomb sites' were my playground and shrapnel was what poked out of our sideboard, courtesy of a 500-pounder from the Luftwaffe. 'Danger' was never mentioned. My parents' generation somehow took it all in their stride, and re-garded a bomb disposal unit as something which turned up as regularly as the rag and bone man in order to take away something unwanted.

Since those world wars, bombs have been part of the landscape of much of Europe. For more than half a century, what was intended to detonate on impact or with a calculated delay some-times just refused to do so. The term UXB (unexploded bomb) is still common, and construction work in Britain regularly unearths large and surprisingly live shells. This is a source of fascination for those who witnessed the huge German air raids in the 1940s and who marvel at the techniques in use today. Along come the remote control vehicles furnished with cameras and microphones, robot arms and sensors which can look, listen and sniff – a far cry from the 'technology' available in the forties. Then, it was a matter of pickaxe and shovel, and a spanner and some string for the awkward bits.

Defusing a bomb is inherently dangerous. The bomb is designed to kill or maim, and its maker may well have added deadly refinements just to make it that bit harder to tackle if it fails to go off first time around. So who would volunteer for such a job?

When there's a war in progress, it is often not a question of choice. People are under orders and pickiness is out of the question. In World War II the majority of the population, both men and women, found themselves directed into work whether or not they had the aptitude or the desire for it. In the services, this was easier to accept. Even so, when you have trained as an architect and dreamed of designing buildings it is a little ironic to spend time in uniform dealing with objects intended to destroy the built environment. However, Stuart Archer took to the task with breezy enthusiasm. He was working in London and had joined the Honourable Artillery Company (HAC), part of the Territorial Army, because he thought it 'the right thing to do'.

'This was about the time everyone was being a little difficult about Hitler. "And what you want to do, old boy, is join the Territorial Army." So I did, around 1937, and in order to join it at all you had to be proposed and seconded and go before a committee to see if they would accept you.'

We sit talking in his immaculate flat. He is the perfect host, with coffee at hand, and has insisted on me joining him for lunch along with the other residents in this sheltered accommodation in north London. He has a bottle of wine ready and a pile of albums and scrapbooks. A tall, spry widower, he is very apologetic that I have walked from the station – at nearly ninety-three, he is insisting on driving me back after lunch. His memory is pin-sharp and, as for so many of his generation, World War II is in bright relief, full of action and challenge, but recalled with an easy, gentlemanly charm.

'I did all my training, marching and this and that, and had gone to a summer camp, and had only just completed that sort of thing when the war arrived. With the war, you had to go and sign up, and they were so full up at the HAC HQ, with everyone arriving at once, there was nowhere to sleep. They said, "Come back in three days' time."

'I said, "May I get married within that time?" and they said, "Yes, that's all right, as long as you're back by Tuesday."

'On Saturday, 2 September I phoned the local town hall to see where I could get a special licence, and they said, "We've given up giving out those licences for the past three hours, because we're full up to the brim. The only place you'll get one is Westminster Abbey." So I went to the Abbey, and the chap was one of these ex-army people. He said, "I've been turning you people away since eleven o'clock this morning. It's no use coming here." Anyhow, because I'd got the HAC uniform on he then said, "Oh, all right. Sit down and behave yourself and you'll be the last to get served." So I got the last special licence in London on 2 September. Then, of course, I had to arrange with the vicar to marry me the next day – he'd never heard of anything like this. But I persevered and I did. My fiancée was rather surprised – but in those days it was possible to get things up to eight o'clock at night, like a wedding ring at 38 shillings and sixpence [just under £2].

'It was a strange atmosphere, but joining up was the right thing to do at that time. Hitler was becoming a bloody menace.' So Stuart Archer was married on the day war was declared, and exchanged a life of designing pubs for an uncertain future in the army.

'I went away with all the chaps who'd joined up that weekend, and we all disappeared to Barton Stacey in Hampshire. Then they started looking at us properly. And when they realised I was an architect, it was really more appropriate that I should be in the Royal Engineers than in the infantry with the HAC. So they transferred me to a Royal Engineers' OCTU [Officer Cadet Training Unit]. I did my four months' course and came out a second lieutenant. They had to post me somewhere, and put me with a Territorial Army Royal Engineers unit as "surplus to requirements" – because they'd got a hell of a lot of young men and they had no idea what to do with me.'

In that casual manner that disguises personal fate, a request from London decided Stuart Archer's future. 'The War Office sent the word round to ask if anyone would like to join a Bomb Disposal Unit. They were glad to get rid of me. I had to join something, and I can't remember if it gave me pause for thought. At the beginning of the war there were really no such things as proper Bomb Disposal Units. They seemed to think we were going to send a chap round with a wheelbarrow and put the UXBs in it and wheel them away. They had no idea of the problem coming. There were something like fifty thousand UXBs dropped in this country that had to be dealt with – quite a task, and by the end of the war they realised that it *was* necessary.'

Techniques, it was true, had not moved on much since World War I, when the main method was something of a 'fishing expedition': you found the bomb, got a rope and a hook, hoiked it up and took it somewhere else. Sandbags figured large in the operation. Not until May 1940 was there a concerted move to put things on a firmer footing, with the formation of Bomb Disposal Sections; however, training for these was not too sophisticated either.

'I did a four-day course on bomb disposal with the RAF at Melksham. All they were doing was saying: "This is the one and only German bomb we've got – 50 kilograms, and this is what the fuse looks like. That's all we've got – but we can show you all the other *British* bombs." Then I went and collected my "bodies" – sergeant, corporal and men, about fifteen altogether – and we were posted down to Cardiff.

'We went into the Welch Regiment Headquarters, near to Cardiff docks. And there was a raid that night. I was woken up by the explosions, then someone came and shook my arm and said, "Look, you're Bomb Disposal, aren't you? Well, we've got an unexploded bomb down on the docks." So we drove in a car about a quarter of a mile, and I saw, for the first time, what I thought might be the hole made by a bomb entering the tarmac. So I said, "Yes, I suppose that *is* an unexploded bomb. We'll come down and dig it out" – we'd got picks and shovels. So we got back to headquarters, woke up the sergeant and the men, and while we were marching there the bomb went off. So that was my Bomb Number One . . ..

'I rang my wife and told her that I'd fixed up a place for her to come and stay. "You'd better come pretty quickly – I'll not last very long at this rate." So she came down in the next few days and I started off on disposal work.'

What no one had foreseen was the blizzard of bombing when the Germans targeted shipping, then ports and docks and airfields, before attacking British towns and cities. Nor had they anticipated the nature of the bombs: many had delayed-action fuses, which meant that hours or even days elapsed before they detonated. The psychological consequences were considerable: when the All Clear siren sounded after a raid, there was no guarantee that the danger was past. Added to this the Germans, who had tested a lot of their ordnance on a civilian population during the Spanish Civil War in the mid-1930s, were well ahead of the game by the time World War II broke out. They had developed mechanisms which were intended to thwart any attempts to make a shell safe: booby traps in the bomb and fuses which reacted to movement near them soon took lives.

Second Lieutenant Archer and his men found themselves in the thick of it. 'Most of the bombs at that time were being dropped on docks, so that was why Cardiff was being hit. We had quite a lot of work to do. It wasn't "high-tech" at all, because when we got to the bomb we hadn't a clue what we were looking at. "We" was the sergeant and I. I'd had four days' training, the sergeant less. All we could see was a bomb fuse with some letters on the top, and that didn't mean a thing. Also some numbers, which were all about what the fuse actually did: either it blew up on impact, or before impact, or waited a number of days.

'We had pickaxes and shovels to dig the bombs out with, because they were nearly always buried or partly buried. Eventually we got quite a lot of digging tools and special timber for lining the sides of the hole so it didn't collapse in on us – so we were really quite efficient at that. All the boys dug down and then left while the sergeant and I tackled it. I'm very proud to say I never got anyone asking to leave the job. They put up with what they were doing, those boys – ordinary young English boys.

'To start with, we had a spanner to undo a very big nut and pull the fuse out, but that was all. Oh, a little thing to clip on to the top of the fuse, so someone could tie some string on it and pull it out from a distance. That's about it.

'Was I worried? Yes, because we realised that there were things that would set it off, if you hit it with a pick or a shovel. Therefore, once we'd got down to where the surface of the bomb was, the digging was very gentle. Normally we would try to get the fuse out where the bomb was, but subsequently we realised that if we pulled the fuse out it was possible there was a booby trap behind it, and as you pulled the fuse out that would force the bomb to go off. So that's why we used the piece of string to pull it out from a distance – 50 yards or so, depending on the size of the bomb. There were no remote systems in those days, you know – and sometimes the piece of string broke. . . .

'Most fuses came out easily, except for one particular one which got partly jammed on impact. I got a couple of pickaxe heads together, like giant tweezers, and levered it out with them. We were asked to send the actual fuse we'd just dug out to the War Office. Everything we found that was new or different we would send, and then it went to a place in Teddington for the scientists to look at. All the time, people were working on this. Then we'd get a message very shortly saying, "Don't do what you've just done!" And that happened to be the sort of fuse that would go off if you banged it around a bit. Most of the things I was able to do were because the fuse was faulty for some reason or other, but I didn't know that.

'But then there were the booby-trapped ones with delayed-action fuses, which were intended to kill the chap trying to deal with it. They had spirit levels inside, and the slightest movement would kill the chap. You needed a steady hand . . . I got out the very first booby-trap bomb successfully and that was a complicated business, because I managed to get the whole of the fuse pocket out of the back of the bomb, not through the side, and there it was in front of me. And I looked inside and thought: ah – what's that? And there was the booby trap – which in fact didn't work, because a little bit of water had got inside, and so it went *wisssst* instead of bang.'

All this is described with enormous sangfroid and great meticulousness, punctuated with laughter at the sheer Heath Robinson aspects of the task. Stuart Archer was both intrigued with and totally focused on what he did. South Wales was taking a pounding and the rest of the country too was seeing waves of bombers most nights. The War Office was desperate to keep up with the inventive German minds that were forever modifying the shells – a cat-and-mouse game that is the hallmark of the disposal business. There was a high percentage of casualties among the members of the early units. As for his own personal safety, he hardly reflects on it and sums it up briskly.

'One of the points about the kind of bomb disposal I was doing was this. If I had been dealing with a mine or something small and it went off, I might lose a leg or an arm or something. But the type of bomb that I was dealing with, 1000-pounders, meant it was either all or nothing. And that, strangely enough, comforted me, because I would go completely and I wouldn't know anything about it.'

His memory is keen, and his scrapbooks and photographs and drawings show the really awkward bombs that burrowed underground, involving a fevered bout of digging before he wriggled his way to them inch by inch. 'Down a hole in a building, just me usually, with a torch and a mirror. And you'd put the mirror down the side of the bomb and be able to see what figures it had on it. Altogether I dealt with over two hundred fuses. . . .'

At this point he breaks off to produce the genuine article, an eight-inch steel cylinder which he plonks on the table. 'This is an electric fuse, which arrived on the ground *live*. In some cases where you suspected this, you didn't withdraw the fuse. You would dig the bomb out, put it on a lorry and drive it away to blow it up somewhere else. I had one of those where there were a lot of fighter planes – St Athan airfield. Four of these 500lb bombs had been dropped near to the workshops and we dug out each one, and I decided that I'd be the one driving the lorry. So we put them on it and I drove a couple of miles away and blew them up.

'The most difficult one was at the Anglo-Iranian oil refinery near Swansea which had been bombed during the night. And on the way down there, from thirty miles away we could see the flames. Anyway, when we arrived there were still four bombs unexploded and the fires were still going on. I chose to deal with a bomb that was right at the side of an oil tank. It was embedded deep down the hole, pointed down. The lads had to dig down to it – fifteen minutes on, fifteen minutes off. I went down head first on my tummy, slid down the shaft. Then, with my hand right inside the bomb, getting hold of the whole of the fuse and booby trap – with brute force and bloody ignorance – got it out. And when I went down the road with it, away from the bomb, the fuse went *phtt . . .* you see, some water had got it in it.'

He's smiling and wryly amused, and still handling the large steel object with interest. However unselfconsciously he recalls these events, his contribution to the overall work of bomb disposal was of acute importance during the Battle of Britain and afterwards, as the latest German technology which he unearthed was examined by the boffins and the information relayed to other units. His own personal courage was recognised in 1941 with the award of the George Cross and he's been a stalwart of that medal-holders' association ever since, keen on meeting the new young members and hearing their stories. He is slightly perplexed when asked about danger and courage, more concerned that his wife must have 'gone through a lot'.

'I am conscious that my wife was with me in Cardiff, in a flat, and she had the problem of not knowing whether I was going to come back or not. Must have been a dreadful strain on her. And one day I had been down to Swansea with the whole section and got out ten small bombs from an attack on the marshalling yards, and my chaps were absolutely exhausted. They came back lying down in the back of the lorry, side by side with the ten bombs. I was driving and as we came over the brow of a hill where there'd been an accident I'm afraid I ran into the back of another lorry which had just been bashed up and broke my leg. The following morning, an officer from the unit went round to my wife and said, "Mrs Archer, there's some very serious news. Mr Archer's in hospital with a broken leg", and she said, "Thank God for that." '

I wondered if he had been a confident young man, even with only four days' training behind him, and he replies that he never thought about it that way and felt 'delighted to have been successful'.

'It was, after all, not a very good thing to join, because somebody worked out that a new subaltern joining bomb disposal only had ten weeks' expectation of life . . . . Was I ever frightened? No. I was very conscious of what I was doing. And it was no use arriving and saying, "Oh, I don't want to do this." You're there to do what you're required to do, and that's what you're going to do. But I'm very proud of the young men who were with me, because they could have said, "I don't like this – I want to leave." But they didn't.'

So he did what he did in the name of what?

'I'm not quite sure how to answer that. . . . Yes. In the name of duty.'

The Bomb Disposal Officer

Bomb disposal was not the stuff of newsreel footage in World War II, nor in subsequent conflicts. Unwieldy film cameras were not made to follow men burrowing towards a bomb. Nor would it have been thought wise to show how much was learned every time a fuse was extracted. The enemy might benefit. The occasional controlled detonation might reassure the public, but otherwise it was work that was carried out either out of sight or at a considerable distance – for obvious reasons.

With the advent in the early 1970s of terrorist activity first in Northern Ireland and later in the rest of the UK, the ticking bomb turned up in factories and shops, cafés and cinemas – not dropped from the sky, but either cunningly planted or randomly left. The TV crews turned up at the very far end of the street, prepared themselves for a long wait, and made sure they were nowhere near plate-glass windows should there be an unexpected event. I spent many an hour staring at cars, vans and lorries that looked no different from any other, except that they had been hijacked and then abandoned while stuffed with explosives (frequently a home-made concoction known as 'Co-op mix'). The press would gossip, the soldiers would lounge quietly against walls and the locals would tsk tsk with irritation as the route home or to the shops was once again blocked. There was little sense of looming danger. So many bombs had gone off that most people managed to push back the sense of personal danger and accept the temporary detours as part of life. And anyway, at some point the ATO would arrive – the Ammunition Technical Officer who would deal with the wretched nuisance. He would also bring with him an odd bit of equipment called the Wheelbarrow – a robot which didn't look at all like a wheelbarrow. But we never got to meet the ATOs. Their world was across the police tape in the area thought potentially danger-ous. And all we often saw of their work was what's known as the Long Walk.

'While I was at Sandhurst I met two very impressive officers from the Royal Army Ordnance Corps, and when I came out I decided I would go with them. They just seemed to do lots of things and it seemed like a proper job, as opposed to digging holes in the ground as my friends in the infantry spent their time, and taking hamsters on exercise and trying not to eat them. . . .'

Alan Taylor can't suppress his laughter. His is a personality which very much reflects the modern army, serious about his profession yet relentlessly amused by its quirks and slightly insane conventions. Regarding the latter, I recall a conversation with him while driving in a convoy in Saudi Arabia during the first Gulf War. Eight hours of crawling through the desert following tiny red tail-lights on a moonless night had produced exhaustion and a strong desire to know where we were going. We bumped to a stop and Colonel Taylor appeared out of nowhere.

'Where are we?' I demanded.

He looked thoughtful, then said, 'Why do you want to know?'

I had rehearsed several reasons in the preceding hours of darkness, dust and negotiating unseen gullies full of rocks in my spring-free pick-up truck, listening to the BBC's precious satellite dish bouncing behind me like a coin in a biscuit tin. The words 'Going to war, facing possible death in the un-known, colliding with the Iraqi front line, being forewarned and forearmed', and the like were listened to by the colonel with the patient expression of a doctor dealing with a raving patient.

'We're back where we started,' he said finally, absolutely straight-faced. And we were.

I just happened to peer out of the window to watch him turn and walk away. He did a little skip in the sand and I could hear laughter.

'I know why he's like he is,' confided the bespectacled and omniscient Belfast Protestant lad who was attached to our unit as a driver. I waited for the usual imaginative tale, but the skinny owl looked earnest. 'He does the real job,' he said.

'Meaning?'

'Bombs. He stuffs the Provos. He's yer man when they try and send us early to Kingdom Come. Bloody marvellous. Got guts . . . which is surprising, 'cos it seems to me that most of yer ATO are missing bits.'

Since World War II there's been a never-ending stream of left-over ordnance, and the rise of low-intensity conflicts and terrorism has meant an expanding role for ATOs every decade since. A Lancashire man, Alan Taylor joined the army with a vague idea that he might develop his language skills – recruitment was strong on 'see the world'. He went to Sandhurst, appeared to have signed on for the Parachute Regiment, applied to study Russian, did neither and, with absolutely no science background, found himself headed for a course on ammunition.

'I was amused at the time, but subsequently found out that we'd lost three ATOs in Northern Ireland in very quick succession and they needed to get more through the course to fill in the gaps – filling dead men's boots. But when you're twenty-four it's quite exciting, really – you don't properly understand it, but it's satisfying.'

At the heart of understanding why and how these men do this job is the training, which they all constantly refer to. It's not just a set of facts and learning the mechanics of explosive devices – it's about self-control and confidence. It's an intense system, taught by men who've been there, done that and survived with the T-shirt to prove it.

'We started with six months at Shrivenham, which, as you know, is the military's second-rate university with an out-of-hand cadet force.' Alan delivers asides with a deadpan look and charges on, delighted that he's led you up another subversive lane. 'And we learned about the chemistry, in very broad terms. With Explosive Ordnance Disposal (EOD) a little bit of it was done in the classroom, but basically you went into the depot near the Explosives Ground, where the blows were done. And it was very hands-on.

'They replaced detonators with electrically initiated fireworks that wouldn't explode, but instead went *phttt*. There was lots of practical work and you were very focused on the job. And of course the instructors had made these devices, and what they lacked in humour they'd gained in nastiness. You were dealing with one of these makeshift devices and you heard the *phttt* – it was as though it had gone off, and you just felt incredibly down. And they booby-trapped devices, like a milk churn or a route to a terrorist command post. If you picked something particularly obvious the instructors would booby-trap *it*, so you're concentrating on a milk churn 50 yards up the road and suddenly you hear *phttt* behind you and you think: oh, shit. There were a lot of "Oh, shit" moments on the course. But it was very well done – it wasn't gung-ho.

'The thing that sticks is the outstanding quality of the instructors. They were senior NCOs and warrant officers. Some, who'd done several operational tours, were very highly decorated. They had "walked the walk" – though it sounds an awful cliché, doesn't it?'

The Long Walk may be regarded as a cliché in the military, but it's a test of resolve and skill: the moment when the remote high-tech gizmos aren't up to dealing with a particular bomb, and there's no option but to walk right up to it and see what needs to be done. And with the Troubles in Northern Ireland going at full pelt, the men on the course knew that the real thing was very near.

'I think we understood that we were doing something special. We knew that at the end of the course – fourteen months of it – we would be going to Ireland. Our training was updated while we learned, because when a report came through that somebody had been killed we would be briefed within twenty-four hours. We had very good feedback – the device and the circumstances would be replicated – and we'd learn. So if something happened on the streets of Northern Ireland, the Defence Research Establishment would be up all night and the next day you'd have a piece of kit to deal with it. Danger was implicit – you were well aware. We got lots of visitors – the police, the Bomb Squad, who of course were all ex-army, scientists – and lots of good equipment. There was a lot of historical stuff as well – lessons from Hong Kong and EOKA in Cyprus.'

All this was a far cry from the four-day course and pick-and-shovel approach of World War II. And this time it wasn't air raids but terrorism, where men at work in garages and back rooms and on kitchen tables devised bombs which killed randomly across Northern Ireland and the rest of the UK. In 1975 Alan Taylor went to run the team in Belfast, where explosions were a feature of everyday life and we reporters spent a good deal of time staring down empty streets at figures doing mysterious work with curious equipment, dealing with what was known in newsrooms as 'another suspect'. It would be a vehicle, a package or just something 'suspicious', disrupting traffic, evacuating houses and bringing a weird ring of quiet into a noisy city. We would corral some pavement space next to the police cordon, focus the camera on the 'suspect' and work out whether someone ought to get sandwiches now, before the shops closed. A couple of anonymous-looking army vehicles would have turned up, and men who certainly didn't intend to give interviews would be doing inexplicable things involving that strange piece of equipment known as the Wheelbarrow. Bomb disposal in Northern Ireland was a high-profile activity with only a few discernible features – a dangerous cat-and-mouse game with the bomb-makers, details of which were not freely available from either party. So we just watched. Not that our presence was lost on Alan Taylor.

'You people used to get me into serious trouble. Whenever I did a job you would film me using one of these lenses which are right up people's noses, and there's a fore-shortening effect – so if I was dealing with a device I could easily be 50 metres from it, but when it went out on the news later I appeared to be right next to it. And I used to get phone calls from my colonel, saying, "What the bloody hell are you doing?" '

Not that our presence impinged on the job in hand. The work was so intense that the media on the pavement were just a blur in the distance. Added to this was the sheer volume of work.

'We used to get a lot of call-outs around five o'clock, because it was rush hour and it would all get on the six o'clock news. You'd be sitting there quite relaxed, as Number One on call-out. Number Two was usually a young Ammunition Technician. The phone would go, you'd check the details, you'd hit the button, and all your team would go down to the vehicles – two or three of them holding six to eight people. They were big armoured "Pigs", as the locals called them, and they *were* pigs to drive – we spent more time on the pavement than anywhere else. The brigade commander reckoned I'd done more damage to sangers [sandbagged army positions] than the IRA had done in four months.

'You're working from the minute you get into the vehicle. On the way to the device, you'd be trying to get information from brigade. Anything in from the police? Any description? Anything en route? Were the bombers seen? It's a short period of intense focus. When you get to the scene there's normally already an incident control point set up by the infantry on the ground, and you'd jump out of the wagon and say. "Where's the incident commander?" He'd make himself known, and you'd say, "I am Felix." As soon as I hit the ground, I was the incident commander – he's always called "Felix" in EOD.

'First of all, you take a look at the area – while people are throwing bottles at you. Or take the Europa Hotel [scene of numerous "suspects" and several explosions] – if that goes up, several tons of glass are going to come down on you. So you look at your immediate environment and your own safety. Then you start taking evidence and you talk to the incident commander and any witnesses.

'You had to be careful with witnesses. A friend of mine had one and asked him if there were any wires going into the device from a small box, and the witness said no. So he assumed it was safe, and carried out his approach. But when he got into the shop he found there was a little wooden box with wires going into the bomb, so he came back and grabbed the witness and said, "You told me there were no wires going from the box into the bomb!" And the witness said, "No, no, no, they were going the other way round. . . ." And witnesses would say things like, "Let me take you. Let me show you," and you said, "No – just explain, just stand here." They'd say, "You see that plastic bag on the floor, about 10 yards away?" and I'd say, "I'm just going out!" because they'd take you right up to the bomb.

'You got perhaps ten call-outs for every real one. And you had to deal with them all in exactly the same way – it's only at the end that you know what you've got. So many suspect devices proved not to be devices that people defaulted on to "It's not real." Whereas *you* always defaulted on to "It *is* real" and I don't care if it's got "BOMB" written on the outside of it' – which one of mine did.

'And then, of course, there's "Ding Dong the Avon Lady". I did a couple of those in one day – blowing up rather curious-smelling boxes left on doorsteps, and none of the team would talk to me because the whole of the inside of the vehicle reeked of this perfume which was blown up. And around Christmas there are lots of Christmas cakes that might be bombs that are delivered and left on doorsteps. And if it's a bad area you're not going to take any chances . . . and you find out when you've blown a few of these things up that nothing smells more like marzipan – than marzipan.

'It's very intense. You're looking around all the time. One of the unsung heroes, doing one of the really dangerous jobs, is body-guard to Felix. We'd always be assigned someone to give us close protection, because there had been times when someone had tried to pick off the ATO. The ATO isn't armed with a personal weapon, and might be wandering round doing a recce. I had a young man with me who was very good: I'd be working on a device and a shadow would fall across it, and he'd be standing next to me. And I'd say, "No . . . get back there," because everything's a one-man risk.

'But sometimes local people might be hostile or just worried. I was attacked by a woman once because I wouldn't let her go through the cordon to her house, which was next door to a car I was working on. She'd actually ducked through the cordon and got to me and said, "Are you in charge of this? You bastard – you come over here, causing all this trouble!" So my close protection man hauled her out the way. Sometimes people lose sight of the default and think it's probably nothing – they just want the streets cleared. And there are times when you could get engrossed in your job and then you'd look around and you'd find the crowd were about ten yards away . . . and they'd sort of crept in . . . If you had a cordon set up by the police, they very often used to look inwards – and I always used to say to the police, "Look outwards – *I'm* all right." I – or my robot, to be precise – actually shot three people because the cordon had crept in. I'd done an approach with my robot, and it went over its own cable and short-circuited and fired the shotgun which it carries down the street. It fires SG, which are balls about a quarter of an inch in diameter, and I wasn't aware of it until I got back and the brigade commander phoned up and said, "When are you going to report these three people you've just shot?"'

I used to wonder about how close we journalists crept in Northern Ireland. When dealing with bombs in London, the Metropolitan Police used to remove us almost to Birmingham. Back in Belfast, we had a ringside seat and were horribly used to seeing bombs explode before the army arrived on the scene. However, I suppose most of us were still obsessed with the James Bond image of the clock ticking and the hero finally realising that it's a matter of red wire or blue wire. Alan Taylor is heartily glad that the reality is different (well, most of the time, anyway).

'Red wire? Blue wire? We had fabulous tools that could do it much better. And you were at a distance. The robot – the Wheelbarrow – was always closer. It could have a small water cannon, which was very safe. The water went through the outer casing into the suspect device, and the wires ripped under the pressure of the water in a shorter time than it took for the electricity to heat up the element. You'd use the shotgun for things like putting the window out of a car so you could put another tool inside the vehicle. Or you might try to cut wires by firing the shotgun.

'Every single device was different, from one painted black with "BOM" written on the outside to a gas cylinder about 18 inches by 12 inches that we eventually discovered was packed with explosives. At the time you wouldn't know that the explosives had been fed in through a tiny hole. You did have the ability to X-ray bombs, but it was a pain in the neck and you never bothered. Though a friend of mine did take such a device into a hospital in Belfast and asked them to X-ray it – seriously – and he married the radiologist . . .

'At some point you've got to go forward, though nine times out of ten, you don't walk to it. The Wheelbarrows were really good. I lost about four, and one of the boffins pointed out that they were jolly expensive and what was I playing at? And I said, "hey – I'm pretty expensive, too." I did one job where I took the robot into a shop, and there was a bomb on the counter. I lined up, went outside, and while I was manoeuvring the door closed on my cable. So I wasn't in the right position. I could still fire the robot's shotgun, however, which might have worked. But it didn't – it set the bomb off and the building came down on top of the Wheelbarrow. I then lashed it to my vehicle and reversed out, dragging it through the rubble. The boffins weren't best pleased because their Wheelbarrow was . . . a little bit mangled.

'But if you do have to "do the Walk" to the bomb, you get kitted up in the bomb suit. The visor is half an inch thick and the helmet alone weighs about 30 pounds. The suit itself is pretty heavy too, and you've got reinforced armour for the chest and the groin. So you're wearing quite a bit, which makes you hyperventilate and you can't see where you're going because you've just taken the suit out of a bag in the back of a cold vehicle and so you've got condensation. As you start walking you're trying to get your hand up to wipe the inside of the visor so you can see where the hell you're going, and you hear radio comms [communications] and your Number Two says, "*That's* not the car – it's the red one." I got to one incident and I'd opened the doors and the boot and the bonnet remotely and I was pretty certain . . . Then I got the suit on, walked up to the vehicle, got on my knees to look underneath it and was toppled over by the weight of the helmet. I ended up on my back like a turtle, thinking the bloody TV cameras were bound to get me . . .'

Getting called out to tense situations, not knowing quite what's waiting for you, might wear a man down perhaps?

'Well, you're not constantly at it. You've got a team there. One of them is looking for radio-controlled devices, another might work the robot much better than you can, and yet another is better at selecting the weapons – you all work together. Say the device is in a shop and the door's closed – and when the man went in and put the bomb on the counter the idiot shopkeeper came out and locked the bloody door (they were always doing that): "Here are the keys, sir." You think I'm going to open the bloody door? So you'd say to your team, "I want a constant sweep, starting now. I'm not moving anywhere until you've done a sweep. What weapons do you think we ought to put on the robot? Water cannon? Shotgun? Anything else? OK, once you've got that sorted I want you to shoot the door out, get me in there, and when you can see the bomb I'll do the last ten feet." Now all that might take several hours, but it's teamwork.'

But what about the team at home? Most people shiver at the very notion of bomb disposal, so how does an ATO's family react?

'I was "unaccompanied" for the first tour – that is, the family didn't come with me. For the second tour I was "accompanied", and that was a bit difficult. I think I tended to underestimate the effect on my family. If your three-year-old daughter looks under the car before she gets in, that's when it starts to hit home. When I came home for R & R halfway through my Belfast tour, my twenty-five-year-old wife and I sat down and worked out funeral arrangements, made sure the will was up-to-date. There aren't many people who go through that sort of thing at that sort of age. So it does have an effect.

'When we were out there for two years, interestingly enough, we made some of the best friends we've got – we were driven together and there was a lot of camaraderie and mess life, and all the women were breeding and there were kids all over the place. But it did have an effect. Sometimes Ros would answer the phone and it would be a senior policeman who'd say, "Is Alan available for a drink?" It meant I had a job. And Ros would be back there with a couple of tiny babies in a house that wasn't on a protected estate (when they blew up the pub across the road Ros had half the staff in the house, giving them cups of tea, while I was actually dealing with the incident). So I think there was an enormous effect on the families. I don't think we discussed the detail of it, but we did discuss the possible consequences. And my wife had been with me all through the course, she knew lots of people in the trade, and she knew some of the people who died.

'But you're working all the time to very high standards. Our reputation is absolutely sky-high and it all comes back to the training, the experience, the technology and the lessons of history. One of those lessons is that, when there's an accident – when a bomb does go off – the majority of fatalities come from secondary injuries and not necessarily from the blast. They tend to come from the fact that the ATO is thrown at 6500 metres a second against a lamp-post. The bomb suit will probably protect you from about four ounces of explosive – well, that's the size of a matchbox. Other than that, the suit just keeps the bits together. So one of the lessons we were given was that when you went to deal with a device you put the toolkit to one side, not in front of you. For if it went off, the shrapnel from the toolkit would add considerably to the damage. Little things like that stick in my mind thirty years on . . .'

Probably thinking about the Hollywood image of fiddly wires and tiny batteries, I kept staring at Alan's hands and wondering if you needed nimble fingers.

'No. You need a very strong sense of survival. And you need an understanding of the mechanics and the electronics and the chemistry. Though, funnily enough, when we had a twenty-five-year reunion from my course, and I was asked to give the only speech of the evening, I said I was dividing it so as to address two audiences from the course: those with ten fingers and the others. Because my course actually did quite badly on the old digit side, and a few of them did lose one or two bits. But that's a measure of success, of course!

'I look back on it as a time when I really feel I made a contribution. I say that, not as the great "I", but in the sense that I feel personally I did something important. I didn't kill anyone while I was doing it, I saved thousands of pounds' worth of property, and I was operating at the top edge of the technology of a very small specialist area. I was conscious that what I was doing was important, I was conscious that we had to get good results, and I was conscious that we had to work to improve it all the time.'

And in the name of what?

'I loved Northern Ireland tremendously – I loved being there, I loved the people there and everything else. And I honestly thought then – and still do now – that I was helping Northern Ireland.

'I mean, before all this started in '69, Northern Ireland must have been the best-kept military secret in the world. There were soldiers over there who went fishing four times a week, hunting three times a week, and then all this started. So when I went over in '75 you were actually meeting people who had been there in the early sixties, and they'd take you to friends all the time, and – you know what they're like over there – the first thing they'd say is, "Hello, what do you do?" You didn't actually *say* you did bomb disposal in Belfast, but they knew – they knew within minutes. And I felt that I was helping them, and seeing them going through the drills and getting searched each time they went into the centre of Belfast I found heartbreaking. I used to wander around the city centre on my day off and just thought it was fantastic, and I wanted to do anything I could to stop the bombs. Also the IRA weren't faceless to me, because I had evidence that these people existed: I didn't know their names, but in some respects I knew their identities from the way they made the bombs, so they were a real enemy. They weren't shooting at me, but they were trying to make life pretty unpleasant for the people of Belfast. That was what I was trying to fight – and I thoroughly enjoyed it.'

Although we journalists saw the work of the bombers in Northern Ireland, we were never privy to the detailed work of the ATO. And I only ever saw the Wheelbarrow robots in the distance because they belonged to that murky grey area covered by 'security considerations'. In other words the Army Press Office insisted they were 'secret' even though any twelve-year-old on the streets of Belfast could give you a detailed appreciation of the Mark 5 model as opposed to the Mark 3. In some ways, these weird machines symbolised all that was different about life in the Province: you were highly unlikely to see one crawling down the street in Bournemouth. To appreciate their finer points (should you be so inclined), there's a roomful of them at the Army School of Ammunition in Oxfordshire. It might be called Dr Strangelove's Mad Lawnmower Collection. They defy definition, except to say that they are highly expensive to manufacture but look as if they've been knocked together in a garden shed. Some have tiny wheels, others miniature tank tracks. They all have dangly bits and bolt-on thingies and lots of wires. They spray water, fire bullets, snip wires, peer into dark corners and acquire ever more specialised bits to deal with the hazards they encounter – and they're still very much in development because bomb disposal is a growth area. Although the image is fading of a wonky machine trundling through the terraced streets of Belfast, its modern little brother is hard at work with sand in its innards in Iraq. And unlike its Northern Ireland predecessor, it rarely gets to perform on our TV screens. For bomb disposal is getting rougher by the day.

This is not the world of the obvious lump of explosive sticking out of the ground, or an awkwardly parked vehicle. It's a scenario of deception and booby traps, where an innocent-looking kerbstone or a dead dog can be the disguise for the 'roadside IED' – the Improvised Explosive Device. These are the weapons that have produced the majority of casualties among British and American forces since they stayed on in Iraq after the second Gulf War. They are harder to identify, often unstable and carry a much higher risk of unreliable behaviour.

And in Afghanistan, welcome to the world of the reusable Taliban mine: the sound of a motorbike carries across the plains of Helmand province quite distinctively, though it's difficult to make out if you're a NATO convoy rumbling near. Two members of the Taliban hop off the bike and quickly bury a couple of the mines they've been clutching – some of the leftovers from when the Russians and Americans piled in supplies in the 1980s' war. Should the convoy miss the mines and continue safely over the horizon, the bike buzzes back and the Taliban scoop them up and buzz across country to try again. And nothing for the bomb disposal team to investigate.

Bomb disposal is becoming a vicious game where not only does the bomb tick, but everything round about conspires to add to the danger and interfere with defusing. The man charged with making the device safe cannot rely on being able to operate in an environment that is under control. However, the kind of people who undertake disposal work don't seem to change. The spirit of Stuart Archer ('It's a job that's got to be done', coupled with a disarming insouciance) lives on with the men who have headed for Iraq and Afghanistan.

Having completed his training and absorbed the lesson that most incidents are best dealt with at a distance, using the latest Wheelbarrow, Staff Sergeant G arrived in Basra in southern Iraq expecting to familiarise himself with the situation and settle in.

'The first day of my tour was a bit of a baptism of fire, and my predecessor had already headed home to the UK. You usually do a handover – a few days with the outgoing operator, get to know the patch, talk about the sort of stuff he's been working with. Then, if you get a "shout" – a call-out – he'll go there and you'll shadow him, because every area's a bit different. Then, having watched him, you get down to all the paperwork he's left you . . . I suppose none of us really wants a shout. It's a bit dangerous, isn't it?'

Sergeant G is grinning wickedly, as if he's describing his first day as an apprentice at the water company and contemplating a burst main in the High Street. However, Basra has supplied a lethal proliferation of IEDs. These are the varied products of terrorist and low-intensity conflicts, and they have an effect above and beyond the local damage they cause. Placed at the side of roads which the majority of troops will have to use at some point, they are a relatively cheap method of spreading unease and fear. Usually a small but powerful device, an IED can take on an armoured personnel carrier and inflict many casualties. And there's not much that the APC can do against it – it's a hidden or disguised box of tricks that will be detonated from a distance using a switching mechanism, a trip wire, an infra-red or electronic signal, or anything else that might be thought up in garages, factories or backyards by its makers. So there's an almost inexhaustible supply, considering that the components of some of these devices are cannibalised from mobile phones and garage door openers. Others contain sophisticated components assembled from international sources. Whatever their construction, they are a classic pinprick tool with which to harass, obstruct and damage a well-armoured modern force. And almost the only way to pre-empt such an attack is for an eagle-eyed soldier to spot something 'odd' – a patch of disturbed sand or soil, a dead animal, a discarded cardboard box or a heap of rubbish – and call in the EOD. And as you have no idea what you might be dealing with there's more reason than ever to operate remotely, getting the robot to take the risk.

All this formed the background to Sergeant G's first day in his new job, which didn't go according to plan. 'First morning, called to the ops room, short brief, sketchy description of what's happened. Out with an escort down there, and on to the ground. Is it hostile? How much disruption is being caused? Just crack on with it.

'Northern Ireland's where people will evacuate their homes and move out of the area. In Iraq, there are people who utterly refuse to leave because they think their house is going to get robbed. So you've got people about 50 yards away wandering about, little old ladies in black. This was at a large road junction with a load of leftover building material next to it. And someone had seen a lump in the sand. Anyway, you take an infantry guy down with you and put him in a fire position about 30 yards away and crack on with it. You've just got to focus on the bomb and not worry about anything else.

'There appeared to be a wire hanging out of it. So in such cases you send the robot down, because you don't really know what you're dealing with. Did that – and it managed to uncover the base of a shell and a radio control pack attached to it.'

Meanwhile, others were gathering to have a good look too. Instead of a calm circle in which Sergeant G's brain could concentrate, a circus was building up: locals agitating, angry young men making threats, children running willy-nilly – never mind the old ladies screeching at each other from their courtyards and the teenagers darting across the rooftops. And there were also quite a number of individuals whose purpose turned out to be to close observation of the operation – in order to report back to the bomb-maker. Additionally, a group purporting to be from the local TV station rocked up and seemed uninterested in the wider picture of an area disrupted by a suspect device. 'Dicking', we call it, says Sergeant G. 'Just filming what *we're* doing.' (I find myself embarrassed at the thought of the media acting as informants for the bombers, but I'm being naïve.) There is a cordon of soldiers to control the scene, but their main concern is to ensure that no one takes aim at the ATO: for the expert is a prime target. Trying to put all this out of his mind, Sergeant G is dealing with his first-ever bomb.

'You have to have a good look, confirm what you're seen on the CCTV camera on the Wheelbarrow, and get a good idea of it. . . . I decided to throw some smoke.' The camera lens and the eyes of the onlookers had spooked the work in progress – too many people had been hoping for information rather than deliverance from a lethal blast.

'I always stop about five or ten yards short and throw a smoke grenade, just to get a smoke screen between me and the crowd. Invariably, the guy who's put the bomb there will be watching. We're all conscious of having certain patterns of operating, so you don't want to make yourself vulnerable. Pop a couple of smoke grenades that'll dissipate in about a minute – it'll give you enough time to get in and confirm what your Wheelbarrow's told you, and you can start work.'

So there's the sergeant with his first bomb on his first day in Iraq. He's got a circle of alert and twitchy young soldiers round him, fully aware that there are those who would interrupt the process of defusing – or seek to learn the secrets of his trade. It's stinking hot and he's not feeling at his best. But he presses on because he has to. The problem is, the Wheelbarrow has no sense of dedication. Somewhere in the last few minutes, either the temperature has gone up or gritty grains of sand have blown into its complicated parts; it's given up the ghost and broken down. So it's a matter of getting down the road and dealing with it yourself. The Long Walk, for real, for the first time. What's on your mind?

'I always wonder what the wife and kids are doing at this moment, while I'm doing this crazy stuff. Then I just focus and crack on, as we've been trained.'

That first day went well, and Sergeant G survived. What helps someone face up to this danger?

'Well, I make sure they're OK – or if they're going to kill themselves.' Staff Sergeant D is responsible for training and testing for operations going to places such as Afghanistan and Iraq.

'It's meticulous training – but not as long as everyone thinks it is. It's six to seven weeks for actual bomb disposal. Now I'm on the instructional staff I realise that you monitor people's capabilities – though if I found precisely what it is we're looking for I'd make a fortune! But I suppose it's credibility. When you rock up at the scene, you want to be able to portray to the infantry commander, to the policeman on the ground, that actually it's all right: "I'm here now – and I'm going to take this problem, the danger that you've got, and I'm going to make it go away. I am Felix!" You've also got to be able to convince people to do what you want them to do. Especially in Iraq, when you're asking infantry commanders to keep their guys out on the ground for longer than necessary – you could leave the bomb there, but then the terrorists could come and pick it up and use it another day. So you want to convince the infantry commander that, although his guys are being shot at, they need to stay that little bit longer so that *you* can make the device safe. You have to realise that the soldiers watching your back are at risk too. And they don't actually see what you're doing – they have to stand around while you do your stuff. And then the van leaves – and it's very hard for them to appreciate that at least there hasn't been a bang. . . .

'I've been in the army for twenty years now, and for the last nine or ten I've been doing this job. My two boys are aged eleven and eight, and when my bleeper goes off they say, "Oh, it's just Dad's job." I've always been aware of the reality: the IRA blew Musgrave Park Hospital up in 1991, and I'd been in there for a very minor operation a couple of weeks before. I drove round the corner, and the ward that I'd been in was no longer there. Quite an eye-opener.

'Why do I do it? It's a sense of pride. Having stopped that bomb from functioning is quite something.

'It's all down to training – and that's unfortunately built on people having learned the hard way. I've got a £200,000 robot which I will gladly sacrifice before myself any day of the week. It's there to do the work. Bomb disposal might seem quite glamorous, but actually all you're doing is putting on a suit, walking down the street and sweeping up the bits and pieces of what's left after you've shot it.'

He's backed up by a colleague, a softly spoken Liverpudlian, Sergeant O. "I'm actually very proud to be what I am. Calmness is what you need. When you get there everyone isn't calm – they're highly agitated, headless chickens – so you have to instill calm in them. But, as I say, it's down to training, which was always geared to what it would be like on the ground.

'What has marked out Iraq, though, has been the relentless pressure – the sheer number of "shouts" and the fact no one else is going to come along and deal with it. You can't back out – it's your responsibility. Every time you deploy, the buck stops with you. You have to have an enormous amount of self-confidence – though I don't tell people what I do. I don't know what it's like for this generation of soldiers, but the IRA used to actively target us, so you don't say. And it's a very difficult habit to drop. I wouldn't lie and say I wasn't in the army – but nothing specific. My family approves – they're very proud – but my wife hates it. I've never been worried about getting killed – but making a complete cock-up of a job and having everyone talking about it scares the life out of me!'

Both sergeants acknowledge that Iraq has pushed the boundaries of their job. The years spent in Northern Ireland taught a lot of lessons, but on the whole they knew what they were getting. Now the internet has enriched the recipes for bomb-making; we're a long way down the line from the *The Anarchist's Cookbook*, the 1971 bible for experimental bomb-makers. Anyone can download the recipe for an up-to-date and lethal cocktail which can cause major mayhem.

So the game moves on, with players on the internet adding to the hazards on the ground. Even so, the classic red wire/blue wire decision which features so prominently in fictional bomb disposal still rears its head occasionally. And inevitably Sergeant G, on his first tour of duty, ran into it early on, on yet another occasion when the trusty Wheelbarrow decided the sun and sand were too much for it and refused to function.

'I was working out of the American Camp Dogwood, just south of Baghdad, at a site where I knew there was a booby trap. It was in the desert, in an anti-tank ditch which had been filled in at various points to allow tracked vehicles over it. And the Black Watch had tracked over it and set a pattern – and when a pattern's set up, it gets exploited by the insurgents. One of the Warrior armoured vehicles had gone over the ditch and one of the guys had looked back from the turret and saw what looked like buried artillery shells, and they called us.

'We went out, but the Wheelbarrow broke down completely right next to it, and I had no option but to do a direct kinetic energy attack – blast it, in other words. So the Warrior had a go with some 30mm high-explosive shells – about five or six rounds into the general area to get rid of it while we were all nice and safe about 100 metres away. That didn't work. So we put some 7.62 chain-gun rounds into it from the Warrior. That had no effect. So we moved on to the last resort which was manual – me. My Number Two had left all our equipment at another location, so I had to walk forward with just a pair of pliers to cut into the circuit, uncover it, work round a pressure switch, find the detonator, cut the detonator off and then finally cut the dead leads . . . It felt a bit surreal at the time. Hey – just like the movies!'

But in the movies the pressures emanate from the bomb, and the hero usually doesn't get shot at while making his life-or-death decision. Not so in real-life bomb disposal. Sergeant G discovered while working alongside the US forces at Camp Dogwood that there was a horrendous time frame being factored into his work.

'You had *no* time on the ground. Within forty minutes of getting the shout and arriving at the bomb you were getting mortared. So it was really quick, dirty, horrible bomb disposal. You didn't have time for planning – just get the job done, destroy your main charge and get out of the area. Even down in Basra and Al Amara, particularly during night jobs, you got shots. You're lit up like a Christmas tree and you're in the middle of a load of guys trying to protect you, and you get shot at. It can take your mind off things.'

So why do it?

'What's first and foremost in our minds is that we're saving lives. I'm in the army, but I like to think of my job as a safety role. Whether people like it or not, I'm going to make that bomb go away. I don't think they properly appreciate what can happen – their property may be destroyed, their wives and children may die. It's not just the safety of the troops, but the people as well. The Iraqi people are absolutely lovely, friendly people. It's just a few of them that don't like us that much.

'If I reflect on what I do, I know that my wife's worried sick most of the time, especially when I'm on operations. It's very hard for her and the children . . . Should I mention that we only get paid £35,000 a year . . .?'

In the name of what?

'Because it's a job like no other. I don't think any one of us who's done the Long Walk down the road to a big bomb could ever work in an office.'

13

The Bodyguard

Reporters may bring bad news to their audiences or readers, who perhaps are numbered in millions. However, it's much more difficult to be the bearer of bad tidings to an individual or family. It doesn't happen often in the trade, for the reporter is usually well behind in the walk up the garden path and the solemn knock at the door. On occasion, though, it may fall to the hack to break the news. And the circumstances may not be conventional.

The small room was lit by the telly, and Saturday night entertainment was blasting away at maximum volume. I fell over a crate of beer, but no one heard. There were two figures in the room: a woman ironing, or rather gently singeing things while her eyes remained glued to the screen; and a man flat out in an armchair, hand now groping for the crate of beer. My camera crew and I wondered whether to announce ourselves formally. The front door of this house in Dagenham had been ajar, and much knocking and polite shouting had produced no response. We had entered, the usual mule-train of television – large film camera and tripod and large cameraman, soundman trailing a cat's cradle of wires, lighting man with mysterious assorted kit guaranteed to fuse anyone's electricity supply, and reporter. We had pushed open the living room door and stood there. I had moved forward and bumped into the beer crate. Nothing had happened.

So I shouted our apologies for arriving unannounced at their home. The ironing person looked away from the TV briefly, but showed no curiosity whatsoever at four strangers squashed between her ironing basket and the armchair. There wasn't a twitch from the armchair. The crew and I exchanged glances. We were quite good at barging into meetings where we hadn't been invited and nifty at insinuating ourselves past unwelcoming door-keepers. Here, we felt a bit adrift.

At least a minute passed. Then the iron was plonked down and the woman yelled, 'Yeah?' I started to explain, but lost out to tumultuous whooping from the box. After some shouted exchanges, there was a grudging swipe at the volume control and a weird silence began.

I'd begun to realise that I was the bearer of bad news that hadn't yet reached this family. Carefully, I stuck to the short piece of information that had come into the newsroom from a civil war in southern Africa.

'Your son's trial has ended,' I said.

No response. I knew we were in the right house, and was 99 per cent certain that these were the parents.

'Your son's been found guilty by the court and. . . .'

I trailed off and experienced the odd sensation that they weren't taking much notice. Oh God, were we in the wrong house?

The 1 per cent doubt grew and then vanished as the armchair said, 'So what's he going to do, then, silly sod?'

The crew were staring at the wallpaper intently, clearly wondering how I was going to dig myself out of this one.

'Um, he could be shot.'

Ironing recommenced. Another bottle of beer was located in the crate.

'But it's possible he'll just get life.'

The silent television was proving more interesting than me.

I realised that this was not going to be a fruitful visit, so rattled off the details of the sentences which had just been announced after a lengthy trial of foreign mercenaries in Angola to these, the parents of one of the defendants. They were resolutely indifferent, and I could only speculate on just what had brought about such a reaction and lack of family feeling. There was no possibility of an interview, and as we turned to leave the ironing board was given a hard bang with the iron accompanied by the words: 'I suppose we could visit him at weekends?' I decided not to delay our departure with a geography lesson.

The mercenary business is murky. Several people I tried to contact, having heard what they'd been up to over the past three decades, turned out to be very elusive. Or, to be honest, still very busy at what they know best, for they're using their military skills.

Many who have been in the military never quite leave it when they return to civvy street. They will give all kinds of reasons: the camaraderie, the sense of family, the ordered life, the challenge, the occasional high drama of conflict. They find work in other uniformed organisations such as the police or prisons. A small number go off to other people's armies for a second bite of the cherry: a grizzled and cheery Foreign Legionnaire with whom I shared a morning's shelling in a burnt-out shop in Sarajevo happily admitted that one army career hadn't been enough for him. He had had two, serving his full-time in the British infantry, getting his pension and straightaway applying to join the Legion, where he was heading for his second pension and his cosy house in Corsica.

Others have slid into the deadly world of the mercenary – an ancient profession, but one in which neither the enemy nor the side you're fighting for value your life. It's very dangerous: you're useful for a particular time, you're paid, and then no one wants to know you. A dog of war.

These days the global business of Security soaks up thousands of ex-service personnel. Some are sleek and business-like, advising on safety and civil affairs. Others are armed and prepared to fight if need be. Governments everywhere are glad to shift the economic responsibility from their own forces to the private sector. And if you don't want to hire a whole company, then maybe you might like your own personal bodyguard?

It's something of a status symbol in the World of Celeb. Should you hang around cool clubs or frequent film premieres, you may have been barged out of the way by a group of gorilla-like creatures who wear sunglasses at dead of night. These guys look good as the flashbulbs pop and magazines get their exclusives. They are basically crowd-ploughs, steering their mini-star into the masses and across the pavement to maximum publicity, occasionally flicking an over-keen fan to the outer limits in the manner of a mobile pin-ball machine. You wouldn't expect them around the Royal Family. With royalty, there's the opposite approach: the quiet and discreet Protection Squad, small in number, endlessly scanning the immediate area around their titled personage, murmuring into a radio occasionally and terribly polite if they ask you to move.

Then there are the Americans, often more obvious than the quarry, shouting up their sleeves to something attached to the curly wire sticking in their ear, loping alongside armoured limousines and rather terse in their relations with the public: 'Don't try anything, ma'am – we don't do jokes.' There are the Libyans, ostensibly a bevy of nubile young women in cute matching combats and berets. But these are intended for the excitement of the foreign press, and Colonel Ghadaffy's real protection is a small group of very purposeful and circumspect men who are amiable enough when relaxed but look as if they could dissect you with a meat-axe should they feel inclined. And there are the ever-growing number of 'security personnel' in the grey world between military and civil forces who pop up, usually heavily armed, in those countries where the local police cannot be relied on and no one is quite sure who is in charge of law and order.

These people's clients are the extremes. In between are a range of worried individuals, who for myriad reasons feel they can't walk the streets alone. They want someone beside them who's prepared to face the danger. So how do you know it's coming?

'What you're looking for is – nothing. Stillness. If there's activity, it's usually OK. But with stillness you can almost feel the apprehension and your antennae start twitching. If it's deserted, and you can hear the silence . . . that's it. Like during a curfew in Ramallah in the West Bank. And I remember an industrial estate in St Petersburg – feeling the nothingness instead of people walking by, or a car or two, or something moving. I was there with a couple of Americans who'd got involved in a bad business deal and they were trying to get their money back. But the Russians knew they were coming – you could feel that everything had been set up because of the unnatural silence. Another time I was in a park in Moscow, just like in a film. Two people were sitting on a bench reading newspapers, others were walking about – in fact in these situations almost everyone you can see is part of it, one of *them* . . . you can feel the apprehension.'

Will Scully is describing these scenes as if he's surveying them again, with keen eyes and quick, darting looks. He laughs as he recalls the slightly surreal events which crop up regularly in his line of work. It's one that he relishes, having dreamed of doing something which would lift him out of a life of routine as a teenager.

'I'm from south London. I started on an apprenticeship in printing, after working on the market stalls in east London, and always had a sense of adventure. One day, sitting there watching the printing machines running, I thought: do I want this for the rest of my life? Someone said to me, "Look at the man in charge, and if you don't want to be him then you're in the wrong business." And I reckoned I didn't want to end up sitting in a small box in a factory. So I went off to find myself some adventure.

'I started reading books about the Foreign Legion, all sorts of stuff like that. I joined the TA, then went into 21 SAS [its Territorial section] for four or five years. I finally joined the regular army and went to 22 SAS – I spread my wings. I wanted adventure, not just the military – that's why I went into Special Forces. There were fewer constraints, I enjoyed it, met some terrific people and did some wonderful things. But even so I never planned to spend the rest of my life in the military – it still wasn't quite enough on the edge for me, because I've got frontier spirit. I'm not worried if I'm on my own, and I like to get out there "amongst it".'

I suggested he should have been born in the nineteenth century, and he laughs and says, 'I'm really a pirate.' He's a very respectable-looking pirate, elegantly dressed, and would pass for a city gent any day.

Scully left the army, went into various ventures, wanted to earn money and was on the look-out for a challenge. He did a little bit of trading round war zones and worked for an aid agency because he knew how to move stuff and get convoys through awkward places – a combination of military training and good market-trader nous. He found that he could be more his own man, pushing the boundaries and with only his imagination as the limit.

'I'm not an adrenalin freak or a risk-seeker – I just love adventure. I'd love to have been with Scott in the Antarctic. I could see myself in the desert, or on top of a mountain in a storm – that's where I needed to be in my mind's eye. I mean, my favourite film's *The Dirty Dozen*, where a bunch of rogues get sent on a mission and have to do everything by the seat of their pants – that captured me.'

He had trained in Close Protection in the SAS and while 'hanging around in war zones' eventually found people approaching him to see if he could use his skills on their behalf, though it wasn't usually in deserts or on the top of mountains. In the first instance it was in down-at-heel premises in industrial Poland. He was shepherding a somewhat naïve American businessman, who had trustingly shipped a lot of equipment into a bonded warehouse in the country and found that the paperwork had been switched and the consignment had vanished along with the payment. Off to meet these not entirely savoury people 'for a few words', he had decided he needed 'a comfort factor', but Will found himself giving advice on how to conduct business rather than worrying about how and where to meet dodgy traders. He learned that you must know about your little lamb as well as watching over him.

He uses the phrase CP (for Close Protection), which is how it's referred to in the army, and describes its function in a very simple way. 'CP is like shoes. You've got different shoes for different occasions. Some are flashy or smart, some are for special occasions, others blend in so you would never notice. But they're always there. You have to be in synch with your client – attending meetings and looking like one of the delegation, or sitting quietly at a distance with your eyes peeled. A shadow.'

If it's a businessman who has called upon your services as a bodyguard, you have to understand what he's doing – in fact, have a special working relationship with him. 'The relationship matters: if you get called up to go to Moscow to oversee someone getting involved in a deal, you fly there, walk round the hotels you'll be using, check if you'll be followed and so on. And if there's obviously going to be trouble, you need to know your man. And vice versa – because if there's conflict you're standing by him. You're not going to throw yourself in front of a gun for a one-off job for one day for a few hundred pounds. You're going to be standing alongside, advising him, moving him around and being professional – but are you going to take a bullet? I don't think so. But if you've got a relationship, if you feel in some way emotionally attached to that person, then you'll push the boat out. And yes, that's happened a couple of times.

'I took a businessman into Ukraine and we had a problem with some of his contacts, who could be described as "heavy" – and they chased him out of town like a rat. We ended up at the station, boarding a train, and they followed us. We stayed in the carriage, and just before the train was due to leave I went into the corridor and they came at us. Three of them in a line. They were going to stick a knife in him. A big fight ensued and I got a few cuts and bruises and things [he gestures at a rather long area of arm]. You see, if you're in a corridor – which I where I chose to be – it's a bit difficult for all three to get at you and surround you. You're fighting one at a time – sort of. It was very brief, and then they left because I'd guessed they didn't want to end up travelling. That's why I'd held back in the compartment until the train was just about to leave – it's all about timing and planning.

'Then you have stand-offs and tense moments, and there was one time in Iraq when I was with the press and we were ambushed by the Fedayin – we came under fire in our car and they tried to kill us. I was with a CNN TV crew and I had no option – I had to pick a weapon up and fire it in defence.'

None of this is delivered in a gung-ho manner, just matter-of-fact. He doesn't sound as if he relishes the fights – it just comes with the turf. If you've been trained for it, you merely employ your judgement and skills. And those skills are broadly based for, despite the popular image of figures abseiling down ropes and blasting their way into a siege, Special Forces are more likely to be sitting quietly observing, blending in with the background, and planning, planning, planning for all eventualities. They have a background in every kind of accomplishment that might be useful in a war – siege, kidnap, intelligence-gathering, communications, medical emergencies and other people's hairy situations. They are identifiable by *not* being the bloke at the bar who bangs on about being Rambo. Frequently they are extremely hard to identify, and that makes them very happy. What all of them share is a quiet confidence.

'I'm not looking to prove anything to myself. However, I was always pushing for adventure and once my wife asked me, "When are you going to give up all of this?"' So he thought, why not give something else a go? He decided to become a journalist. 'I bought a professional camera, and learned the basics from a friend – how to take shots for news and so on. I read the paper, found a war, bought a ticket and went. Said to my wife, "See you when I get back."'

This is the sort of thing that 'old hands' used to recall got them a cracking story at the first attempt having just got off the boat. *Scoop*, in fact – the sort of thing that someone might have achieved back in the 1930s in a far-off land of which we know little. Surely you can't do it today?

'You see, Rwanda, eastern Zaire, was kicking off. I landed in Kigali and made it to the front line with some specially printed press cards. I was in a hotel in Goma, along with the rest of the press, with very little money, pretending that I knew much more than I did. At that time there wasn't usually anybody doing security for journalists – this was the mid-nineties – and some of them were a bit dubious about heading into the action. So I said, "You've got a car? I'll drive it – can't be difficult to find our way."'

If this seems a very casual way to operate, it's the norm in chaos. Put together thousands of refugees, mix in several groups of armed tribesmen, sprinkle with a horde of journalists and place in a location with little accommodation, poor communications and regular bouts of panic and desperation, and life gets very informal. Those with experience and their wits about them thrive.

'So off we went and ended up in a bit of a conflict situation – kids with guns shooting across the road and so on – and eventually they chased us and tried to throw a grenade into our car. I was spinning the car round, driving backwards, doing all the stuff you do in CP – and there were some pretty surprised journos in the back. I was rumbled, but then we became great friends. But I was hooked on journalism, and for a year I worked in Kigali as East Africa correspondent for Associated Press. Lot of work – stills, video and copy. Almost too much work, but I enjoyed it. What then happened was that the more I ended up in conflict areas, the more people asked my advice, and I was doing more consulting on security than journalism, so I sort of rolled back into the security business.'

We've both got vague memories that we may have bumped into each other briefly somewhere, among a million or so people on the move in circumstances of total confusion in Rwanda. You remember the useful people who seem to have a few facts and a grasp of what's going on, who are much more valuable than 'important' people keen to deliver a statement to the visiting media.

Travelling around eastern Rwanda and crossing into the Democratic Republic of Congo (DRC), there was hardly anything that resembled a functioning state. Shops and businesses had been looted, hotels were wrecked, roads littered with burnt-out vehicles. An assortment of military people from various countries popped up every so often, but there was little that could be made orderly and safe. For the countryside was littered with corpses from the massacres of the Tutsis by the Hutus. Meanwhile, both tribes had unfinished business and were either vengeful or fearing for their lives. There were guns everywhere.

As journalists in such circumstances, you are going into the unknown. You have to rely on decency and humanity and hope that you take sensible decisions. However, at times you find yourself in the middle of hellish scenes: as we crossed from Rwanda to DRC, having witnessed the French Foreign Legion seal the border with brutal effect, we ran straight into trouble with Congolese troops who were almost out of control. Later on, having wriggled out of one nasty incident, we were deluged by an immense tropical thunderstorm which churned the town of Bukavu's dirt tracks into a mud river. Precisely then, a crowd of refugees were dumped into the town as the border opened for a brief period. They ran aimlessly in all directions, falling in the mud, and turned out to be the contents of one of Rwanda's mental asylums. It was a scene which Breughel might have painted. At such times, reporters have few skills they can offer. We record the scene and try to stay alive, but not much more.

People like Will Scully are much more effective. The training and discipline make staying alive a much more logical task, and the pragmatic approach can be used to help others. None more so than in Sierra Leone, where he found himself in the middle of a rebel uprising of great ferocity, in a hotel overflowing with a thousand terrified refugees under attack. How he single-handedly dealt with the threat is the stuff of *Boys' Own* adventures and not a little courage, for which he was awarded the Queen's Gallantry Medal.

He had arrived in the country just over a week earlier, to join a protection team for a group of geologists prospecting for gold. When the rebels moved on the capital, Freetown, he planned, organised and then conducted the defence of people he had only been with for a few hours, holding back several hundred fighters for twenty-four hours until the US Marines came in like the cavalry. Which underlines his relationship to anyone he has to protect.

'When I was in the hotel in Sierra Leone, I felt obligated – there's a point when you commit yourself. I don't necessarily have to know the person for very long, but you eventually feel connected to him and you feel you can't walk away. I should have done in Sierra Leone – the plan was that I was going to leave. But I couldn't walk out on those people. They trusted me, and when I've given my word that's it.'

So how did he feel, going into a dangerous situation?

'I do get tense – I get butterflies. But mostly it's that tingle when things aren't quite right. It starts like something electric across your back and you start paying much more attention to certain things. Your brain's going so fast that things start to go in slow motion. You're calculating the options at great speed just as things are about to happen.'

Scully only works abroad. Security in the UK is either for pop stars or the rich and young. 'You get some little jerk who wants bodyguards around so he can be a twat. And they get him out of trouble – and some of them provoke, to see what happens. They're the worst. They want to be a name, a celebrity, and create something round them.'

He loves the variety of his clients. 'You see princes and paupers. You do everything from protecting someone among the dirt at a gold or diamond mine in Africa to being at the very top – yachts and helicopters and beautiful country houses and so on – but you do only *see*. You're not a participant. And you meet some very interesting people. There are times when you're with someone and you get to know them – not as a confidant, but you realise that most people are human, and many are very different from the public person.

'But all the time it's like being in a queue, and you've got to keep pushing towards the front. And when you get there you'll eventually find your adventure, and the further you go the more you're valued. My only regret is what I haven't done – yet.'

In the name of what?

'In the pursuit of adventure – I've picked up skills, and I've become . . . well, a protector.'

14

The De-miner

In Bosnia in the early 1990s, it was known as the dinner plate problem. Lying upside down in the road would be a dirty green flat dish, the size of those large plates which, for reasons unexplained to customers, waiters in posh restaurants whip away just before the meal starts. As you approached a small village lying suspiciously quiet in a landscape devoid of cattle, you felt that mischief was afoot. No farmer had thought it safe to put the animals out to the sweet grass. The only wisps of smoke came from smouldering houses torched in the name of ethnic cleansing. And your vehicle had had an uncomfortably clear run for several miles, encountering no other traffic – but endless obstacles.

Roadblocks were a fact of life on every track and trail. They popped up in open countryside where their defensive or strategic purpose was utterly incomprehensible. Occasionally, as on the edge of Sarajevo, they grew into small forts of jumpy gunmen, hostile to the very idea of anyone travelling along their highway. In valleys laden with plum orchards and ungathered sweetcorn, each village sprouted its self-important boundary barriers.

The edge of the village was usually marked by those who were territorially minded, otherwise unemployed and in possession of an AK47. Young men lounged around in a jumble-sale of army surplus camouflage from all corners of the fighting globe, topped by black woolly hats which gave them uniform low brows. They would be slumped on broken chairs or propped against trees, and the appearance of a lone vehicle had the effect of a fish tweaking the line of a sleeping angler. For a BBC vehicle, even a battered armoured Land Rover by the name of Miss Piggy, presented an opportunity for . . . what? Well, something to enliven a day of wartime tedium, with no frightened refugees to harass, no local score worth the effort of setting fire to a barn. A BBC vehicle, all alone on the road – ah, something stupid this way comes, providing an opportunity for a display of militia power, a satisfying bit of shouting, perhaps even a nice little earner. . . .

Peering through the windscreen, we would try to work out whether this particular 'roadblock' was likely to cause serious trouble. Men would lurch up like drunks and sling a metal pole or a couple of oil drums across the road. Like drunks? They *were* drunk. Bosnians may be Muslims but there's a very, very big brewery in Sarajevo. During nearly four years of siege in the early 1990s, the public water supply frequently ceased to function; the brewery did not. In fairness, it should be added that the Croats and Serbs would claim to drink any Bosnian Muslim under the nearest table, preferably while the sun was still rising.

As the makeshift roadblock was hurriedly erected, our slothful Miss Piggy would lose a little momentum while my cameraman and I made a quick decision on how to treat it, centred on irritation (with the locals) and fear (of the dinner plates in the road). Those green metal discs could be mines – the mangled remains of unidentifiable traffic littered the Balkans. One evening we had watched a 35-ton Warrior armoured vehicle 20 yards ahead of us leap into the air and lose its tracks as a Chinese dinner plate flashed white-hot beneath it. Luckily, all the Warrior's armour worked, but the bang nearly took away what hearing I've got left. Our appetite for putting our own vehicle through such a test was negligible – aid workers, colleagues from the Reuter's news agency and soldiers had all had terrible experiences in Land Rovers, and not all had survived to tell the tale. However, there were very good odds that the dinner plates were just bits of metal about as lethal as a Frisbee.

Given Miss Piggy's pathetic acceleration, the decision point – whether to stop or to treat the roadblock as a crashable fence – was about 20 yards from the barrier. If the decision was to go for it, holding our breath, foot flat on the floor, we'd target the obstacle like a carthorse cantering towards the high brick wall at the Horse of the Year Show. The poles and oil drums pinged off us. A blur of uniforms used to fall back into the hedges, giving vent to the belated yells common to those who are rat-arsed by breakfast time. And with luck, there was no bang.

The alternative, stopping at the checkpoint, would involve argument, demands and possible threats as fighters with drink met journalists with determination. Admittedly, money was rarely extracted. There seemed to be an unwritten rule that this was unworthy of those defending their history, their honour, their farm and their cache of slivovitz. However, cameras, batteries and even clothes seemed to qualify for acquisition. And as a TV crew, we had strong views about hanging on to our equipment. Food was another bargaining chip: militias initially seemed to believe that we carried whole roast sheep on which an entire unit might feast. They were puzzled, indeed tetchy, when faced with our small stack of handy war zone provisions, leading to a difficult moment when cameraman Nigel Bateson presented some huge thug with a Pot Noodle. Nevertheless, whatever the messy encounter there would always be one glorious moment awaiting us: Bosnian mine clearance. Having allowed us passage, the heroes of the roadblock would stiffen the sinews, wave us on our way and deliver a thunderous boot to the dinner plates, which then skimmed into the grass verge.

For much of my early life I had never really given a thought to mines. On the seafront in Sunderland in my childhood there had been a large object which resembled a giant tomato with golden prongs sticking out of it. It had a slit in the top and appeared to be a charity box for a maritime organisation. That this was actually a mine dredged up from the North Sea was never mentioned: the shining brass horns were no elegant decoration, but in their time could have triggered enough explosive to scupper one of the sturdy

World War II cargo ships leaving the River Wear. Not until I went to Afghanistan in the 1980s did I encounter the real fear that mines induce.

Trudging across a snow-blown plain north of the Khyber Pass with a volatile group of mujahadin, I had been gazing at the extraordinary architecture stuck to distant hillsides to displace my thoughts that the muj were not the most confidence-inspiring guides. They leaped about, waved their rifles, shouted and giggled a lot. The idea that Russian bombers and helicopter gunships could heave into view at any time was regarded as laughable, and the ground was simply the place where they prayed. The idea that those gunships had been scattering tiny but lethal anti-personnel mines randomly over the landscape for many months gave rise to disdainful shrieks that their almighty would protect them.

As we crunched and slithered along the trail, we saw a crimson blob ahead of us. A slippery mound of shredded camel lay in puddles of blood, still steaming. The muj thought it hilarious; I remember feeling very frightened. Until then, I hadn't grasped that mines could be *anywhere*, even underneath a well-used track supposedly clear of such objects. While the Afghans were celebrating the poor beast's demise by mindlessly banging away into the ether with precious ammunition, I was having a definite case of funk. And turning back wasn't an option either, because the return route would surely have included bits of path which hadn't been trodden on before, so that was almost as risky as carrying on.

However, I managed for most of the day, then did very badly at nightfall when it came to lying down full length. As for the possibility of turning over several times while asleep – well, it's a wonder I got a wink. Anyway, the next morning, the threat of what lurked underground receded, because we got badly bombed from the air and there were two fewer mujahadeen to fire rifles pointlessly at unseen aircraft 20,000 feet above us.

One of the more depressing aspects of Afghanistan is the amount of mines still in the ground years after the Russians left – and that many can still be detonated by children playing in the dust, or by women sent to work in fields known to be dodgy because their loss is considered of less consequence than that of men. And Afghanistan is not the only country where old mines continue to cause grief. De-mining is not even contemplated by some governments because of the cost and manpower involved. It is left to international agencies and charities to intervene.

It is a fact that mines also cause social and economic injury. In Sudan, one mine clearance team worked intensively on key roads linking major towns. Everyone near the roads spoke of the threat and kept well clear of them, making long and uncomfortable detours. Yet when the team surveyed the roads they found not a single mine – and the roads had been closed for twenty years. In the Balkans, villagers stuck placards declaring '*Minar*' into fields of cabbages and rows of sweetcorn. In most cases it was an improvised defensive measure, warding off ethnic encroachment from the next village. But after some villages had emptied, there was no one left to affirm or deny the presence of real danger. The placards remained to lay waste the productive earth.

In the Falklands, great tracts of land remain out of bounds more than a quarter of a century after the Argentinian invasion. It is a worldwide problem, with over sixty countries affected by between 70 million and 100 million mines, but greatest in Africa, where the legacy of numerous conflicts is compounded with poverty. Those countries which are very fertile, such as Rwanda and Uganda, find that 'denial of land' is very much a weapon of war. And most of us would prefer not to walk on land where there was the slightest suspicion that the earth might erupt without warning. So de-mining demands determination – and a constant search for the most efficient and cost-effective method of clearance.

Part of the answer may lie with Fly, a Belgian shepherd dog, keen and energetic, but not renowned by those who work with him as an especially intellectual canine: 'If brains were explosive, he wouldn't have enough to clear his ears. . . .' But he loves to play. He leaps and bounces, every muscle straining, eyes bright with anticipation, longing for his daily 'game'. Which takes place in a minefield.

Fly is part of the team trained at the Dirk Ridge Dog Centre at the International Mines Action Training Centre in Nairobi. Kenya

– which doesn't have a mine problem – is nevertheless best situated to provide a 'centre of excellence for Africa' – it is relatively stable and has good communications, and can therefore attract business from other African nations. This joint Kenyan-British initiative, begun in 2006, is funded mostly by Britain, and staffed by the British army, and the Dog Centre itself is run by an NGO from Guernsey, the Mines Awareness Trust. Ben Remfrey, the Trust's operations director, is a large, energetic man who has not led a dull and quiet life:

'I enjoy a challenge. I joined the army as a young soldier at sixteen, was educated as a junior leader, went into the Royal Engineers and was very fit then, skied, did the biathlon, trained as a diver, then went to commando forces and did all sorts of different things – diving, jumping out of aeroplanes, Arctic warfare, all the things young guys like to do. Then I woke up one morning at twenty-six and thought, "I want to do something else", and left the army for commercial diving. I fell into this business in the aftermath of Gulf War 1, getting involved with Royal Ordnance doing bomb disposal, leading a team in the oilfields, clearing routes for the fire-fighting, Red Adair, all those good guys. That was a massive challenge and one where we took a lot of casualties. But safety was a major thing.

'My life's been a whole lot of this, that and the other, and I'm certain that if I was to leave de-mining tomorrow my CV would show itchy feet. But it happened, and what I'm doing now is what I think it's all led up to. I'm not a religious person – the world is my religion, people are – but I was in Bosnia and I saw the effect of landmines on people, and I was back in Guernsey when the Kosovo thing kicked off and I said to my wife: "Do you mind if I get a Land Rover, drive down to Kosovo, raise a bit of money and give some education to some kids?" And she said, "Fine – how long are you going to be there?" and I said two months. That was in 1999 – The Mines Awareness Trust was born – and we're still in Kosovo today. Also Eritrea, Sudan, Sri Lanka, Congo, Uganda, Rwanda and so on – we've evolved.'

And de-mining evolves all the time, with everyone looking for a safer and more efficient way of finding mines and getting rid of them. It has been described as 'landscape gardening crossed with archaeology', although the British army team at the training centre is keen to point out that it's 'professional equipment and credibility, not wellies and the garden rake'. A rather monstrous machine called a flail can prepare the ground remotely, getting rid of tripwires and blastmines, but it's regarded as an 'expensive lawnmower with Playstation controls', and after it has done the initial work human beings have to start searching and probing.

On the human side, over a thousand de-miners have been trained at the centre in its first two years, most of them military personnel who take an intensive course before returning to African countries which have often had no unit of their own to undertake de-mining. Even so, they will all have found out that there is no 'magic bullet'. Manual de-mining is slow, time-consuming and tiring; it takes diligence and concentration. But the extra help is getting ready in the next door Dog Centre: several keen animals who have undergone much longer training – up to a year in some cases – but don't treat it as work. They're the sort of puppy that you don't pick out of the litter if you want a quiet life. The handlers, all qualified de-miners, are quite clear on that: you need the boisterous, aggressive, smart one, not the nice-but-dim floppy-eared shy creature. All his efforts go into his work – to him, play – which starts the moment he leaves the litter. Lots of play-training with a ball, stuffed with harmless explosive: the ball's thrown, he scents it, it's all a game. Then he moves on to learn detection techniques – again, all a game, with lots of reward.

Then it's back to a very spartan pen – just a wooden pallet under cover to sleep on and a water bowl. This is deliberate, so that the dog has nothing to interest him other than getting out to 'play'. And are they keen to go! When the handler approaches, they yip and jump and wag and tear around the pen. Their handler often spends the night in the pen with the dog because there has to be real interaction – not just feeding, training, but sitting and staring together. The dogs are in peak condition, fed high-energy food, checked daily for ticks and with vets in attendance for any ailment: if you're going to be worth $25,000 when trained, you can expect the best. There's the occasional observation that they live rather better than their handlers . . .

Every morning it's into the training area on a long lead – into the long grass which is divided up by tape into lanes, just as a real minefield would be during clearance. The dog goes first into a test lane to see how he's behaving that day. If he's off-colour, or a bit inattentive, then he doesn't work. But if he's fine, then it's two hours up and down the lanes of the training minefield, or less if it's too hot, too windy or there's heavy rain – all affecting his ability to sniff out the explosive. He is trained not to paw or touch what he's found. He stops a yard short and then looks at his handler – who he knows has got his favourite toy or reward. Up goes the handler's hand to indicate 'stay', while the position is marked by a cross-reference of stakes. The moment that's done the dog is led out of the area, back the same way he entered, and gets his toy.

I watched Fly, then another dog named Asta, pushing fast through the grass. Each was utterly focused, nose down, tail high, very intense and methodical. They go at their own speed, which happens to be ten to twelve times as fast as a human mine finder. In ideal conditions, a good dog can clear 10,000 square yards in a day.

I wondered if there was any part of the training which familiarises a dog with explosions, and got a very firm reply from Ben: 'A dog should never hear a detonation. Ever. At the end of the day a dog's an animal – a person understands a detonation but a dog doesn't – it comes as a complete surprise. Engendering fear of detonations would be bad for the animal and we don't want them to get spooked. It'll affect their performance. So after mines are found and marked and excavated, the detonations take place when the dog is well away and can't hear. For him this is a game, and he has no need to know the properties of a mine. And the dogs have to have complete faith in their handlers, because they can always scent fear in a human. That's why all the handlers are formally trained in de-mining, so that they won't give any indication of fear.'

However, dogs are just part of the operation – what the army briskly calls 'a tool in the box'. And they are only brought in after the manual de-mining has been done, to be used as final-stage 'quality control' – making absolutely certain that there are no devices left in the area and it is safe for people to go back and walk there.

The dogs I was watching were headed for Rwanda, to snuffle around in the sweet-smelling tea plantations near Ruhengeri in the north-west. I was there during the appalling killings of 1994, when the country was in chaos and Ruhengeri almost a ghost town. Hundreds of thousands were dead, and much of the remaining population was either on the move towards the borders or in hiding. Now there is relative stability, but the intervening years have seen more conflict, especially near the eastern frontier with the Democratic Republic of Congo, and the legacy is a patchwork of minefields. Ruhengeri is now a bustling centre for the emerging tourist industry, with posters beckoning to the volcanoes to the north, home to the huge and enchanting mountain gorillas. But Rwanda is still desperately poor and very densely populated. Land is precious and every little plot is productive – drop a seed in the ground and it will bear fruit. However, drop a mine in the ground and there will be years of wasteland, especially on the steep slopes of the tea plantations.

The landscape is breathtaking: ochre-coloured soil seeping into terracotta rivers, lush valleys and hillsides thickly carpeted with emerald tea bushes. And that landscape is full of people: tramping along remote paths, negotiating lumpy tracks, clustered around roadside kiosks selling single razor blades and sticks of chewing gum. The problem is poverty: jobs are scarce and existence has to be scraped any old way. Children fetch water and firewood, balancing heavy loads as they plod along the only decent road, built by the Chinese. And though the women wear colourful wraps, they conceal worn clothes and little ornament. The luckier ones have bright yellow plastic tabards – tea pickers, who are paid 300 francs a day – about thirty pence. Looking thoughtfully at a hillside full of whispering eucalyptus trees is Jean Nepo, the manager of the tea factory. One thousand five hundred extended families rely on it for income – probably over ten thousand souls –

but at present many will not come to work there, however desperate. Mines were laid among the fast-growing eucalyptus, which supply the wood for drying the tea. Although local people had been aware of this, it didn't stop children foraging for firewood. One child was killed and five have lost legs. Five cows also died. The mines are a blight on the economy. The manager sighs.

'Everything suffers,' he says, with rumour and fear spreading more trouble. Some of the hillsides are worked by villagers with their own small plots, but talk of mines makes them too afraid to tend their tea bushes or to walk to the factory with their baskets. And the eucalyptus has to be brought from further away, disrupting the factory's schedule.

Going to see the source of the trouble is a sweaty business. Ben and I put on heavy protection garments and helmets with thick plastic visors before starting down the steep slope below the tea factory, slithering into trees and getting entangled in bushes. The wood has been divided up, with lanes marked out with tape. However, it's not easy to keep to a straight line, and just over the tape to our left is the unexplored part of the minefield. Rwandan army soldiers trained in Kenya are quietly searching the ground with odd-shaped probes and detectors. It is very different from the flat field in Nairobi. The mud is deep, the vegetation knitted together, the heat oppressive. Wooden markers, tipped blue and red, are sprouting as the unit moves forward, inch by inch. This is the manual search – it would be impossible to use machines here. Earlier in the morning, one small mine has been exposed. We peer at it, cream-coloured, ridged and round, a few inches across, while watching where our feet are planted. It doesn't look impressive or particularly dangerous. The soldier next to it thinks differently: 'It's in perfect working order,' he says, 'and it was put here thirteen years ago.'

I am reminded of the Afghan camel and the dinner plates in Bosnia. However, having been through a couple of Rwandan army briefings that morning – a mixture of English, French, Rwandese and army-speak – and seen the diligence with which the de-miners are crawling over the wood, I feel more confident that the next time

I put my foot down there won't be a dreadful bang. It's curious, because a mine is an inert and rather ordinary-looking object which doesn't tick or flash but just sits in the earth and waits for a passing foot. However, one tiny disc of plastic can paralyse a whole area, never mind just one curious observer – and I did find myself staring into the mud, breathing rather heavily. It's a reaction which Ben Remfrey knows well:

'Everybody's perception of landmines is clouded by danger, and most people don't really understand what they are and what they can do to you. Yes, we've seen film and we've seen the bits and pieces according to Hollywood, but it's not actually like that. It can be quite boring, because people can work for weeks and weeks, even months and years, without finding a mine – and then suddenly come across a whole row of them. So you have to keep focused, you have to be well trained, well equipped and well led. And you keep to the guidelines, adhere to the Standard Operating Procedures – ours is five hundred pages long! If people step outside of that, they can get fired on the spot. What we don't want is casualties. It's not dangerous . . . as long as you *respect* the threat.'

We're standing in the minefield which the dogs will finally clear when the manual search is over, speeding up the local people's return to the land. And though they've only been introduced into de-mining quite recently, they're proving their worth. But they've got competition. Further to the south in Tanzania there's more scampering through the grass, but there isn't an Alsatian's tail waving in the air. Instead, on the end of a long lead is an animal feeling very much at home: the African pouched rat. Sensitive and smart, the rat can actually scratch away to indicate when he's found something, and is so light he doesn't set off the mine. His reward is a banana. He and his fellow rats are also deployed in Mozambique, where there are estimated to be around half a million mines. There are advantages to using this animal – he doesn't crave affection like a dog, he runs on bananas and peanuts, and he is said to enjoy a whole day's nose-twitching that gets a reward. Rats, according to their handlers, apparently don't get bored.

They also come in large numbers and are very cheap, and their handlers only admit to being 'quite fond' of them. However, they are not as thorough as dogs and tend to scuttle this way and that, sometimes missing mines. And there's a cautionary tale from the early days in Mozambique when a trained rat team in its little crate was inadvertently left for three hours at an airport. When the handlers returned, they discovered that the locals had roasted them for lunch . . .

Dogs, rats, flails, water pressure, even experiments with bees in America – the hunt for the most efficient clearance operation goes on. But modern armies are keen to plant yet more mines. A short distance from where we watched the Rwandese soldiers patiently working through the eucalyptus forest, another unit of the Rwandese Defence Force was on the border with DRC because of continuing trouble from warlords. They are deployed behind another minefield – one still regarded as 'active and useful'. Warrant Officer Mark Livingstone, who trained the Rwandese de-miners, previously spent years in the British army using mines as a soldier:

'From a military perspective they're a very good weapon – very cheap, very effective. They stay in the ground for thirty years – you don't have to pay them. However, from a humanitarian point of view they're a dangerous weapon, and the trouble is that we have armies that aren't well trained in laying them, and also leave minefields unmarked. They're not recorded in any way and confrontation lines move, so it all causes a major problem when the conflict finishes. The impact on the civilians after the fighting's finished is massive.'

For Ben Remfrey and his colleagues it's an uphill task, because putting a mine in the ground costs so much less than removing it. But he thinks it's worth it: 'It's not rocket science, humanitarian mine action, and there's some very good guys involved in it for the right reasons. Land is the most important thing to people in the developing world, and if you deny people land you deny them their lives. And the biggest buzz I ever get on a project is when a bit of land is handed back: to think that this area in Rwanda has been denied to its people since 1994 – and if the rains hold off this will be cleared in two or three weeks, and then the land will be handed over. Of course, there's never enough money – but you keep battering away and you get it done.'

In the name of what?

'I do it in the name, I think, of those who are unable to do it themselves – through my life I've gained skills, also along with the people who work with the Trust. And we have the ability to help others.'

15

The Missionary

The White Horse is a source not only of danger, but of dispute as to what he symbolises. False peace? False belief? But his rider wears a crown, which suggests a conqueror. What is indisputable is that belief in itself can be dangerous – the history of religion is violent and the means of spiritually driven death often frighteningly inventive, as illustrated in every major art gallery. Believing in a particular god can be lethal. Not believing in the same deity as the majority can be equally dangerous. Not believing at all – well, you're asking for it. In the realm of the secular, holding strong views, following a particular code or trying to uphold certain principles may bring on trouble from both believers and unbelievers alike. Thinking for yourself is regarded in some quarters as a very subversive act. No wonder the White Horse sets out to conquer your mind.

The book I shall not be taking to a desert island is *Fox's Book of Martyrs*. It sat at the top of the best-seller lists for a couple of centuries, and was essential reading for pious Protestants. Today it would probably be called '101 Horrible Ways to Kill a Human Being' and carry a health warning, since it's a gory and detailed compendium of torture, murder, execution and every kind of violent death that could possibly be invented in the persecution of Protestants by Catholics. First published in 1563, it no doubt reflected the short, brutish and nasty aspects of everyday life then, but even so it's still an eye-watering read, dwelling on imaginative use of the hatchet, the stake and the rack. It had a lasting impact on British attitudes to Rome and its religion, although these days it's not likely to appear on a course of comparative religious studies. However, it still has a grip among Christian fundamentalists, recommended on their websites as a magnificent record of 'heroic lives' and 'triumphant deaths'.

The Christian martyrs were killed for their beliefs, and there was no sense that this was a quick route to heaven – unlike some modern Islamist martyrdom, which gives those who blow up themselves as well as others instant access to their paradise. And fundamentalist beliefs across many faiths embrace violence and an unquiet end as if they were to be both admired and desired.

I have never been able to find much sympathy for determined martyrdom. Admittedly, many of the Christians were powerless to avoid their fate, and died with courage. But there are also those who appear to have walked willingly towards the danger, cocooned in their belief, ready to face danger and death, even perhaps inviting it – and they don't tug at my heartstrings. It's not the faith I find difficult, but the discarding of life for . . . for what? An example to others – what, to march towards the flames as well? Surely you don't have to be murdered to prove a life well lived? Or perhaps it's a form of suicide. No, I'm not going to join those who applaud, or even look on with awe. However, I'm curious. Does belief land them in danger these days? . . .

I was standing in the rain on the deck of a clapped-out river boat, watching the River Paraguay swirl by and wondering if, Humphrey Bogart-like, I might have to dive overboard and push this South American *African Queen* through a shoal of piranhas. Why was I smothered in mosquito repellent, nervous about dengue fever, and avoiding a loo open to the elements where one false move means an early meeting with said piranhas? Because this is missionary work, this is. And there's an element of danger – but not from the usual direction. And it all began five days ago in Raleigh, North Carolina, USA . . .

People were coming over for a 'prayer evening'. Not familiar with such an event, I manoeuvred myself into the kitchen. And they were also bringing food – not only as a social gesture but because it sustained Lindsay and Danny, who had no income since he had given up his job in telecommunications to become a full-time pastor, along with his wife, English-born Reverend Lindsay. An array of fried plantains, dips and cookies appeared. A guitar was being strummed in the living room where ten people were already gathered. There was small talk peppered with 'The Lord will have the answer' and 'We'll need to pray over that.'

I was doing a peeping Tom act, creeping my head round the kitchen door, unsure of my role and beginning to have a very British sense of embarrassment. In this modest house, sitting shyly between the grand porticoed new-builds of Raleigh's well-rewarded IT workers, there was a lot of sound. Voices were singing to the guitar. 'Praise to God, praise be, praise be,' came from a woman who was now being hugged by a little group, while 'Thank you Jesus, thank you Jesus,' was being shouted relentlessly in no particular direction by a tall, middle-aged man with a sunshine-yellow toupee. He was the man whose opening remark to me had been, 'You know Lindsay – you're in her Church in England, of course?' I came clean and said, 'No, actually.'

His expression was one of puzzlement, with just a tinge of suspicion. 'You *are* a member of a prayer group there, I hope?'

'Er, no.'

The expression changed to that of challenge, as he realised he'd lit upon a Lost Sheep. 'Do you not have Jesus in your heart?'

I recognised one of those moments where there is a choice of answers, some of which might cause more trouble than others. So I retreated into lightly frosty Englishness, replying that such questions were considered rather personal where I came from. He was reaching for his Bible as I slid back into the kitchen.

Now, as I watched him double himself with passion while calling upon the Lord, I realised the whole room was in a rhythm of emotion, driven by repetitive phrases and the excitement of inhibitions let loose. The hugged woman was sobbing, Pastor

Danny was on his knees Calling upon the Lord at full throttle, and a young black African, who had told me he had come to the USA to study but had since decided to be a missionary, was delivering at the top of his voice a rat-a-tat of invocations for Jesus to save him, us and indeed everyone. It was like an intimate tribal ritual that would be mildly ridiculous in a public setting.

Meanwhile Lindsay, her face suffused with happiness, was waving a huge gold flag. I stared at this tableau of divinely directed emotion and backed further into the kitchen, watching the fantastic fireflies in the wood outside – I'd never seen such a display as they flared and danced. Come to think of it, I hadn't seen such a display as was occurring in the living room – though a couple of faint memories stirred.

One of the benefits of being brought up in a large industrial town was the rich choice of religious denominations. In Victorian times, when shipbuilding and mining flourished in Sunderland, there was clearly deep concern among the rich that the poor needed saving from Hell rather than Hunger. The Nonconformists were the most successful, smartly targeting the suburbs with grand churches, the terraced cottages with chapels and the riverside slums with missions. The Church of England didn't have the same clout in a town awash with pubs, as the Noncoms pursued souls on the wagon of Temperance, pitching virtue against Vaux's Brewery. However, the Roman Catholics, mainly Irish labourers, were regarded as beyond the pale and blatantly ignored. The Methodists came in many guises – Independent, Wesleyan and Primitive, as did the Baptists – Strict, Emmanuel and Bethesda. And they all had a serious building programme, aiming to grab a plot before the Congregationalists, Unitarians, Spiritualists and other individual shepherds looking for a flock beat them to it. Nearly every street had God's house on one corner versus the public house on the other.

Christened Methodist, I was early aware that others did things differently, for faith and ritual were bones of contention. However, even the pews of our own church occasionally shuddered with dissent. Prayer was personal, a matter for quiet mumbling in a demure crouch – anyone on their knees would be whispered of as 'heading for Rome'. Even so, in broad Geordie the quiet contemplation was sometimes interrupted with a loud cry: 'Lord, hear my prayer'. This used to provoke shuffles of embarrassment and disapproving glances as I popped up above the pew to see where this interesting diversion was taking place.

It was usually at the back, where sat a number of gentlemen in their ancient Sunday Best – a silk muffler for the pitmen and a waistcoat with brass watch-chain for the shipwrights and welders. They were Victorian men, steeped in 'witnessing', and with grandfathers who might have remembered the Wesleys as they crisscrossed the counties with their revivalist message. To sit quietly all through the service was, to them, to show inadequate respect for the greatness of their God. Witnessing, though, had gone out of fashion. It wasn't quite in step with a more affluent congregation that ran the yards and the coalmines, rather than labouring in them. Was it education and a better grasp of complex religious ideas that brought this about? Or more sophisticated social behaviour and the belief that good manners included a degree of polite reserve?

Not only religious observance changed. During the days of Empire, many of Sunderland's Methodists appeared to have set off to convert the world. The evidence remained in the modest bungalows of elderly couples: in front rooms with a few twee ornaments on the mantelpiece, a child's eye was drawn to large and rather moth-eaten things on the wall. Was that a spear – with hairy, dangly bits? And a shield – clearly clothed by some wildish animal with moulting problems? There were a few photographs, too – fading groups of black or brown people in front of small thatched dwellings. It had been hard work, I was told, but 'rewarding'.

No one seemed to have disappeared into a cooking pot, however, and I was hugely disappointed. Surely being a missionary involved danger – an obligatory dramatic scene, where the spear-waving mob indicates that lunch is overdue and still very much alive and would it mind popping into the bubbling stew? The mild-mannered Methodists recalled battles – but were referring to termites eating hymn-books; Armageddon involved termites and an entire piano.

That set of early memories from north-east England was complemented by another memory from the Arctic Circle. Spending a year teaching in northern Sweden while reading for a degree in Scandinavian Studies, I had to find a suitable subject for a thesis. Most students chose to delve into obscure corners of literature. I veered somewhat off-course, having been intrigued by a fellow teacher's description of her family as 'spiritual head-bangers'.

It turned out that they belonged to one of the many revivalist Protestant sects that flourished in the early nineteenth century: Laestadianism. It was characterised by a Puritan lifestyle, plain dress and, for some obscure reason, a dislike of curtains and potted plants. Under Pastor Lars Levi Laestadius, various 'worldly' practices were shunned – drink, dancing, card-playing and, later, television, pop music and contraception. My teacher friend, finding life somewhat dull, had escaped to the city to indulge in curtains and lots of potted plants. However, the most embarrassing bit of the family's behaviour had been, she hissed, *liikutuksia* – a Finnish word conveying the idea of being inwardly moved.

'They used to squeal and weep and throw themselves around,' she confided in a whisper across the table in a smart coffee shop. 'Just the sort of thing that Swedes find very un-Swedish. Some old biddy kicks off first, calling for forgiveness. Then it gets very noisy and not one of them seems to realise it's induced by pressing all the right emotional buttons. They just let themselves go. Granny even used to do the talking-in-tongues gibberish.' She cringed at the memory. Being modern and progressive was the social norm in Sweden in the 1960s, and *liikutuksia* summoned up the dark backwoods of Lapland, shamans and all.

And *liikutuksia* was what I had seen in North Carolina. Re-reading my rather pompous thesis, I could at least recognise the age-old mechanics of induced ecstasy: repetition, excitement, a crowded space, the emphasis on emotive words, the appeal of shared sentiment, the claim to an exalted state. Every 'ism' finds it useful. And I'd nibbled at the new research in the sixties about glossolalia or talking in tongues, as scientists probed the area of the brain that enables reason and self-control. Subsequently, evidence has emerged that when the frontal lobes – which make you feel in control – shut down, you rabbit on meaninglessly. And rabbit is not a known language.

After childhood, for a very long time missionaries did not figure in my life. Few people seemed inclined to pack a canoe and head for mosquito-infested river-banks. They rarely got into the news, except when held hostage by grumpy regimes; even then, they were singularly ordinary folks who didn't attempt much conversion and stuck to good works and friendly comfort: non-threatening folk, unlikely to provoke danger. But then I hadn't realised that the mission spirit had crossed the Atlantic and been given new life in the form of money and modern marketing.

Not until I spent time in the United States did I become aware of the surge of determined evangelism that comes with affluence and the availability of television as a pulpit. In the mid-eighties, the televangelists were doing a roaring trade. Sunday mornings were wall-to-wall images of yelling, exhorting, hallelujahing orators. Sometimes they wept, sometimes they had enormous choirs of satin-robed hymn-belters, almost always they asked for your money. Most of these shepherds of the faithful came to a sorry end, often involving remarkably impious behaviour with younger members of the flock who possessed impressive boobs. Or else they couldn't keep their paws out of the collection plate. As part of my job I was dispatched to find out what was going on in the suburbs of Charlotte, North Carolina. Not that I was hunting a low-profile, shy couple. Jim and Tammy Faye Bakker hosted a TV channel that delivered their own special Christian message twenty-four hours a day via their own satellite.

It wasn't difficult to find their lair: Heritage USA – a mammoth theme park just over the state line at Fort Mill, South Carolina. You merely followed the crowds, estimated at over 5 million a year. Both Bakkers had embraced fundamentalism early – little Tammy recalling that she 'felt the glow of God's love' while attending an Assemblies of God church at the age of ten. Both took to the idea of showbiz religion like ducks to water. They had millions of viewers – although if theirs stood out from the other religious programmes, it was mainly because it starred a man whose wife displayed the most spectacular amount of mascara ever seen on TV, notable for the way in which it ran in thick wiggly rivers whenever Tammy wept. Which she did frequently, usually when asking people to send money. The audience sent in millions of dollars believing their gifts to be solely for the furtherance of the ministry – which was later revealed to include several lavish homes (among them a condominium in Florida with gold-plated bathroom fittings, referred to as 'The Parsonage'), his 'n' hers Rolls Royces and an air-conditioned kennel for their pooch. However, no one was taking much notice of these trifling indulgences while the show was so popular, and when people's dollars also bought 'lifetime access' to the swanky hotel and apartments at Heritage – 'a truly gospel theme park'.

We turned up there on a Saturday afternoon and stood in the grandiose hotel lobby, all white and gold and scarlet. A man in white evening dress was tinkling at a glossy white grand piano on a dais. I thought I had heard most of the familiar favourites that provide irritatingly soothing background in such places, but it was some time before I identified the smooth flow of hymns. The receptionist not only wished me and my crew Have a Good Day, but added The Lord Be Your Guide to the Park. Typically, we wondered where the bar was, and were frostily informed that Such Places of Sin were not to be found at Heritage: 'We're all Christians here.' We lifted our eyes to the heavens – and were rewarded with a chandelier-hung ceiling embellished with biblical quotations.

We explored: there was a fake mountain towering over a vast water complex, with hundreds of happy people rafting down the falls and channels. A lifeguard looked on and I asked him if he was a Christian. He looked a tad shifty, then said, 'I'd rather not say, but it seems kinda odd that if all these folk on the water are Christians – why do I have to be here to save them?' There were Olympic-sized swimming pools and lots of easy-peasy gentle sports facilities – all catering to the crowd which was not only large in numbers, but individually rather hefty too: roly-poly Holy Rollers. These were overwhelmingly poor whites, and all were overwhelmingly thrilled by Heritage.

Much of the time they went shopping. Heritage boasted a faux-Victorian arcade crammed with goodies to 'brighten and bring a breath of the Lord to your home'. There was a riot of piously twee knick-knacks, all stamped, embossed or embroidered with virtuous sayings. You could come home to welcome mats inviting you into a Home to Happy Believers, and go to bed with pillows saying you'd be Safe in the Lord.

As the visitors ambled around in a state of seeming bliss we vox popped them. They relished the high standards of accommodation and leisure facilities, topped by the ultimate icing: 'It's in the Lord's name' . . . 'God wants us to be here' . . . 'There's no cussin', swearin' and drinkin' – who could want more?' Well, the Bakkers could.

The next day we went to the heart, or rather the engine, of the operation. Not exactly church-shaped, it was more a barn with aircraft-hangar pretensions – and it was crammed. The TV broadcast was in full swing and we could just about make out two tiny figures at the far end as they gave their all, while willing their viewers to give a bit more (dollars please).

Out in the sunshine, we yet again faced the question of. . . . No, to be honest, a dozen questions. Here were thousands of people, their faces beaming with delight, full of innocent joy, excited and revelling in a sense of shared emotion, responding eagerly to a pair of pious sharks. You didn't have to be a cynic or an atheist. You just had to wonder what was going on, and where the line was between pure faith and blind faith. The Internal Revenue Service soon drew its own line, and asked for rather a lot of tax. Fraud and conspiracy charges followed, along with the little matter of a one-night stand with a future star of *Playboy*'s centrefold, whom Reverend Bakker tried to buy off with a quarter of a million dollars in hush money. Jim went to prison; Tammy dabbed at her mascara and divorced him. Heritage is now partly redeveloped, partly derelict.

The televangelists went through rather a bad patch, with a number of them revealed as energetic sinners in the most traditional manner. However, not all their flocks were disillusioned. In the same way that some Americans have rigid convictions that aliens keep abducting their fellow citizens, many of the religious right refuse to believe that any of their leaders have strayed. It's all a conspiracy gotten up by the Devil, they maintain, aided by his Imp, the media – so let's be steadfast and keep on spreading the word. And by golly, they do. Like Reverend Lindsay, they get out the atlas, pray over it and head for the airport. For many American evangelists, the end of the Soviet Union was akin to an archangel's trumpet blast. Tickets were booked to Kazakhstan and anywhere else that sounded vaguely Commie. Africa, mired in poverty and conflict – time to bring aid wrapped round a hard kernel of belief. South America – well, there's only One True Path and the Roman Catholic Church is kinda off-message. Iran – now, there's a challenge . . .

Since the turn of the century there have been numerous reports of American missionaries venturing far afield and frequently getting a hostile reception. Maybe not the cooking pot, but certainly prison, violence and sometimes death. Changing the way people think, altering their priorities and principles, can be taken to be just as threatening as an invasion or assault. Not that Americans are targeted exclusively – Christian Koreans have found the Taliban in Afghanistan less than welcoming, while the Chinese government frequently throws out any proselytising foreigners and gets nasty with home-grown enthusiasts too. But the Russian Orthodox Church, the Israeli government, Hindu fundamentalists, the Burmese military junta, Islamic zealots . . . all have form when it comes to dealing with evangelising Protestant missionaries. A quick glance across the globe suggests that the battle for souls claims rather a lot of casualties even beyond those occasioned by internal squabbling about the true path of belief. And joining the fray is the growing determination of fundamentalist Islamists to impose their beliefs through force and violence. The naïve American Holy Rollers are now fishing for souls in waters where Islamists are sinking lethal depth charges.

Not that any of this bothered Danny and Lindsay back in North Carolina. Hope Chapel, their local church, operating under the umbrella of the massively wealthy FourSquare Baptist Church, is a huge warehouse throbbing with comfy-sounding middle-aged rock 'n' roll and full of pamphlets and newsletters about its forays abroad. There are missions to Ecuador, Cuba, Mozambique, Sumatra and Ghana and many other dots on their map, all under the banner of 'Wheresoever Ministry'. Large people in shorts ambled about clapping, pausing to browse at the free coffee, donuts and peanut butter table. Quite a bit of huddling went on – three or four people, heads down, clutching each other and emitting a few sobs. I read some pamphlets in which readers were typically informed that 'thunder and lightning are not really understood by scientists – they're just part of God's Plan'. Total reliance on Wikipedia also showed a touching faith. Facts and history got a good mangling, and Darwin didn't get a look in.

It's a brick wall of spiritual confidence which accepts no argument, licked round with little flames of racism and xenophobia. In their own closely knit society, it's comforting. There's no intimation that it could bring danger or harm in another setting. And nothing intrudes on this confidence: TV is dismissed as sinful, the radio ditto. Newspapers are considered full of lies, and the only books to be found are devoted to religious themes.

'Listen up: we're gonna dive into the Book of Acts. . . .' On stage, the pastor was revving up for a high-octane examination of Pentecost and the rushing mighty wind which blew in the exciting subject of speaking in tongues. The donut-chomping congregation was nodding in unison, shouting 'Yeah', and clearly had no time for neuroscience. I read on, as the literature began to tackle things like the need for converting Jews, the necessity of healing gays ('They're very sick') and the ever-present spectre of Communism. It was time travel with attitude. Any mention of Islam was avoided: according to members of the congregation, any problems in that direction were being dealt with by the state through its 'war on terror'.

After church, the house filled up with prayerful friends. Reverend Lindsay's impending missionary journey needed to be 'prayed over'. Her supporters were fretting about the wider world and its needs: 'Africa's big, ain't it? I guess they don't have air conditioning either' . . . 'Why don't they get our message? . . . It must be Communism. . . . And there's witchcraft too, right?'

The ignorance was blithe, the confidence in the American way of life total (except for unpleasant areas where homosexuality, equality and secularism appeared to have besmirched the flag). But all problems were met with the rolling phrases of belief: 'The Lord told me' . . . 'I'm filled with the Spirit – I don't need science nor nothin'. . . . 'I know what the Lord has said to me – and *you* can't understand.'

Reverend Danny was off to Mozambique while his wife was pursuing her mission: 'Basically, we're going to pray over the land. We don't understand the language or the culture, but we go to a village and praise the Lord, dance African style, then we tell the group about Jesus. But God specifically told us to go to Africa – and isn't it interesting that we're so often called to former Commie countries? We go in, stir things up, then all of a sudden they're all exalted. . . .

'In Africa there is a tremendous urgency because of HIV and so on – and we need to get Jesus into their lives, as they're dying like flies. We do care about clean water, orphans and widows and we have plans. However, others are taking care of that, so it has a lower priority for us. We bring people to Christ, and we plug them in to some organisation or church or at least get a pastor to minister to them. You know, some of these pastors have a small view of life – and we're saying, there are gonna be *hundreds* knocking on your door, for we baptise people *all* the time. We don't start churches, we're a ministry – we need to be a catalyst to get other churches to get their act together. Our spiritual message is this: Jesus Christ cares for you, and if you repent of your sins he'll forgive you. So you have to feel sorry if you're going to be forgiven. It's not that you must be good – you must just love Jesus. Then the goodness will come naturally.'

It's all about repenting sins and being exalted, and it's spelled out in a huge rush of conviction. I put it to Reverend Danny that this all seemed to be aimed at poorer people who live in countries with sparse education and health facilities. It doesn't seem to take place in Europe. He replied innocently, with a giggle, 'Yes, I don't see this happening in Europe. . . .'

His wife had learned her destination while praying over the atlas: it was to be Paraguay. And not just anywhere in this South American nation, but a tiny dot on the border with Brazil called Bela Vista.

I asked, 'Why Bela Vista?'

'I've no idea,' she said. 'But God knows. As soon as God has named the country and I know it's Him talking and nobody else, not some nice idea I've had, then we start praying, and I get a map of the country and start praying over it and finding out what's going on there, what the people are like, and what their spiritual needs are – just knowing and understanding that God has got his eye on some bunch of people over there and that he's got a plan. And if I follow it, if I actually go in with what He's doing, then I know that things will happen and people's lives will be changed. People *will have* emotional healings and there *will be* physical healing as well.'

I wondered what sort of people had their lives changed. Were there specific kinds?

'Every trip is different. But, yes, we often finish up with the poor, if you like, and a lot of the people who don't have access to doctors, hospitals, you know . . . it tends to be with them. But on other trips we are definitely on the other end of things – we are ministering to people who are probably well-to-do. But God has no favourites. He actually cares about everybody.'

Paraguay seemed an interesting choice, as the area boasted traditional attitudes to missionaries as far back as 1515, when the Spanish conquistador Diego de Solis was given a warm welcome by the Charrua Indians, then chopped up and eaten. The Guarani Indians, on the other hand, ate each other, and then a decade later tasted the first Portuguese to land on Paraguayan territory. Aleixo Garcia and his son intended to show the heathens the error of their ways and extend the dominion of the Catholic Church. Unfortunately, the Guarani couldn't resist foreign food. Ten years on, and another ship's captain, Juan de Ayolas, also went into the pot. Subsequently, the Church returned with greater firepower of the non-spiritual kind, but not before several Jesuits had also provided lunch. Admittedly we're now five hundred years down the line, but what is it that makes missionaries head for Paraguay?

Every time I ask the question on this South American trip there is a serene smile, and the answer involves direct communication from God. I feel disconnected from the spirit of the journey. However, I'm heartily relieved that it's not one of last year's trips, which was to North Korea. Initially, I thought I'd misheard. Surely South, not North? The North has a grim and slightly deranged regime headed by men called Kim. Kim Jong-Il (the present Dear Leader, as opposed to his father the Great Leader) is regarded as a kind of god (or as near as you get in fanatical Communism) and any deviation from Kim-worship is reputedly met with little forgiveness. Meanwhile the country has problems with semi-starvation, forced labour and isolation, and its long-suffering people are rewarded with the promise of being a nuclear power. Conventional religion, mainly Buddhism and Confucianism with some Christianity, has difficulty functioning under state control. And some of that state's propaganda has the Kim family arriving on earth from heaven and popping down on Mount Paektu, where they assumed human form. Closer observation of the dynasty reveals a great deal of interest in lavish parties with large numbers of nubile young women, also a string of mistresses alongside several wives. There are several little Kims in the official biographies, so maybe heaven's not always involved.

But none of this fazed Reverend Lindsay, who trotted off in the guise of a tourist and felt that her trip had been well worth it: 'You see, we don't aggressively go against things. We try to take in the love of Jesus. And then *they* see. I didn't go into North Korea as an evangelist. I just went in and blessed the land . . . and when I came out, the officials said: "*You're* different. We don't know why, but you are."'

The greyness and misery of this authoritarian nation, its denial of human rights, prison camps and dependence on foreign aid to feed its people are not the preoccupation of evangelism. Engagement takes place only on the spiritual level, so I wondered if it was possible to gauge any success.

'It would be hard for me to explain it to you, because you'd need to understand the work that we're doing, the *spiritual* work. . . . It's not something that you *see* – but *they* knew I was different from others that had been there. And there were many people praying for that land, and I was able to say to one person, "There are a lot of people out in the world who really care about your situation here . . .".'

So perhaps Paraguay might yield a little more achievement, especially as I was clearly not yet quite on the right wavelength to appreciate success. And so it was we found ourselves on the most rickety of boats, heading up the Paraguay River. The *Cacique* had looked rather enticing as we saw her at dawn being loaded up for her weekly trip from Asunción, the capital, north to Conception. However, let's be honest, if you get change from a $10 bill for a thirty-hour voyage it's reasonable to assume you're not heading for the *QEII*. Half her deck was covered with bags of cement, vegetables, chickens, steel cables, racing bikes, a bed and a large fridge. The lower deck looked like a street shelter busy with insect life – I instantly dubbed it the Cockroach Saloon – and above were cabins resembling cupboards. Still, for $9 who's complaining? The narrow companionway boasted several large dog-eared pictures of a mournful Virgin and Child, wearing huge crowns and radiating rainbow beams: over 90 per cent of Paraguayans are Roman Catholics.

But the North Carolina missionaries, of whom there were now three, remained undaunted by the Catholic 'opposition'. Reverend Lindsay had been joined by Millie, a lively Puerto Rican American, whose Spanish proved useful and whose ten years in the US army seemed somewhat at odds with her present vocation. And for communication in Guarani – the second national language – there was Betsy, a middle-aged dentist with a nest of flyaway black hair and never without a beaker and straw of terere, a bitter tea, and rather a lot of baggage. Travelling light was nigh impossible, because of a huge hold-all containing the coloured flags and poles which would be used in 'religious dance'.

In our first two days in Asunción I had been introduced to this concept following a rather thinly attended evening prayer meeting in an evangelical pastor's apartment. There was some half-hearted hugging and a bit of weeping among the dozen meek and rather listless members of the congregation. Most people in Paraguay which is rather unkindly regarded as South America's backyard, are extremely poor, below a very thin top crust of those who run and own everything. The national business appears to be smuggling, daily life is regulated by corruption, and the legacy of General Alfredo Stroessner's appalling thirty-five-year dictatorship still infests political life. We had driven through gloomy streets lined with tacky shops, only enlivened by the enchanting confection of the capital's Gothic railway station. It has a splendid collection of ancient steam trains and, tacked to the archway where the railway lines disappear under tarmac, a notice which proclaims, 'Abandoned, pending further funding'.

So, after an evening of rather uncharismatic response which seemed to reflect our surroundings, it was time to spread the word further, aided by dance – and if the faithful failed to draw nigh then we could always corral an audience where there was literally no escape. The Central Women's Prison in Asunción had a scruffy courtyard in which scores of young women sat gossiping as we arrived. The head warder grumbled about overcrowding and implied that it was all down to democracy.

'Twenty years ago there were only forty women here. Now there are two hundred and fifty. It's all because of the government. When we had a *strong* government, we didn't have any delinquency. Things are now out of control.' Her complaint echoed those laments for the rule of Stalin that are heard in the former Soviet Union. Dictators are often fondly recalled for their ability to keep petty crime at bay and run the trains on time, and there's amnesia about the monstrous side of the deal: General Stroessner, who regarded opposition as something to be shot, has benefited from such forgetfulness. The warder glared at the skinny teenagers huddled in the thin sunshine, before yelling at a depressed-looking group of women with small children.

'What are they in for?' I asked.

'Homicide,' she snapped, 'with firearms.' She went on to paint a picture of gun-toting toughs on the prowl, ruthless muggers and thieves.

Appearances can be deceptive, but the courtyard didn't seem to exude an air of latent violence. The women now staring at us had not an ounce of menace among them. However, as about eighty were now gathered, along with a few visiting fathers of their children, the three missionaries had their congregation. Others could not be coaxed out into the sharp air because they had no warm clothes.

Tinkly, New Age music wafted from a portable player as Millie began by explaining in Spanish that they had a message for everyone and would be telling a story – in dance. The congregation looked bemused but clearly didn't get much entertainment in jail and decided to hang around for a bit. Christian dance ensued from Lindsay, narrated by Millie. The miming and flag-waving, a child's guide to good and evil and the search for the meaning of life, represented by different coloured flags, produced furrowed brows and the boyfriends sniggered. The chief warder poked her head out from the gatehouse, glowering. She had already sniffed suspiciously round the motives of her visitors, growling that 'This is a Catholic country', and was clearly not impressed by the protestations about their 'all Churches' ministry'. In a city where the Mormon headquarters, surmounted by much gold leaf, are a great deal grander than the Paraguayan Presidential Palace, there is a definite sense that a kind of invasion is in progress – and that a Trojan Horse could well take the form of a dance.

The music twittered to a stop, the show was over, and nearly all the women wandered off without a hint of being touched by anything spiritual. Two or three seemed undecided about approaching the missionaries but their indecision was swiftly swooped upon, and within a minute there was a huddle of hugging and shoulders to cry on. The chief warder looked as if the Inquisition might be reinvoked. I was drawn to half a dozen who looked as if they wanted to talk rather than hug – and soon I had been baldly informed about the country's justice system.

'We have no worth,' said twenty-eight-year-old Rosa Alba. 'Women have no value here. We're poor – and we have no jobs and we get into drugs. You don't feel anyone cares about you. And men just use you. Life is dangerous.'

Rather than committing random murder on the street, all these women had been involved in domestic violence. They insisted this was the pattern for just about every woman in the prison. And even within its walls there was both rape by male guards and organised prostitution from which officials profited, attested to by inmates and several international reports.

'It's dangerous to be poor and a girl in my country,' said a pale young woman holding a baby conceived in prison. 'Your family throw you out because you don't bring in any money [she had ten siblings], so you go with a man, get pregnant, he's into drugs, there's trouble, and you're guilty.'

Next was twenty-one-year-old Lilian Duarte, shivering in disintegrating denim. She was serving a twenty-year sentence. Her boyfriend had killed her boss, she explained, an elderly woman she had worked for since she was fourteen. 'I was in the kitchen when it happened. I heard the shot. I ran into the living room. But my lover wouldn't say anything during the trial, so here I am. I didn't do anything – my conscience is clear. I don't feel safe in here, but sometimes I think I just might get out before the twenty years are up . . . but I don't have any money for a lawyer to make an appeal.' She had a baby – by another man – who was one of nineteen infants in the prison at that moment.

Three of the women – who had never met before their imprisonment – were in for the same crime: the appalling kidnapping in 2004 of a former president's daughter, Cecilia Cubas whose father Raul ran Paraguay for nine months at the turn of the century. The thirty-two-year-old woman was found dead five months after being abducted and, although all the public fingers pointed at a left-wing political conspiracy, Asunción was rife with rumours that both the police and the Catholic Church had meddled disastrously in the kidnap negotiations. A number of men alleged to be connected to left-wing guerrillas were arrested. As were their partners. Rosa Alba was seven months pregnant when the police arrived, and she protested that she had no idea where her husband of a year was or that he had ever been 'a rebel'. He is still on the run and she hasn't heard from him since; meanwhile she herself is serving five years.

None of the women seemed to find this unusual: 'Justice sees women involved with men who are criminals – so women are always considered to be in on the crime too. And if they can't find the man, they charge the woman. Because we don't matter as people.'

Considering their situation, it's surprising that just two are now weeping in the arms of the missionaries, who are giving thanks for the appearance of these stray lambs. However, it is only the 'hurtin' inside' that interests them. They shrug sadly at the tales from the cells, but justice, equality, human rights and the consequences of poverty are not on the evangelical agenda.

Reflecting that anyone who begins a visit to a country with a prison visit and a prayer meeting has a narrowed view, I stared over the rail of the *Cacique* and hoped for a more general set of impressions as the boat shuddered out into the river. From a distance Asunción looked more like a conventional capital city, with high-rise flats and several industrial areas. But its shops had displayed racks of the cheapest and tattiest clothing, the flats were jerry-built and the slums were redolent of African-style poverty. Nestled like caged jewels between the rotting colonial villas were mansions of appalling splendour: mini-palaces with emerald lawns and bulbous statues outside, giant chandeliers flashing above ornate furniture within. All were surrounded by huge steel fences bristling with electronic devices. The rich in Asunción are conspicuous, and so are their bodyguards. But a certain lassitude, helped by a climate of oven-like summers and regular bouts of deadly dengue fever, combined with a historic predilection for corruption, seems to maintain the status quo between rich and poor. So what might the missionaries target? They weren't here to relieve the poverty or effect a revolution, as Reverend Lindsay confirmed.

'In Cuba, Ecuador and Africa we're taking basic over-the-counter drugs. But not on these exploratory trips, like Paraguay. We take just what can be left behind, "bits and bobs" – clothes and so on. But the main thrust is evangelism. And we'll just be talking to people, meeting people and just seeing how we finish up here and there.'

Although our destination was Bela Vista, the town on the Brazilian border to which Reverend Lindsay had been 'steered' when she opened her atlas, the journey too presented opportunities. Millie chatted to the passengers trying to doze in the Cockroach Saloon, gently pressing upon them the possibility of being saved. Reverend Lindsay had already been sounding out the crew, and Betsy meanwhile had begun to make subtle moves to track down my soul in the narrow companionway. Or not so subtle. Having a woman sing 'What a friend we have in Jesus' at full throttle one foot away, and furthermore in Guarani, is not an approach that I find particularly appealing. I had nodded on hearing the familiar melody, and this had proved hugely encouraging to her. She flourished her Guarani hymn-book in front of me and pointed hopefully to something with many verses. When I looked blank, she launched into what was recognisably 'If you're happy and you know it clap your hands'. A couple of the crew squeezed past, clearly wishing not to know us. I got an inkling of the determination needed to 'witness' as a vocation.

The river was bereft of other traffic, and there was little of interest on the banks. Occasionally the scrubland gave way to a well-ordered *estancia*: often a grand country mansion with neat paddocks and lively horses. Here lay the riches of the beef and sheep farmers, but most lived in the capital and many were foreign owners who rarely visited at all. The *Cacique* dropped off fruit and crates of building materials, and took on the odd family and more chickens and dogs. Eventually we landed at Concepcion via a single long wobbly plank. Dogs, chickens, cement bags and missionaries nipped across: the word 'piranha' motivates people.

Bela Vista was still over 100 miles to the north, and we growled up the road in a decrepit bus for three hours before getting off at a crossroads with a sprinkle of kiosks and a café. The route onward was a rust-red track, but the local café owner was helpful and negotiated for a fat teenager to drive us in a small pick-up truck. Betsy and Reverend Lindsay pluckily elected for the open-air ride with the teenager's two sisters, who had apparently decided to enjoy an evening of potholes and dust and whose only comment on the scenery was, 'Jaguars live there.'

At dusk, the chosen spot on the map was reached. A teeny air of anti-climax pervaded as we sought accommodation. Bela Vista is a border town on the River Apa, curious for having no sign of the border except for the river. There was a customs post, which had obviously not been open for business for a long while. The long, straggly mud streets lined with modest bungalows did not contain a hotel and it was suggested we stay over the river in Brazil – 'More to eat.' But eventually we got a couple of rooms at the back of a general store and picnicked on the remains of the supplies of cheese and peanuts we had munched on the boat. There had been a very definite decision that heavy expenditure was not part of the mission. The Church funds for the trip were to be meticulously accounted for, and food seemed to be something of an extra. I cast my mind back to the multi-million-dollar activities of the Four-Square Church and its behemoth of a temple in Los Angeles. Clearly, missions work on the principle of the widow's mite rather than the corporate budget, and Millie was instructed to bargain hard for cheap dinners with café owners who clearly lived from hand to mouth. Indeed, the unwillingness to part with any money among a population on the bread line was a notable feature.

The next morning revealed a town that either goes to work across the bridge in Brazil or stays at home to grow marijuana. The place seemed to have been forgotten by Paraguay (the dust road should have been paved, but the money 'disappeared') and it had latched on to its neighbour. The locals therefore spoke Portuguese, some of their children went to school across the river and Brazilian money was preferred in the shops. Smuggling was a way of life, and the marijuana provided what little income the town acquired. The centre was a dusty square of small hedges with a central monument commemorating the day in 1987 when General Stroessner himself granted electricity to the grateful inhabitants, most of whom now sported about two light bulbs per home. A simple but elegant Catholic church presided on a hilltop, while a plain shed housed the local evangelicals further down towards the river. With much of the population abroad (as it were) during the day, there had to be other means to reach ears and win souls. A large antenna stuck up above a small bungalow: Radio Frontera. The missionaries spent a happy hour proselytising on air to a DJ who was very glad to see some guests. For my part, roaming the streets confirmed that poverty ran deep: many families lived in shacks with mud floors. The petrol station had a padlock on the pumps. A keen young lad on a motorcycle told me that Bela Vista had been the site of a great battle: sadly, Paraguay's history has been full of battles that had little point and were usually lost. There were plans to bring tourism to the area, but even he was unsure why anyone should come. When the road was built? I asked. He shrugged and said such plans had been laid before he was born.

Reverend Lindsay was walking the muddy roads purposefully, 'praying over' the town, before talking to the local evangelical pastor who offered his building for an evening meeting. For one and a half hours there was dance and exhortation and much waving of flags. The children enjoyed the flag-waving. There were four of them and a teenager, with four adults. It was a strange session, with the missionaries in full flight in English, Spanish and Guarani, and the tiny audience round-eyed and rather unresponsive. Afterwards there was a sense of achievement, bolstered by conversation about how people they had bumped into during the day were 'full of love for the Lord' and amazed that the missionaries had turned up 'just at this moment when they needed to hear about God's love'. Certain 'healings' had happened here and there when somebody knew someone who had turned to God in their hour of need and been rewarded. These exchanges fired up the women, who gained genuine satisfaction from incidents which to an unbeliever were a mixture of coincidence and hearsay. 'But this is what Jesus wants us to do,' they exclaimed, stressing that all of this pointed to a confirmation of their Purpose.

Another day of wandering the town produced an intense scene in a two-room wooden shack, the home of a middle-aged woman with advanced uterine cancer. I remained outside as the missionaries entered to pray over her, but was drawn in as voices were raised to a near shout. The missionaries were all around her on a couch, hugging her, almost smothering her, praising the Lord at the tops of their voices and relentlessly delivering their words of comfort two inches from her ear. For the first time, when they spotted me in the doorway, I had a fleeting glimpse of sheepishness; but afterwards I was firmly told that the patient had derived great comfort from being prayed over.

Eight adults, three teenagers, seven children and two babies came the next night to the evangelical hall. For competition, there was a Catholic celebration of a local saint in the small stadium off the main street. Theirs was a noisy disco with some speeches and lots of kebabs – contrary to the missionaries' whispered suggestions that 'pagan rites' were known to be celebrated at such events; they had even hissed the word 'witchcraft'. It was a word I had heard in North Carolina, and used of several countries. It was uttered with a patronising tinge, and with the open acknowledgement that most of the people who were targeted by a mission were poor, uneducated or in some other way very vulnerable. None of this caused the teeniest expression of doubt.

And so we left Bela Vista. Had the purpose been fulfilled? Reverend Lindsay was confident that, just by reaching the town, 'something had happened'. All three women chewed over various chance encounters and snippets of talk with the locals, detecting good omens and the furthering of God's will. This is what they have devoted themselves to: a relatively uncomfortable life away from home, but one which gives them great satisfaction. Betsy in particular was reluctant to return to Asunción: she had quietly indicated that her domestic background was tumultuous and mission work gave her stability. Millie was much more open and confident, although ten years in the US army, trying to build a solid career, had included a great deal of racism and obstruction. She was now delivering her energies into spreading the Word. Lindsay was a middle-class Englishwoman, whose drive seemed to originate back in childhood.

'It was a journey. I think the first thing was when I was fourteen and about to be confirmed in the Church of England. They suggested we went into the chapel for prayer, and when I came out I just *knew* that God existed. That was a big moment. Then, at some crisis point in my life years later, I just felt I was being taken care of. And that was when I went looking. Who is God? Why would he take care of me? And when I met Danny I felt this was a god of second chances, and I wanted to understand that. Why is he a god of second, third, fourth, however many chances? And something very odd happened in a church in Winchester. This man just came and said he was an accountant, and that he had gifts of healing. And that really touched me – that so many people are really hurting deep inside, not just physically but emotionally, and have so much pain in their lives. And it would be just wonderful to be able to help people.'

The chance encounter, the inexplicable moment – and the avoidance of psychological analysis – is something we all know. Maybe a Road to Damascus moment. Although not everyone takes it as a catalyst for irrevocable change.

Lindsay was reading her Bible, which was endlessly bookmarked and annotated. She reads nothing else when travelling and offered biblical quotations in response to several of my questions, especially those about how others see mission work.

'We're very *accepted* by other denominations. That's not to say everybody – some people are very set in their ways and don't want us to come in and talk to their fellowship . . . but it's very rare that we meet opposition. I did once get an invitation to speak in a church I hadn't expected to – one with different views. But I thought, Jesus would have ploughed in there, so I went. I think existing churches expect that people will come in through their doors. But many people won't – they think they're going to be struck by lightning. They don't understand that God is just there for everyone, that there's a *relationship*. You know, we're very good at letting ourselves down as Christians, and non-believers often tell us what we should do and what we should be.'

'Non-believers' is a term which seems to cover almost anyone who doesn't share their own evangelical Protestant beliefs. That this might bring them into open conflict with other faiths is ignored. There's a blithe indifference to the more militant aspects of Islam, preferring to see Muslims as people 'in darkness' or 'on the wrong road,' motivated by politics rather than faith.

This fits snugly with their wholehearted support for American military operations in Islamic countries. That they might one day find themselves facing a battle about beliefs – a real fight, as violent as any faced by missionaries in the past – is never addressed. Nor do they consider that their own beliefs might well be classed as extreme by other Christians. They're heading out, in large numbers, to a world increasingly sensitive about religion, regardless of the notion of 'religious conflict'.

With regard to martyrdom, I wondered if she ever felt she was a voice crying in the wilderness.

'I know that there are times when I am certainly alone. That can be hard, when you go out to do something that you totally believe you're supposed to be doing. But I know I am also never alone.'

Her voice warms at this point, and I catch a touch of pity that I'm not quite in the cosy fellowship, which then turns into an affirmation of her commitment. 'That companionship, if you like, is the thing that carries me through, whatever and wherever, and why the fear which I had in many areas of my life has just gone.'

There is no elaboration about the fear. In fact she has set aside any fear when considering how far she would take her faith, especially in the face of great danger.

'I've had to think that through because of the circumstances abroad, and what if the plane fell out of the sky – that's one thing. But if I'm face to face with such a thing, then I'd just have to stand. I would die for it. And I don't say that lightly. Someone was once talking about such danger – in a country where there's persecution – and that's when it hit me. How can I pray for these people if I'm not willing to take that step myself? And when I work with young people whom I love and respect, I know that somewhere down the line some of them will be martyred for their faith. And when you're in that situation I don't know how one reacts, but I'd like to think I wouldn't back down.'

I wondered if she had any thoughts about whom she would leave behind. I was met with a look of frank surprise.

'In what way?'

Family?

'But the family know, and the family understand. They stand with me on this.' It was a very matter-of-fact remark.

And she does it all in the name of what?

'In the name of Jesus, and of pleasure. I think he's done the most incredible things in my life, and I just want him to touch as many other lives as possible.'

16

The Ulster Policeman

Before I went to university, my knowledge of the police force was non-existent. I grew up in a highly law-abiding area where there was an unspoken belief that if the law was not upheld, feral creatures would dominate the earth. Respectability ruled. There was little major crime: gang warfare and murder somehow bypassed Sunderland. Poverty and drink drove most of the cases in front of the magistrates. A police inspector lived in our cul-de-sac, but the family kept themselves to themselves and their children were regarded as having drawn the short straw: 'They've *got* to be well behaved.' No one at school ever considered the police force as a career option – first, because my generation wasn't even expected to have a career, and secondly because female police officers were rumoured to have to deal with 'not very nice women', as it was put. It was thirty-five years after I had left Sunderland that an old schoolfriend pointed out that our dancing lessons were held next door to the biggest brothel in town.

I was a student in the era of demonstrations, and protest brought quite a few brushes with the law, mainly at ground level. Either you fell over when colliding with a line of constables, or you were towed away from a 'sit-in' (having lined your jeans with newspaper). There was little animosity, the Newcastle police having an all-encompassing phrase for students: pests.

As a reporter with a film crew and the prospect of hanging around for several hours to get some pictures or an interview, the main hazard was finding yourself accused of 'obstruction': a fine old law which generally meant that you were standing somewhere a policeman thought you shouldn't. Like a pavement. The way round this was to shuffle about a bit, and chat up the constable who had noticed you were a woman. Real riots, such as Southall and Brixton, placed you between opposing factions: uncomfortable, but it avoided the risk of being identified with either side. You never saw the police as your protection, and you didn't hide behind them. (This was particularly true of forces abroad, where colleagues advised three strategies: run, hide, offer them money.)

During an exceptionally difficult time during industrial strife in the early 1980s, TV crews frequently found themselves in the role of ping-pong balls between the demonstrators and the law. You expected to get thumped by both. This still surprises people who fondly imagine that journalists live in a protected bubble or carry special privileges.

'Surely no one hits you?' enquire those who have never encountered a crowd of very angry citizens.

'Like to see my scars?' is the only practical reply. I have the X-rays as well.

There's genuine disbelief that the forces of law and order, too, might raise their hand against the press, which probably shows a comforting, if rather complacent, confidence in the constabulary. However, observing the police dealing with drunken youths, violent domestics and motorway pile-ups imbues most journalists with a grudging sympathy for them, which forgives the occasional thump or two.

And happily they mostly tolerated us – except during terrorist bomb incidents. Then we were often dropped to the status of 'less than normal civilian' and herded into distant corners behind tape while local people moved freely up and down the street. All through the seventies and eighties reporters and camera crews refined methods of crawling over walls, worming their way into back bedrooms and shinning up trees in order to get a better view of a 'suspect object' from way in front of the police cordon. Not that we wished to be blown to kingdom come. We had merely spent day after day in Northern Ireland, where packages, abandoned cars and lengths of metal tubing exploded with regularity – and we had worked out how to keep a safe distance *and* get the pictures. And in Northern Ireland we had met a very different police force. Their view of the visiting press, right through the Troubles, was: 'If you want to walk down that street, that's fine by us. Your life's your own. By the by, it's a very, very big bomb. . . .'

This was a force which bore almost no resemblance to any other in Britain. Not only was it remarkably tolerant of the press when streetfuls of rioters were busy, it was armed and operated alongside the British army. But it also had its own particular problems. Indeed, at the end of the century when Chris Patton, the former Governor of Hong Kong, described it in his report on its future, he wrote: 'Policing cannot be fully effective when the police have to operate from fortified stations in armoured vehicles, and when police officers dare not tell their children what they do for a living for fear of attack from extremists from both sides.'

The history of the Royal Ulster Constabulary is entirely bound up in the origin of the Province itself. Loyalties, motivation and religious affiliation have all been shaped by the population it serves – and its divisions. Those RUC officers who served in the last thirty years of the twentieth century experienced a life as far from *Dixon of Dock Green* as you could get. And ever-present, life-threatening danger was inherent even in wearing the uniform.

'When I left our house, turned on the radio in my Vauxhall Viva, this thing was coming through: "One dead, two dead, three dead . . . the Paras are . . . ." And it seemed to me that all hell had broken loose in Northern Ireland. As a result of listening to this, I got slower and slower, driving down to the depot . . . When I entered the depot the sergeant who was to take us in wasn't there, because he was grieving for his son, Raymond Carroll, who had just been shot dead in Ardoyne, on the Cliftonville Road – just half a mile from where I lived . . . because when I was driving down to the RUC Training Centre on 30 January 1972 – it was Bloody Sunday.'

Brian McCargo had a baptism of fire the day he signed up for full-time membership of the police in Northern Ireland. And as he drove to the depot in Belfast, he also knew that he wasn't just any sort of new recruit. He was a Catholic. To those of us who arrived to report the Troubles from what was called 'the mainland' (a forbidden term in BBC-speak) the divisions in Ulster (another forbidden word) society were almost invisible. Names often sounded Irish or Scottish, or both. Ginger-haired freckled lads could turn out to be Northern Protestants just as well as Irish Catholics. Schools all seemed to have saints' names, and accents were broad and their nuances undetectable to an outsider. Admittedly, there were maps which indicated the sectarian divides – but many areas were still relatively mixed in the mid-seventies, and how were we to know that a short pipe sticking out of the first-floor brickwork of a terraced house indicated that a Protestant was in residence? (The pipe held the Union and other flags on the high days of Unionist celebrations.)

Over the years I often heard the prejudices and vicious jokes about how you told the two communities apart. But there was never enough evidence for an outsider to be certain there was substance to the suggestions. However, those born there seemed to have lightning-rod recognition of the origins of any individual in Northern Ireland. And of their religion. And it mattered – often to the point of being a matter of life and death.

Brian McCargo just wanted to be a policeman. But there was no getting away from his background, even though when he was young there was a mixing of loyalties which seemed to him perfectly natural. 'I was born and bred in Ardoyne during World War II. And there are two ends to the Ardoyne – Old Ardoyne and New, which people refer to as Glenard, which was a new estate built in the thirties. Not built for Catholics, I would suggest, but Catholics moved into it. What you got was a very mixed working-class estate, not supportive outwardly of the police, but when you consider all my contemporaries later joined the services – army, navy – that was replicated in all the streets of Ardoyne. And I was one who didn't. In those days – and this was amazing when you think of it – all these guys returning on leave walked about in their uniforms. Irish Guards, air force, navy, up to the churches. Also in those days the local police officers would have gone to mass at Holy Cross church, in full uniform. That was accepted – there was no big problem in that. But what I always wanted to be in my life was a police officer. It seemed the thing to do, and I loved the whole idea.'

Brian McCargo is recalling a Belfast where divisions were recognised but not a cause of isolation. His speech is that of someone used to precise descriptions, but peppered with little interjections – a low-key rhetorical style which has a natural rhythm and grace which softens the Belfast sound.

'My family come from two sources. Although my father and his brothers were Catholic, some of whom were very strong Nationalists, the other side came from Protestant roots, Orange Order and so on, very strong. My grandfather was a County Grand Master of the Orange Order! So somewhere along the line, things had got a bit crossed.

'But I had always had this idea that I wanted to be a police officer. I wasn't getting the encouragement, though – to join anything. But on TV at the time it was *Z Cars*, and I thought I'll maybe have a go in England. So when I was a young lad in my teens I applied to join . . . Merseyside, was it? But I didn't get in. Then at twenty years of age I went to America, and while I was there I thought I'll join the NYPD. I was told I couldn't do it until I was five years there and became a citizen. But it was the time of Vietnam, and if I joined the army I could get out and do it quicker. I applied to join the US army, but was put back because I had a touch of gangrene in my leg prior to going to America – fell on a broken bottle practising for Gaelic football. And they wouldn't allow me in until it had recovered properly. And I came home and never went back to America, because the girl who became my wife – forty-odd years ago – I met her within a week of getting home. So then I stayed in Belfast and got my old job back – I was a weighbridge engineer – but I still had this hankering to join the police.

'Which brings us almost to the Troubles, because the Hunt Report, coming out in 1969, called for more Catholics to join the police. The Nationalist politicians and the Catholic Church said more Catholics were needed, and they started this thing called the Police Reserve. So I thought maybe I'll apply for that – it seemed the right way forward. No point in criticising the police – and the B Specials as was then. You're given the opportunity to do something about it – so you don't do it. So I says, I'll be a good citizen and I want to join. I was a Catholic too – but it turned out to be everything that I had hoped for.

'I was living in Ardoyne, and there were riots between the Catholics and Protestants and people being put out of their homes, and the police couldn't cope. On 14 or 15 August 1969, the British army in their NATO helmets marched past Holy Cross church. I remember the banners: "Disperse or be shot".'

When he put in his application form, he was fully aware that the rumblings of discontent and protest were growing louder. There was already widespread rioting and the city of Londonderry had erupted – but the full intensity was yet to come.

'In my family I think there was a bit of a disbelief: "He can talk, but it'll not happen." And people said, "Why not join the Metropolitan Police or the Garda?" But I said, "That's not my home. *This* is my home." My wife was very supportive – she comes from a very quiet area, the Ravenhill Road, not Ardoyne, and she couldn't understand why people wouldn't join the police. Great encouragement from her. But at that time they weren't shooting and killing so much. So I decided to join the police, the Reserve.

'I was a very well-known Gaelic sports person. Played for the local team, which had just won the League. I was held in high regard in Gaelic circles – played for my county as well. And I knew that I was going to be thrown out of the GAA, under Rule 21.' Rule 21 of the Gaelic Athletic Association had been in place since 1886, and specifically forbade members of the British army and the RUC from joining. Names of entrants to the RUC were published in the local press. 'I remember going up to play a match, and we met in our clubrooms, and by this time there was publicity given to me in

274

the *Belfast Telegraph*, and it split the club. One half thought, "Thank God, it's good to see this", and the other half just said, "Hang on, there's Rule 21, so as a police officer you can't. . . ." Anyway, I was told that I couldn't play any more Gaelic football from that day.

'My mother had just died, which was bad enough, and that was the second blow – it was my life. But I'm a great believer in principle, and sometimes there are bigger things in this life that you have to achieve and you have to sacrifice some things. I wasn't going to take a back step. So I decided, irrespective of what they were going to say, that I was going to put my application in. And I was accepted by the police. I made an impact in the police station where I was in the Reserve, and the guys encouraged me. It was everything I'd hoped for.'

In December 1971 he decided to apply to join the RUC full-time, and was selected. But his firm, based in Nottingham, asked him to work on for a while, so another six weeks elapsed before he could report to the training headquarters known as the depot. And that was how he found himself driving to his first day of training on what turned out to be one of the most significant days of violence in the Province. Bloody Sunday, as it became known, still resonates today, and it certainly influenced the work that twenty-seven-year-old Brian McCargo was about to embark upon. At the time he was more concerned that his decision had attracted publicity, which had immediate consequences: 'Somebody had informed the press that I was joining, and my wife and my daughter – well, "they" threatened to kill them if I didn't pull out.' He runs on, saying, 'I don't know if she knows the half of this. . . .' But it's so much part of the life he's lived that he doesn't pause.

'So that was the start to my career in the police. Had I a decision to make? Well, the commander called me in and said, "Brian, this is the threat, and we'll be keeping an eye on the house – don't worry." Which they did. And I carried on. During that period there was internment and the replacement of the Stormont government – all these things, making the entire situation worse. But I thought, a year will do this, and then it'll all be over.'

He laughs as he recalls his optimism, but there are no regrets or ruefulness. 'My wife – she was keen on me joining, and I said to her, "I'll give you an undertaking: by the time I reach retirement, I'll have made superintendent. I'll work hard." I'd taken a big reduction in salary, given up sport, did all that to join the police, so I was willing to put my money where my mouth was. Later people said to me, "Oh, only in it for the money?" Absolutely not. Fifty pounds a month was my first salary.'

Nevertheless, he soon learned that he represented what you might call a tiny minority: the RUC was 9 per cent Catholic at the time, and later went down to 8 per cent. There were only two Catholics in the forty-strong squad which started training. 'The guys were very, very good, and I won the baton of honour. Absolutely, positively *not*, was I treated differently. In fact, with my personality I would have taken it as a challenge. And I went in to show people that I was a rather capable individual. You could let things eat away at you – but with me there's no bitterness. When I joined, I knew my bridges were burned and I had to get on with a new life. For instance, when I was thrown out of Gaelic football I went into Willowfield police station – as if these things are meant to happen by design – and they were looking for anyone interested in playing rugby. I'd loved the game, but wasn't allowed to play it in those days, because you weren't allowed to play "foreign" sports if you were a Gaelic player – Rule 26 said no soccer, hockey or cricket. But one door closes, another opens, and I played rugby with the RUC, ending up captain and chairman of the club. I've now been involved in rugby at the highest level for thirty-seven years.

'So maybe I worked harder than some, and I received the Queen's Police Medal and was Deputy Chief Constable of Belfast. I remember one chief constable saying, "Brian, you're too old to go to Bramshill", the police staff college, and yet I ended up doing the job he thought I possibly wouldn't achieve.'

Ambition and determination were evident at an early age. However, these weren't ordinary times. He was from a Catholic community which was fully involved in the escalating violence.

And he was on the street as a policeman. 'With the name McCargo – not too many people in Northern Ireland have it – I was singled out. In Ardoyne it was a bit strange, a bit like the Gaelic Club. There were those who fully understood what I was trying to do, and would love to have done it themselves, but didn't out of for fear for their families. *I* couldn't go home to my family, my relatives. I couldn't go to births, deaths, marriages, couldn't go to my daughter's school, because it was in the Falls Road. That was a big sacrifice. For instance, going into court, you can't hide it – I'm a police officer. Some would have spat in my eye, had they got the opportunity, and looked upon me as a traitor – others said, "Brian, it's good to see you." And over the years, those who have known me have always known they could phone and get my advice. And later there were more threats – and my wife doesn't know the half of this. There were a number of IRA ceasefires and I'd hear it said that, "The IRA are going to shoot you, before the ceasefire comes in." I lived in East Belfast – a mixed area, with good neighbours, and a Catholic church with a massive congregation then. But there was no guard put on my house, no support, no moving house, because there was nothing like that in those days. Just "Be careful when you're going home. . . ."

'Some of the hierarchy in the IRA who knew me would stop and have conversations with me – about sport and the rest of it. But if *they* didn't mention it to me directly, some of my family was being stopped and told about threats – so you got the meaning. . . . At the paramilitary Irish National Liberation Army (INLA) super-grass trial I was in charge of security, because there were disturbances in the court, and threats came through that "the inspector in the white shirt would be shot". And "they knew his home". Special Branch called me, and said, "They didn't say the name, but it looks like it's you."'

At this point, as frequently, he laughs easily. 'On a number of occasions, I had to ask myself: do I shift my home every time somebody makes a threat? I decided no, I wasn't. But I wasn't going to tell my family – they'd have worried themselves sick. I was like any other police officer: I had to check under my car, under my wife's car, and be careful not to set up routines when I picked my family up. My daughter went to a Catholic grammar school, because I wanted her to have a Catholic education, and the only one was in the Falls Road – [President of Ireland] Mary McAleese's and my wife's old school, St Dominic's. Did she ever say what her daddy did? No.'

None of this can have been easy, but these were years when everyone in Northern Ireland was touched by the Troubles. Riot, murder and bombing were part of daily life. And daily life was unrecognisable, with hi-jacked buses, handbag searches in shops, and streets patrolled by armoured Land Rovers with rifles poking out of them. Brian McCargo must have loved the job to stick at it.

'I never lost heart. I'm not built that way. I've been in situations where I've been shot at. The more they would threaten, the harder I would work at the task. And I'm still a very strong Catholic. Through all the Troubles, not only was I a Catholic in the police but I wasn't afraid to talk about it or show it. This is what I am, and this is what you are, and we can get on well and work together. When I went in to clear a bar or a shop where there's a bomb outside, like Bloody Friday, I didn't look to see if the guy on my left-hand side was a Catholic or a Protestant. All that mattered was that he could help me clear this. Or if we went in to clear a fight in a pub, you know – can this guy help me? – that's all you're interested in. You become friends. And to this day I have great friends who are not Catholic, and I spend time in Protestant churches – births, deaths, marriages and so on . . . which I find fine. But I still have my Catholicism, and my family, and I came through it. Look – Catholic and Protestant are used as a label. Then, I would have known people who were strongly motivated Republican IRA – not good Catholics, by the way, and you wouldn't find them attending mass. Many of them were Marxists. Same with the other side – very few seen inside a Protestant church until, as Gerry Fitt used to say, they're caught.

'What was good about the job was that, when I was in Donegal Pass police station and other places, I went to mass on Sundays. And sometimes my work, when I was on an early turn, didn't permit it. But the guys in the station knew that, and would cover for me: "Away you go – and we'll see you in an hour." And I was a big sportsman of course, and when I wanted to go it was "Yeah, go ahead." And these are *Protestant* guys. So here you have friends, loyal friends, and you grew up in the police with these guys. You were in the worst circumstances you could be put in, and you became dependent on each other. So there was a *goodness* within the guys themselves, and a camaraderie.

'And then there was the idea that we were trying to do something here. We're trying to hold the middle ground and stop these people slaughtering each other – Catholic, Protestant, Nationalist, whatever you wish to call them. And to go and make sure you can prevent these bombs flattening the entire city of Belfast you were putting yourself in harm's way, but you felt you were doing it for a very good reason. It was in the hope that you would give politicians room to come to terms with what was going on here.

'And if anybody let the people of Northern Ireland down, it was the politicians. They should have resolved this a lot earlier than they did. People ask me, "Do you give the IRA credit for calling a ceasefire?" I say, "Absolutely not – they shouldn't have started all this in the first place." I've no doubt that the Troubles, irrespective of discrimination, having witnessed it in this city, would have disappeared anyway through the EU and regulations and affluence – I mean, three and a half thousand people didn't have to die. . . .'

At one point in the early 1980s, the international police organisation Interpol announced that Northern Ireland held the dubious record of being the 'most dangerous place in the world to be a police officer', beating El Salvador into second place. The number of Catholics in its ranks stayed resolutely low. However, on the streets they were always a distinctive presence, never yielding their authority completely to the soldiers, which might have happened in many other countries. From a distance they seemed to us journalists a phlegmatic, solid bunch, with extraordinarily thick necks rising out of green belted raincoats. On freezing street corners they were usually chatty, though wary of divulging much information – perhaps because they knew so much of the villagey gossip which gave reason and drive to the event they were attending. As a 'foreign' reporter, I came to realise we understood very little of the internecine feuds and neighbourhood dealings which lay behind incidents which we simply labelled 'sectarian'. We could rarely unpick ordinary crime from 'political' violence.

When the RUC searched a burned-out house one morning, with screeching neighbours throwing the charred furniture into the street, the official line indicated a straightforward 'cleansing' of a family of one denomination to another area. Ten minutes of conversation with two wry-faced officers opened up a mare's nest of community shenanigans: family of mixed denominations in- volved in protection rackets, teenage son suspected of trying to get local IRA boss's daughter in the family way, meanwhile wife being 'knocked up' by owner of nearby illegal shebeen [drinking den] who owed a lot of money to . . . and so on. The idea that in Northern Ireland there were simple lines and straightforward motives crumbled every time you peered a little closer: underneath lay complex rivalries and old scores and sheer criminality. All of which were an active undercurrent to a scenario which – on TV screens at least – looked like a simple civil war. Though the war- like atmosphere was real enough, as Brian McCargo recalls.

'How often have you seen guys marching down with bands and going to be wiped out? I mean, it's the same as going to war. It's true, too, that there was the excitement. You would be a liar to say certain circumstances didn't give you a buzz. There was some- times a thing like that in Northern Ireland. The difference in Northern Ireland is that it went on for thirty years. I'm not a person who's easily got down, but one of the things you'd have said, particularly now, is "Oh, Jesus, are these parades going to start again?" Because it starts off a cycle of street violence for weeks, and you were going to have to get in between people and take the bricks and the bottles and the abuse again and again and again. All you're saying is, can people not see reason here? Why do they have to march down *this* road? Or if it's a small parade, then why *can't* it march down this road? And you feel, here we go again . . .

'Bear in mind I'm having to stand *between* Protestant and Catholic crowds. And the abuse is: "Get out of the road and let us get at these people – you're holding us back. Just give us twenty-four hours." Quite often I used to say, "Go ahead." I mean, *not one* of them would have budged' – again he laughs heartily. 'Then on the other hand, Catholics were saying, "You're part and parcel of the whole organisation and institutions which allow all this to happen." And you get the abuse. I used to have to go in the early hours of the morning to raid homes and arrest people, looking for guns and things – and you got the abuse from *both* sides. One of the things when you're doing ordinary policing is "Can I see your tax disc?" And you get: "Oh, you wouldn't do this up the Falls" and so on. You're always accused of being afraid to do that – which is totally wrong, of course. But that's how they saw it – the Catholics. And the Loyalists saw it as: "We're your *friends*, you can live in our area . . . *we're* not putting you out of your house." Which is true, because if I couldn't have lived in East Belfast, where could I have lived?'

The RUC statistics of injuries and fatalities back up the Interpol assessment: over three hundred murdered and nine thousand injured. And where else might you get a summer garden party in the grounds of the imposing Hillsborough Castle, attended by Princess Alexandra, which includes prayers and the reading of a Roll of Honour and a line of weeping widows and their children? I hadn't realised that all the people in their hats and best summer frocks were heading for a memorial service. But no one else thought it odd. Life in the RUC was dangerous. Every minute, according to Brian McCargo.

'Being in the police, doing your duty in those times, was dangerous in itself. Bearing in mind my entire life – round the Border, in South Armagh, into West Belfast – I've had people talking to me one minute and heard of their death in the next sixty. I remember the captain of the rugby club, Norman McCabe, asking me one day coming out of Castlereagh police station if I would ensure that certain players from there would be up at the ground because he had to go over to Springfield Road police station. When I phoned the players to tell them one of them said, "Have you not heard the news? A police officer's been shot dead." I didn't ask, but I knew it was Norman McCabe.

'Or you're down in Armagh, where you're speaking to a young fellow who's been in hard station for years, and you're saying to him, "Look, I know you're getting married. We'll ensure that you get a station which is reasonably good – out of harm's way a little bit." And two weeks later he's being buried from a church right beside where I live.' There's a long silence at this point. I remember the sombre RUC funerals that I went to, with lines of slow marching men, uniforms and a terrible silence on all the roads to the church.

The memories come in a rush: 'Or you've guys killed in a helicopter crash, and you're leading the way saying, "Guys, let me get on the next helicopter, because if I don't do it . . ." – you know, you've got to lead. You've got to put things in the back of your mind and get on with it. And it was not just a question of terrorism, deaths and people injured, but it was the lifestyle of many police officers that killed them. Some of them you were talking to, and the next thing they were committing suicide, or being killed in car crashes, as they were driving home exhausted. You can either dwell on that, let it get you down, or be determined and get on and do a job and put all these things in the back of your mind and lead. . . . I never counted how many colleagues I lost.'

All through these terrible times he lived in a Protestant area with his family. He has two daughters, one in her early twenties, the other in her mid-thirties. 'Well, my young one is hardly aware of anything. Where we live, she's never seen trouble. She does know what it's about and she does know I was a police officer. Both of them – and the oldest one in particular even to this day – are very guarded about saying I was a police officer. I used to lecture and do things for the police service at university, and I studied for a Master's Degree in Civil Law at the University of Ulster, and I used to tell them, "Just say your father's a law lecturer" – I thought I might as well pick a half-decent profession. And they used to come and ask me to talk about it!

'My wife *never* ever said what I did. She was worried sick. As Catholics we were in the invidious situation that, if we asked someone to do work on our house, we had to take down the picture of the Sacred Heart and so on in case they were Loyalists. And we had to remove everything in the house related to policing in case they were Nationalists. You *couldn't* have hung your police shirts out on the line – in the old days when I was a constable, a sergeant, they were green and quite easily spotted. You just had to be careful. So your family was indoctrinated to lie, basically. But I have no regrets, not at all.'

And he did it in the name of what?

'To serve the community. And that's all I ever wanted to do as a police officer. Talk to people, help people. I still do – that's why I do so much voluntary work. And then when I saw the way things were going, it was to see a day when Northern Ireland would settle down and peace would break out. And that's where we are, just at the moment. We're on the verge of history – for the whole of Ireland.'

17

The Campaigner

'Come and see how our new politics are working,' said Galina Starovoitova to me at a media conference in Turkey in September 1998. She was a bundle of energy, a leading female deputy in the Russian parliament, with untamed red hair and an eclectic dress sense. 'Come to Petersburg – come now.' She was passionate and articulate, and at the heart of the fight for a fairer and more democratic Russia. She got out her diary and insisted I make plans, and I looked forward to going to stay with her, for it was the old Leningrad that I had seen almost thirty years before. Exactly eight weeks later, when I had identified a weekend that would suit us both, she was found in the stairwell of her apartment with several bullets in her.

In Sri Lanka in 1989, the urbane and Oxford-educated Lalith Athulathmudali handed me a large gin and tonic in his elegant Colombo garden and shrugged when I suggested that political life in the otherwise magical island was an ugly litany of murder and massacre. 'Absolutely true,' he replied, then added with breathtaking frankness and no sense of irony, 'but we are a violent people.' We were sitting in a cloud of insects at sunset, with Lalith, a former cabinet minister, sprawled rather awkwardly in a large garden chair. He had been caught in a bomb blast in Colombo's parliament buildings a couple of years earlier, but survived and continued his political campaigning, interrupted with bouts of surgery. It was a time of great unrest, with several factions using both assassination and mass murder by suicide bomb. Lalith was philosophical; a former Minister of National Security, he was inured to personal safety precautions, attacked several times, and was widely quoted for remarking, 'In a terrorist war, a few fellows can still do a lot of harm.' Four years later, a young man approached through a large crowd at a rally he was addressing and killed him with two bullets.

Having reported from much of eastern Europe under Communist rule, I used to return full of blessing for our own democratic political process. As a journalist you were constantly stopped by policemen demanding, 'Papers, papers' – only to realise that the rest of the population was equally harassed by this, the simplest form of control over ordinary citizens, and always abused. Then there were the political prisoners, the 3 a.m. arrests, the censorship and the pervasive fear of being found to be critical of the system: all demanding a great deal of courage from dissenters. I can still hear the animated voices dropping to silence as we knocked on the door in Prague where we had been taken to meet Vaclav Havel before Czechoslovakia had its 'velvet revolution'. All eyes were on us as we entered. It was a frozen moment before they accepted that we had come to hear their political plans, not to haul them off to jail and destroy them.

It is also extremely common these days to deploy international observers to check that elections are carried out in a proper manner. Violence and intimidation are regular guests at some polling stations, and corruption embedded in the process. Democracy has to be nurtured and defended, and is often a risky business.

Luckily, politics in Britain doesn't usually involve much in the way of physical danger. The hustings, in their present form of carefully choreographed exchanges, have little of the red-blooded energy displayed in elections a century ago, where a good riot and a personal attack on candidates often substituted for a frank exchange of views. But, having no traditional party political blood, I have always been much more interested in individuals who take on campaigns for social justice, or those who stand up for the minority, or people who raise their voices against authority or convention. When I joined the national newsroom in London I never caught the excitement of party campaigning, spending several general elections on weird Bus Tours with Attitude, where teams of enthusiasts pushed nervous ministers into photo opportunities with people who had no idea who they were meeting. At the end of the day, no one in London wanted to know what had happened to our political bigwig unless it chimed with the topic that the other parties were arguing about. The only hope of getting your quarry on the national TV news was if he or she was tellingly heckled or clutched a particularly odd-looking animal or object. Watching a party worker imploring villagers in a Yorkshire beauty spot to produce 'at least one sheep pleeeease' to complement the shepherd's crook the minister had borrowed didn't ignite any desire in me to concentrate on political stories.

However, if you combine charisma and a passion, back it with courage in the face of danger and then have it collide dangerously with politics, that's more intriguing. Add wildlife, and you get Richard Leakey. Who has something of a family tradition to live up to.

The Victoria Cross has often been awarded posthumously since the valour displayed has included laying down one's life for others. The only VC won in East Africa in World War II went to a sergeant in the King's African Rifles. Nigel Gray Leakey was born in Kenya, and when he was twenty-seven found himself fighting in Abyssinia (now Ethiopia) in the campaign to end Mussolini's fascist occupation of the region. The Italians lost ground in hard fighting; the capital, Addis Ababa, had already fallen and Emperor Haile Selassie had returned. But in this vast and mountainous country there were still a number of Italian troops resisting.

On 19 May 1941, Sergeant Leakey was with two companies of the Rifles near Collito, having reached the River Billate, when Italian tanks suddenly emerged from the bush and opened fire. His citation reads:

With complete disregard for his own safety and in the face of withering machine-gun fire from the enemy's ground troops and from the tanks in front, Sergeant Leakey leaped on the top of the tank which was coming in from behind [the British] position and wrenched open the turret. With his revolver, he shot the commander of the tank and the crew, with the exception of the driver, whom he forced to drive into cover. Having failed to get the cannon of this tank to fire, he dismounted calling out 'I'll get them on foot!' and charged across the ground which was being swept by machine-gun and shell fire from the other enemy tanks, which were advancing and causing casualties to our infantry. In company with an African CSM and two other askari [enlisted men] he proceeded to stalk these tanks. The first two tanks passed but Sergeant Leakey managed to jump on to the third tank and opened the turret and killed one of the crew before the fourth tank opened fire with a machine-gun and shot him off the tank . . . the superb courage and fighting spirit which Sergeant Leakey displayed, facing almost certain death, was an incentive to the troops who fought on with inspiration after witnessing the gallantry of this NCO's remarkable feat. . . .

'And all while stark bollock naked.' This observation is not in the citation but comes from a man more than familiar with the need for courage in the face of opposition. Richard Leakey has led a life full of adventure. His father was the cousin of Nigel Gray Leakey's father, and his tale of the VC includes a few details that only families tend to know. The Italian counter-attack was so sudden and unexpected that it caught some of the Rifle company washing in the river. There was no time for fretting about being properly dressed. Sergeant Leakey advanced with just his revolver, nothing else, and one can only imagine the last image the Italian tank crews were given.

He tells the story with delight and laughter, in a swift and compelling manner. Everything about him delivers a message that he's forthright and confident and hugely energetic. A tall, well-built man, often called 'Africa's Wildlife Warrior', he exhibited no sign of his disabilities as he strode to greet me. He takes everything, including two artificial legs, literally in his stride.

The Leakeys are a remarkable family and have left their stamp on our knowledge of several disciplines. Louis and Mary, Richard's parents, were outstanding archaeologists and palaeontologists, contributing to our knowledge of human origins through their discoveries of fossils while excavating in the Rift Valley. Richard, the second of their three sons, had the kind of childhood in Kenya which might have been ascribed to a young Indiana Jones.

'I grew up in an environment that had adventure round every corner. When I was at secondary school, one could get home and ride a horse in what is now a national park. Within twenty minutes of home, you could be seeing rhino and lions – and we were unsupervised. Coming back one evening as a teenager from seeing a girl, having borrowed my parents' car and gone a few miles, I parked the car, walked through the property, heard the metal gate clanking and put on the flashlight – and there's seven lions trying to climb over it.'

But despite the thrills, he felt it hardly compared to his father's young life. 'My father was born in Kenya in 1901 and he had an even more colourful childhood. There were very few kids of European extraction in the country at that time, so he joined young warriors and went on all sorts of trips. I used to be hugely jealous of his adventurous lifetime and set out to have as much fun as I could, just to try to keep up with his stories.'

To many it would seem a rather hazardous existence, but the boys revelled in it and fear wasn't an issue: 'I don't think we felt any danger from nature. I was old enough to have recollections of Mau Mau [terrorists] and the efforts to push the British out of the country, and everyone who was older seemed to have guns. We were very nervous about getting home in time and we had guards outside the place – there was a sense of danger there, but not particularly alarming to a ten-year-old.'

However, there were already signs that he was prepared to stand his ground and take an independent line, even at school. He seemed to relish dealing with opposition and I wondered when he first became aware of this. 'I went to a school in Kenya which was still run on the English lines of very serious discipline, meted out by both schoolmasters and senior prefects. And it was physical punishment – beatings and exercises to the point of exhaustion and stupid things like that. A lot of the boys in my year didn't do very well under it, and they left and went to other schools or had personality crises. I seem to have revelled in it. And it taught me, early on, that you did what you wanted to do. If you thought a rule was stupid, you broke it, and you didn't cry if you got punished for it. I think the school had a huge impact on my ability to see ahead, decide what I wanted to do and do it, irrespective of the consequences.' That streak of ruthlessness has served him well. It has enabled him to take on a challenge, push through a plan, let criticism bounce off him and come back for more trouble.

Richard was initiated early into the world of fossils, accompanying his parents on excavations and getting a practical rather than an academic schooling. But, anxious not to follow immediately in his father's footsteps, while still a teenager he started his own safari business. He trapped wild animals (but didn't kill on safari), led expeditions and became an expert on bones. He taught himself to fly, which led to his curiosity being awakened by a fossil site he had seen from the air – and then he was back into the family passion, leading an expedition to the shores of Lake Natron. However, he realised that his lack of academic qualifications excluded him from any credit for what was found, so he took himself off to London intending to read for a degree. But he was soon back in Kenya, earning money from a photographic safari business, fossil hunting and taking on the directorship of the Kenya National Museum, which gave him his first taste of the manoeuvrings needed to cope with public office in Nairobi: 'I never really felt, for a number of years, in trouble in any dangerous sense. But I suppose at the museum we started doing things that raised eyebrows, recommending changing the rules, because rare fossils were being exported.'

He was hugely busy running the museum, beginning to tussle with corruption and still excavating. And within a few years his fossil finds changed the landscape of the origins of man. Skulls and bones of the earliest traces of upright human beings were unearthed, including the almost complete skeleton of a *Homo erectus*, dubbed the Turkana Boy, who lived one and a half million years ago. Richard was famous, featuring in the media, and he might have continued to hunt for fossils. But throughout the eighties you couldn't be in Kenya, with a love of its landscape and an intimate knowledge of its animals, without realising that you were looking at a country in serious trouble. The bones in the museum were being rivalled by the bones of animals poached for their hide and horns and meat. A far-reaching and vicious trade was in progress, not in the obscure reaches of Africa but in the National Parks. And Leakey was vociferous on the subject.

The most obvious decline was in the number of elephants. Ivory was fetching rich rewards on the international market, and in fifteen years Kenya lost 85 per cent of its elephant population. The National Parks became a graveyard for more than fifty thousand elephants and countless rhino. Nor were they safe for humans: what should have been the jewels of the tourist business were turning into dangerous places, roamed by poachers armed with semi-automatic rifles.

When the tourists stopped coming, the Kenyan government was forced to act. To the surprise of everyone, President Moi called on Richard Leakey to tackle the problem. The surprise extended to Leakey, who heard of his proposed appointment as head of the Wildlife Service via the radio. His response to this new challenge was not that of a mild-mannered palaeontologist worried about statistics.

The poachers were well armed, numerous and ruthless. So Leakey declared war on them. The sky over the National Parks buzzed with helicopters and spotter planes. On the ground a fighting force, imbued with Leakey's principles of good leadership and resolve, and equipped with vehicles, guns and plenty of ammunition, was trained in aggressive action. Intelligence gathering was instituted, and the order went out that poachers were to be shot on sight. This was not quite what had been expected, and was clearly going to cost rather more than had been envisaged. Unfazed, Leakey turned to international sources and raised $150 million, mainly from the World Bank.

Publicity was a weapon too, with his announcement that this would be 'an opportunity to see and film dead poachers, rather than dead animals'. At first he had great success – over a hundred poachers were killed. But soon there were murmurings: did he value animals more than humans? So he set his sights on those who ran the trade in ivory, castigating those who 'bought trinkets and baubles' in the rest of the world. Then he dreamed up a publicity stunt which still symbolises the size and awfulness of the trade. A huge pyre of tusks was built: containing 12 tons of ivory worth $3 million, it represented 1800 poached elephants. The President was invited to light the fire, the TV cameras rolled and the images of the blackening shapes of precious ivory poking skywards through the flames went round the world. The price of ivory fell from over $100 a pound to $3, and in a matter of months the 'trinkets and baubles' industry (mainly in India and China) had declined by 85 per cent.

His success, with the return of tourists to safe National Parks, generated envy, and his forthright manner didn't please everyone. He had also come near those who had made a pretty penny out of the trade through their contacts and influence: the politicians and businessmen. The loudest noises came from government ministers, who whinged that Leakey would only deal with the President; it dented their dignity, they said. What they didn't say was that both politicians and officials wanted a piece of the action.

Leakey was unimpressed with those 'who wanted to get rich on public funds'. 'I came up against people who were obviously making money out of what they were doing, and I was trying to stop them. I received what are referred to as ominous threats:

"People are going to shoot you, people are going to kill you . . . you're going to regret very quickly what you're proposing" and so on. But it always seemed to me more bluff than reality. It certainly was never something that I took home and discussed with the family or really thought a lot about – except how *irritating.*'

The threats continued. In 1993 his single-engine plane lost power and crashed near Nairobi. He was badly injured, and both of his legs had to be amputated below the knee. Sabotage was suggested, but he himself says, 'Who knows?' and concentrates on his convictions: 'I think most people have a pretty strong sense of their own – it's probably a pretty stupid position to take – of their own invincibility. You have a conviction you think you have thought through, and you believe it's unassailable in terms of morality, or in terms of the needs of a particular situation. I certainly found that once I had that sense of commitment, the rest didn't really bother me at all.

'And I grew up in a country where there was masses of wildlife which gave me enormous pleasure. I have a strong feeling that natural space, natural ecology, natural habitat, natural animals are a valuable asset for a country and for a people. And its needless destruction by greed and negligence always struck me as something you should try to stop. I guess I'm not fatalistic, but I really don't think we can afford to wipe out wildlife on the planet at this stage. And I think far too few people try to stop some of these things that are going wrong on the planet. I think we should all make a bigger effort to try to correct some of the wrongs and make the world a better place. Not just leave it as we found it, but try to improve on some of the awful things that *Homo sapiens* has done and continues to do.'

Other men might have left it at that. Richard Leakey, forced out of the Wildlife Service by the very politicians who appointed him, decided that if you can't beat 'em you join 'em and started his own political party. There he ran into more trouble, for his platform was that of 'open and honest' government and he launched it straight at those who were on the take in public life: 'Corruption is rampant at all levels in the public service. Not just the big people taking commissions on contract, but everywhere. No person, when in the service of the people, should be beyond scrutiny, reproach or discipline. Standards are falling. The people are being cheated. Something must be done.'

He was elected to parliament, but his party, Safina, regularly came under attack. Had he expected life as a politician to be so rumbustious?

'Well, I'm not sure that I'd really thought about it. But certainly being chased by police in unmarked cars, and having every phone call listened to, and having police follow me if I went to a meeting of more than five people when we were setting up the opposition party, and having the police teargas them to stop it. . . . It became rather fun, really, to see if we could outwit them. And I never thought of it as dangerous.

'Certainly, when I got into trouble at one of the meetings I was beaten rather severely, and I think an attempt was made to kill me – but it didn't work. It had been announced on the national radio the day before that I shouldn't proceed to my destination, because there was trouble expected. Some of my political colleagues said, "Are you sure you want to go?" because it seemed to them that the government was determined to stop the meeting. And I said, "No. Let's go earlier and let's get the trouble out of the way and get on with what we have to do." I felt that if you give in to threats you might as well get out. You can't proceed with leadership if you get put off.

'Many's the time in my public life, and in government, that there were bomb threats in our offices. And they were clearly aimed at destabilising my position. I thought most of these were simply threats, and I stayed in my office and said, "We've got work to do and we can't keep running out of the office every other day just because somebody says there's a bomb threat." And maybe it was foolhardy, but I didn't take the threats seriously. The police did – but there was never any bomb found. And after a while it became boring for everybody – and they stopped it!"

In the upside-down world of Kenyan politics, it happens that the President describes a man as a foreigner, an atheist and a racist; then appoints him head of the Civil Service, to clear up corruption. Leakey made some headway and improved Kenya's standing with international financiers. But the roots of corruption go very deep and spread widely, and trouble was bound to occur. Nevertheless he stuck to his guns: 'There are probably an awful lot of people who feel privately more strongly than I do, but I'm always frustrated by the unwillingness of people to stand up and be counted. In my experience, people have a far stronger interest in preserving their status quo, and rocking the boat is something they don't wish to do in public. When it comes to leading, to putting your name or your life on the line, they're very reluctant. And I find that a little irritating. You know, I believe very strongly that certain things should be done in certain ways, and if it requires someone to say it, and someone to fight that position, I'm quite happy to do so.

Eventually Leakey made too many enemies and stepped down, saying he wanted to grow grapes on his farm in the Rift Valley. . . . But he is now prominent in the climate debate – everything he sees about him in Africa spurs him on to speak out, whatever the controversy he stirs up.

'The indifference is very worrying. I'm somewhat incredulous at times that people fail to see the obvious signs of climate change. The implications for our species are enormous. It's not something we can deal with overnight. We need to position ourselves as far ahead of time as we can – at least to slow down what's already started to happen. And I guess I'm puzzled by the unwillingness of intelligent people to think this through and look at the consequences of what's happening. And yet in another sense, quite suddenly attitudes do change – in the last five years, particularly in North America and in the conservative elements of Europe, there's been a rapidly changing awareness, which is very positive. But I don't think this comes about unless people go out and talk a lot and make the statements – and yes, you do get ridiculed at times, accused of over-reacting, regarded as a bit fuzzy-wuzzy in the way you look at the world. But so what? These things have to be said.'

There he goes again. Speaking out. And the grapes can't be getting too much attention, because he's once again grasped the nettle of corruption and is Kenya's representative on the anti-corruption body Transparency International, in a country which is still a byword for graft. So what on earth sustains him?

'I'm not sure. I think it's partly a sense of enjoyment, of adventure. I think that when the adrenalin's flowing, and things are looking challenging, and you get the satisfaction of coming out the other side, there's a sense of almost a missionary view. I'm not at all religious and I've no time for faith-based systems – but then again I have a sense of trying to get things done the right way, things that are beneficial to other people in the community. I think there's a zealousness in that . . . that probably drives missionaries and other do-gooders. My mother always said that I had a missionary gene! But not from a religious point of view.'

He's laughing and has confidence in what he does. And he gives out that slight amused restlessness that hints of seeking adventure.

'Yes – and it seems less and less easy to find when you get middle-aged. But listen, I *do* enjoy adventure enormously.'

Was he still looking for trouble? Again, he laughs a lot.

'Yes, if possible. But I've just accepted this anti-corruption job. And an awful lot of people have raised their eyebrows and questioned my wisdom in taking it on. But by the same token, *someone* has to get up and say what's happening and, if there's a risk, be prepared to take the risk and present the evidence. And certainly *I'm* prepared to bear the brunt of whatever criticism arises from exposing mass corruption. It's fine by me.

'It's an adventure – but it still has to be done, and maybe younger people who've got kids at school and who are starting their careers can't afford to do so. But I've had a very full and complete life – I've got international stature of some kind. The world needs people who can afford to be bumped off, if you like, in the cause of what's *right*.'

And he does it in the name of what?

'In the name of Kenya. I would like to see Kenya come right, become a moral country in the continent of Africa. I would like to see some of the stupidities dealt with firmly and let the majority of people enjoy a stable country where due process of law and a future are guaranteed. I'm an old-fashioned nationalist. I would put country first, before anything else.'

18

The Idealist

In a decade, China has become unrecognisable to seasoned travellers. The streets are gone that I ran through in 1989, when the Chinese army was mowing down its own citizens in the violent end to protest in Tiananmen Square. Beijing's little alleys and traditional courtyard houses have been bulldozed in the name of progress. At night, a spiky skyline of glass and concrete, prinked with marble and garishly lit, has replaced that slightly sinister view of an orderly city, under ugly orange lamps and very much under control. A Ferrari costing tens of thousands of bicycles is the admired mode of transport. Tens of thousands of bicycles have been dumped for modest family runabouts, and the air is thick enough to eat.

Shanghai is crane-heaven, the population in the region swollen to uncountable numbers as Chinese Dick Whittingtons set out from their medieval villages in search of their fortunes. Occasionally a decrepit fireworks factory goes bang, or a tiny band of peasants confronts the all-powerful party-business machine as farms and shacks are mulched into the ground for yet another high-rise statement of affluence. The dividing line between state, party, army and private business is difficult to discern. Millions are entering the brave new world of consumerism. A billion more are wondering when – or if – they will get their chance.

Much of history would tell us that it's inevitable that civil society would be undergoing a parallel revolution alongside the economic tsunami. But the Chinese imperial-Communist bureaucracy has centuries of resistance to draw on. Press freedom, human rights, individual justice at law, freedom of speech, openness in government – indeed representative government: none has been invited to the economic feast. All are deemed either irrelevant or an enemy of progress. Great cunning is employed to control information from the wider world, and threat is used to prevent ordinary Chinese people joining an international conversation.

Every so often, there's a squeak of protest from campaigners for justice, religious groups, internet users or dispossessed peasants. Gauging the spread of discontent, the numbers who dissent from the party line, is difficult. All nations have their fair share of weirdos, whingers, pests and trouble-makers, many prone to exaggeration. However, the investors who flock to get a slice of the economic feast do not enquire closely into the sounds of pain and repression from under the table. And the vastness of the land and the traditional need not to 'lose face' discourage outside investigation.

Even so, some strands of individual – and apparently provocative – behaviour have emerged. Not a few tourists staring across the grey killing-ground of Tiananmen Square have been diverted by a minor rumpus nearby. Seemingly innocuous middle-aged people who had been waving their arms mildly in the air, as if they were swimming through pleasant treacle, suddenly get the kind of treatment reserved for a bunch of would-be suicide bombers. Screamed at, pounced on, beaten, kicked and eventually hurled into a van by some kind of officials, these little groups are carted off – and not only the tourists fail to learn their fate. Another instance of the peculiar reality of Falun Gong.

Halfway across the world, in a much smaller country also experiencing great change, Zhao Ming sits in a modern apartment complex which the Irish government likes to think is the symbol of its new-found prosperity. It's all bright brick and big glass balconies, which the rain over south Dublin was gently washing as Zhao walked gingerly to the door. He is thirty-six, but not as athletic as he might like: his beliefs and the Chinese government have seen to that. He is happy to see me, although three other Falun Gong practitioners whom I contacted were nervous about talking.

'Yes, we're monitored – by the Chinese authorities, who'd like to make trouble for us,' says Zhao. 'But Western countries are governed by law, so I don't think they could do much.' In the living room is a portrait of a Chinese man, with several fresh flower heads arranged below it. Zhao makes coffee, produces a large plate of biscuits and begins to talk in a very soft voice, only hunting very occasionally for a precise word in English. I've read some of the literature, handed out by the activists who keep a permanent silent vigil opposite the Chinese Embassy in London. But I'm still trying to understand exactly what Falun Gong entails. Is it a religion? A cult? A set of harmless keep-fit exercises? Whatever it is, it's very Chinese. And Zhao says, 'It has made me a different person. Changed me utterly.'

To call it 'self-development' would be to use a rather inadequate phrase for something which covers a long Chinese tradition of blending moral philosophy with a set of physical meditative exercises. Known as Qigong ('energy work'), it has many variants, mostly intended to improve health and 'harmony of mind and body'. It has cousins in Yoga and T'ai Chi, and in many parts of Asia it's common to see groups of people quietly going through gentle stretching movements early in the morning in public parks.

'Cultivating virtue' might be one way of describing the philosophical side, which marks out Falun Gong from mere physical exercise. And here it draws on a mixture of Confucianism, Taoism, Buddhism and not a little extra-terrestrial belief. However, the emphasis is on moral principles – living your life with truthfulness, compassion and tolerance.

For Falun Gong practitioners, as they call themselves, there is no central organisation, no membership, no fund-raising, no political agenda, and the founding figure, Li Hongzhi, is not worshipped. Zhao Ming has a picture of Mr Li, 'the Master', in his living room in Dublin, but it's more a reminder that he's an exile far from home – as is Li, who is now in the United States.

Zhao has just finished his master's degree in computer science at Trinity College – but it has taken him almost seven years, because of the intervention of the Chinese government in his life.

'I came here in March 1999. Before, I was working for five years in an IT company in China, after graduation from university in Beijing. I was born in Chang Chun in north-east China. China, as you know, is a developing country and it's a common dream for people to get abroad, and even stay outside, because life in China is difficult, both financially and in terms of freedom. My family's academic – my father is a retired professor, and my mother was a fellow student of his. She worked in the Automobile Design Institute in my home city. It has one of the biggest car plants and has a research institute attached. They're now in their sixties. I was born in 1971, during the cultural revolution – so, luckily, they were not old enough to be victimised. Chairman Mao wiped out intellectuals who were in their forties and fifties. Their generation was totally brainwashed by Mao, but also very aware of how you can get into trouble with the government.'

And so Zhao, like many of today's young and ambitious Chinese, might have studied abroad, perhaps settled for a while, but always intending to go back to China. What got in the way was his health: he was the weedy kid who always caught everything that was going around. 'In my childhood and as a student I wasn't a very strong person physically, often feeling tired, got colds easily, with poor digestion. I was just not well, and my parents worried about me all the time. My two elder brothers were stronger than me.'

His parents' fussing about a young man starting out on his career coincided with a period of massive change in China. The abrupt espousal of a capitalist ethic by Deng Xiaoping, brushing away decades of grinding sacrifice by declaring 'to get rich is glorious', was overwhelming for millions of citizens. In the early 1990s, many felt bemused or betrayed as the party machine headed off in the direction of a free-market economy. What were they supposed to believe? One consequence was the return of the Qigong exercise groups to the parks – they had been suppressed under the Maoist regime. In Chang Chun, Zhao's family took an interest.

'My cousin's husband was a Qigong fan, and he told my mother about Falun Gong after he went to a lecture and heard the Master, Li Hongzhi. Many Qigong schools were spreading throughout the country at the time, and Li Hongzhi actually comes from my home city. My mother was suffering from high blood pressure, heart trouble and diabetes, and she had to take medication every day. Immediately after she started her blood pressure improved, and after practising Falun Gong for two years she gave up all her medicines. In 1993 I graduated and started work as a software programmer in Beijing. But I'd spend hours trying to get to sleep, and was worn out at work the next morning. And my digestion was poor – I just couldn't finish my meals, no appetite at all.

'So then I went to a public lecture given by the Master, and I tried to practise regularly. The physical effect started *immediately*: I got to sleep, I regained my appetite, and physically I changed totally. That was one aspect of the effect.'

Zhao doesn't talk as if a miracle has taken place. It merely seems logical to him that this should have happened. He's more animated about the change to his thinking and all he had been taught at school and college.

'The other aspect was what the Master *said*. After the cultural revolution, when Chairman Mao persecuted the intellectuals, put them into labour camps and killed them, teachers were despised. So the traditional culture of China was lost, and the new textbooks were completely Communist, atheist and without any of the old Chinese way of thinking – the philosophy, the culture. So what the Master said was interesting and fresh to me: I'd never heard it. It seemed so convincing to me. Later I began to understand how enormously effective it was.

'I've gone deep into the philosophy. When I was working in my first year after graduation the country was developing economically, people were all struggling to make money, excited about it: "It is glorious to be rich". Bill Gates wasn't as rich then as he is now, but my college friends and I were reading about him and thought that was what *we* wanted. And then I heard this lecture which made me realise that the true meaning of life doesn't depend on money, and that we are predestined – that the wealth of the world is limited and not everyone can become a billionaire, that it is just fate whether you can be wealthy or a high official. Then I changed. I realised that in the pursuit of money people do a lot of bad things, ignore the principles of fairness and don't treat people in the traditionally moral way. I thought this wasn't how one should lead one's life. It's a very big change.'

His conviction is obvious. He speaks with warmth and glances round the apartment he shares with two couples and their children. He appears to have, or want, few material possessions. Zhao wasn't in any way alone in his ideas. Falun Gong grew quickly and attracted huge numbers of adherents – 70 million were estimated in China. Senior party officials and intellectuals took it up. Then, after a few rumblings in the official press about superstition and false science, a vituperative article was published which declared that Falun Gong was actually a risk to health. A group of practitioners who protested in the city of Tienjin were arrested and beaten up by the police. The response was not what the authorities were expecting. Over ten thousand people gathered silently outside the Communist party's headquarters at Zhongnanhai, on the edge of Tiananmen Square. They sat there from dawn until late at night, sending in a request for those arrested to be released. Then they gathered up their litter and left without incident.

The last time such a demonstration had taken place was during the pro-democracy rallies in 1989. To a Westerner like me it had seemed a very orderly, rather prim event amid the lengthy protests in the nearby square, with neatly dressed students sitting around debating social change and stuffing their litter into carrier bags. However, afterwards it was reported that the old men in Zhong-nanhai were both frightened and outraged at this 'show of strength' on the doorstep of their private enclave next to the Forbidden City. And their subsequent response – indiscriminate slaughter on the streets of the capital – reinforced their reputation as ruthless guardians of their own power.

Zhao had seen some of the articles trickling out of official sources in the previous few years, and hadn't been concerned: 'It didn't worry me much, because Falun Gong was such a critical part of my life – I thought it was *right*. So it wasn't worrying me to hear that others thought differently. My instinct told me I was right. It was so different from what I'd learned when I was young. It's about the right way to treat people. I went on with my exercises, for an hour every day. There's no requirement for them to be done in public, but in China no one wants to stay at home! We don't have big apartments, so it's natural to go to the park – early morning, *everyone*'s there. And I never ran into trouble before the persecution started.'

And anyway he was off to Ireland, taking up the prized chance to study abroad. 'I came here in March 1999, and the persecution began in July that year.' He had been in Dublin just four months when the Chinese authorities declared Falun Gong an 'evil cult'. It's a phrase which doesn't imply merely disapproval of something, but the determined intention to stamp it out. A total ban was announced and a major campaign got underway. Media campaigns, demonisations, arrests, beatings, imprisonment without trial, torture and the removal of organs from live prisoners – all have been documented since. And Zhao found himself one of the statistics.

'When I went back at Christmas time for a holiday in 1999, I went to the central government's Appeals Office to speak up for Falun Gong. The police arrested me there. They said, "The government has declared Falun Gong illegal." But I replied, "The law isn't like that. There's no such saying in the law that Falun Gong is illegal, and no one's entitled to say this. I've done nothing illegal, and I'm entitled to practise."'

Zhao's voice rises, and he spits out his words with all the vehemence of the innocent. The Chinese have a complex bureaucracy, and there's a sense that every citizen should lay claim to it working according to the law. The dogmatic system of education leads to a thoroughly dogmatic insistence about how the state should behave. Despite the frequent horrible examples of government ruthlessness, there's a dogged pursuit of a Communist citizen's rights which more imaginative and worldly minds in democratic societies might find somewhat foolhardy.

So Zhao had decided to stick up for his fellow practitioners. He now has a much better understanding of what the appealing-sounding Appeals Office actually does. 'The Chinese Communist Appeals Office is a place set up not to listen to people's complaints but to provide a convenient way of arresting people who have different opinions to the official ones. You expose yourself if you go there.' He still sounds rather surprised, or even exasperated, that this might be so. 'Their way is to let the protester's local police come to Beijing and take you back home. So two Chung Chun police arrived and handcuffed me and took me to an area office in Beijing. Then four or five other practitioners were brought there. We stayed overnight and then were taken back to Chung Chun by train. At home, they separated us and interrogated us. I repeatedly said to them: "I did nothing wrong, nothing illegal. I just intended to talk to the government official there." I saw that they could threaten the practitioners who came from rural areas and were not very educated – they were easily intimidated and confused. But I was very clear. I did nothing wrong. And they found they couldn't arrest, without any reason, a person who'd studied abroad.'

He laughs at the memory. Even officials have their limits, he realises, beyond which they wouldn't be foolish enough to go. 'One of the higher officials was present when a young policeman threw me on the ground and threatened to beat me. But it wasn't effective, and late in the evening they informed my family and let me go. However, in the Appeals Office you have to identify yourself and fill in a form. I'd had to give them my passport and they'd given it to the police, who later confiscated it. So I couldn't return to Ireland.

'In March 2000 I had little to do, and my fellow students and practitioners were all in Beijing, so I went back there. And at that time they were repeatedly going to the government to protest and try to stop the persecution. And every time they did this, they were arrested and detained for a short time. And it happened over and over again. In May I was arrested again. In fact I was kidnapped by the plainclothes police, in a friend's dormitory at the Science Academy. Five of us were chatting and they came in and ransacked the place, and pushed all of us into two cars. We were taken to the local police station and separated. That night I was put into a detention centre, then sent to a labour camp. And this time I was not released easily. I came out twenty-two months later.'

I wondered about the law. Surely there was some form of trial?

'No trial. In China, a labour camp means being imprisoned without trial. Their procedure is that the detention centre's police sign a form and they request a labour camp sentence from a committee from the local city council. And this committee approves it – there's no chance of defence at all. "Disturbing social order" – that was the reason for it.'

Given China's size, I had always assumed that a labour camp would be in a remote province well away from public view. Not at all.

'The camp is in a suburb of Beijing – just a yard with big high walls around it. And there are several four-storey buildings. For non-Falun Gong practitioners, ordinary criminals, it's just a resource for the labour camp police to make money. The detainees are slave labour. You can be used any way they like. The police do their best to find contracts like folding advertising material, or making small paper boxes – fiddly, intensive work for which no one gets paid, or perhaps just enough to buy toilet paper. But us Falun practitioners – mostly they didn't let us work. They used all kinds of brainwashing techniques to force us to give up and recant. No sleep as they tried to break us with beatings. And there were beatings from other detainees – gangsters who'd been sent there for serious crimes. And the police used electric batons a lot. Also pressure squats, and just handcuffing you outstretched to a bed for a month, so your back suffered a lot. Torture. They'd get us to watch government videos, and at one twitch or lapse of concentration the gangsters would get to beat us. Some practitioners would try to resist the torture by using their exercises – but they got tortured more.'

The labour camp system is known as something of an oubliette: prisoners disappear into it, relatives have no official means of obtaining information, and many prisoners refuse to identify themselves for fear that their families (often from the same city) will suffer hostile behaviour from neighbours or police. It's an effective vicious circle of threat.

'At the beginning my family wasn't informed where I was. They had no idea about me. But while I was being shuttled between detention centres before being sent to the labour camp my family found out, because I'd landed up for a bit in my home city's detention centre before being sent back to Beijing. Then they lost track of me again. So my elder brother, who works in Beijing, went to all the prisons and asked about me, and he came to my labour camp a few times, until, by chance, a policeman coming off duty mentioned he knew of me. Until then I'd just disappeared. It's the system. They hide what they do.'

However, some statistics emerge: there are hundreds of labour camps and detention centres, some with a capacity of a thousand each. At least eight hundred Falun Gong prisoners have been either beaten or tortured to death since 1999, and the actual number is reliably thought to be nearer two thousand. Zhao Ming was fortunate.

'The original sentence was one year, but they prolonged it for another ten months. My case was highlighted in Ireland a lot, through my fellow students at Trinity College. They made great efforts campaigning to get me released. Later Bertie Aherne, the Taoiseach, raised my case during the Chinese premier's visit to Dublin, so it was very high-profile. Eventually the regime couldn't produce any real reason why I was being held. They tortured me badly before they released me, with electric shocks – and I did sign something. But my mind was very clear, and I never gave in and believed what they said.'

He was extremely lucky. And only now does he fully realise that he avoided one of the worst excesses of the present regime. 'I feel numb in my feet all the time, because of the nerve damage, the beatings. Both thighs went dark and I couldn't walk for over two weeks. But the boss stopped the gangsters from beating me on my upper body. Afterwards I realised that they were avoiding my major organs – because they harvest these organs from living people, and mostly from the practitioners of Falun Gong.'

Evidence is emerging of a major industry in China which is very much part of the great economic shift towards profit. The socialist underpinning of health finance has diminished rapidly: hospitals now have to look for other sources of income. China is now second in the world league table of organ transplants, just after the United States. Curiously, China has no organised system of organ donation. And a professed cultural aversion to it. However, vital organs are readily available, sometimes to foreigners who would otherwise face a long wait in their own countries. It is acknowledged that one source is the bodies of executed prisoners sentenced to death. But there is a huge discrepancy between the statistics from such official sources and the number of transplants, which runs into tens of thousands. And only Falun Gong prisoners have their blood tested and organs examined when they enter the prison system. All the evidence points to a grim system of 'harvesting' among the prisoners of conscience, of whom the authorities have a particular hatred.

But why? What are they frightened of? It's the same fear which gripped the old men in 1989: a challenge not only to the ruling body, but to the accepted way of thinking. Is there a conviction that the whole country must be unified in thought? Any single deviation seems to terrify the bosses, who seem determined that an alternative set of values or principles must not be allowed to flourish, however small or apparently harmless: others might follow, and unity would be breached. The party has no intention of granting permission to see life in a different light. It is difficult to appreciate this rigidity of thought and to understand why people espousing a non-violent, non-political set of values, accompanied by a lot of gentle arm-waving in public parks, should be persecuted so determinedly. When I voice my thoughts to Zhao, he laughs uproariously.

'You will never be able to understand them! Western people are always expecting that Communist officials have a normal state of mind. They have not. Low-level officials can never give any reason. They know themselves that they are telling lies. But they are pressured by higher officials, and promised a bonus if they could break these people. And they *know* that the practitioners are good people, very moral people.

'I reckon it's just Communism. And it's been running China all the time like this, giving people no freedom or independence. And no other social or independent group with a different kind of thought system – political, religious – has ever been given permission to exist. And now the problem is that we want economic change – but there's no other change coming with it.

'You know, I suffered for my belief. But I believe it's right – the right principles. And I don't want to live without it.'

I was in Tiananmen Square in June 1989, on the warm summer nights when thousands of students were camped across the huge expanse, nattering and laughing and debating and wondering if their efforts might bring about some change. Zhao was there too, but he felt ill on the 2nd – his health was letting him down once again. So he stayed away the next day, thus escaping the onslaught of the army as it shot and mowed its way into the city, showing utter indifference to its own people. But he was still prepared a decade later to challenge such a regime. In the name of what?

'Truthfulness, compassion and tolerance.'

Those who choose dangerous work have a common thread of purposeful determination, which includes neither fatalism nor impulsive behaviour.

We can all understand something of the courage it takes to face up to daily danger, because when the unexpected happens, we recognise our own limitations. Covering news stories I watched all kinds of people face unexpected danger and react in a hundred different ways. Time and again, there were surprising and unexplained acts of bravery – rescue, protest, help and protection – and I could only wonder how people had found the courage – and why.

I saw the slight figure in a white shirt in front of the Chinese tank on the edge of Tiananmen Square as the Chinese army moved menacingly along the streets of Beijing. Protest had been crushed violently the night before by a furious government. He must have known that he was walking into trouble. There've been stories and speculation about him and his motives for two decades. Maybe he just shouted 'Why?' above the roar of the armoured vehicles. We may never know. To the watching world, he was an ordinary man prepared to walk straight into danger.

A spur of the moment spark of courage.

Consider what it is like to find that spark everyday at work.

Everyone can find a way to face danger.

Picture Acknowledgements

©Kate Adie: 1 top, 6 top and centre, 8 top and bottom. Stuart Archer GC, OBE, ERD: 5 top left. AP Images: 5 bottom (photo Peter Morrison), 8 centre. ©BBC: 2 bottom. ©Nrinder Dhudwar: 2 top. *Gazet van Antwerpen*: 1 bottom. ©Getty Images: 3 top and bottom, 5 centre, 6 bottom (photo Tom Stoddart). ©Imperial War Museum London: 4 centre (CH15185). Estate of Avis Parsons MM: 4 top. ©Reuters Television Library: 7 top. ©Rex Features: 7 bottom (photo John Reardon). *Yorkshire Post*: 4 bottom.